TEACHING OF MATHEMATICS

By
Sudhir Kumar
D.N. Ratnalikar

ANMOL PUBLICATIONS PVT. LTD.
NEW DELHI - 110 002 (INDIA)

ANMOL PUBLICATIONS PVT. LTD.
H.O.: 4374/4B, Ansari Road, Daryaganj,
New Delhi-110 002 (India)
Ph.: 23278000, 23261597
B.O.: No. 1015, Ist Main Road, BSK IIIrd Stage
IIIrd Phase, IIIrd Block,
Bangalore - 560 085 (India)
Visit us at: www.anmolpublications.com

Teaching of Mathematics

Second Revised and Enlarged Edition, 2003
Reprint, 2004, 2005
Reprint, 2006-2007 , 2008

PRINTED IN INDIA

Printed at Mehra Offset Press, Delhi.

Contents

Preface to the Second Edition

We feel happy in presenting the second revised edition of the book. All errors/misprints, crept in the first edition are rectified. Additional information is added here and there.

We hope, teachers, prospective teachers and teacher-trainers will find this book informative and useful. We are grateful to our learned readers for their suggestions. Suggestions/Constructive criticism to make this book more useful are welcome from the actual users. We are also thankful to M/s Anmol Publications Pvt. Ltd., for bringing out revised edition of the book meticulously.

Author

Preface to the First Edition

In the present times Mathematics occupies an important place in curriculum. The 'Teaching of Mathematics' is one of the important subjects at B.Ed. level. In this book an attempt has been made to cover up most of the topics included in the B.Ed. syllabus by Indian universities. This book covers the syllabi of Regular and Correspondence courses of Indian universities.

The book has been written in a simple and lucid manner and is uptodate in its contents. To illustrate theory some model lesson plans have been given.

It is hoped that the book will be appreciated by teachers and students alike. While preparing the book, material has been drawn from works of different authors, periodicals and journals and the author is indebted to all such persons and their publishers.

All suggestions for improvement of the book shall be thankfully accepted.

Author

Chapter—1
Introduction

1.1 WHAT IS MATHEMATICS?

The term 'Mathematics' may be defined in a number of ways. It is an exact science which is related to measurements, calculations, discovering relationships and dealing with the problems of space.

According to *New English Dictionary,* "Mathematics—in a strict sense—is the abstract science which investigates deductively the conclusions implicit in the elementary conception of spatial and numerical relations."

In Hindi we call mathematics as *'Ganita'* which means the science of calculations. It is a systematised, organised and exact branch of science.

In the beginning our knowledge of mathematics is based on our observations of physical and social environment i.e. it arises out of practical applications. We form certain *intuitive ideas* or *notions* known as *axioms* and *postulates*. These are self-evident truths.

Starting from *axioms* and *postulates* we proceed to build up the structure of mathematics by a process of deductive reasoning. "Mathematics in the making is not a deductive science; it is an inductive, experimental science and guessing is the experimental tool of mathematics, mathematicians like all other scientists form their theories from bunches, analogies and simple examples. They work out their rigorous proofs only after they are prety confident that what they are trying to prove is correct and in writing these, they use only the bulldozer of logical deduction".

Mathematics is also called the science of reasoning. According to Locke, "Mathematics is a way to settle in mind a habit of reasoning." There are only a few premises on which we base our reasoning. Reasoning in mathematics is of two types: (*i*) inductive reasoning and (*ii*) deductive reasoning.

Inductive Reasoning

When statements containing mathematical truths are based on general observations and experience, reasoning is called inductive reasoning. In this type of reasoning we argue that a particular property is true in a number of cases, so it will be true in all similar cases.

Deductive Reasoning

This type of reasoning is based on certain postulates or axioms and in this the statements are products of mind. We try to compare and contrast various statements and then draw our conclusions from such a comparison. Essentials of a deductive reasoning are as follows:

(i) Undefined terms

(ii) Definitions

(iii) Postulates and axioms.

(*i*) **Undefined Terms.** As in other branches of science so also in mathematics we come across many terms which cannot be precisely defined. In modern mathematics we accept certain undefined terms e.g. point, surface etc. in case of Geometry and set, number and variable in Algebra.

(*ii*) **Definitions.** We define many a technical terms in mathematics only with the help of undefined terms for example, "If A, B, C are three noncollinear points then triangle ABC is the union of the line segments $\overline{AB}$, $\overline{BC}$, $\overline{CA}$." Thus to define a triangle we have used the terms collinear, point, union and line segment.

(*iii*) **Postulates and Axioms.** Early Greeks considered *postulates* as *general truths common to all studies* and *axioms* as *the truths relating to the special study at hand*. However, later on modifications were made and *postulates* are considered *as permissible constructions* and *axioms* refer to *all other initial assumptions*.

In modern Mathematics the two words *postulates* and *axions* are used synonymously.

1.2 SIGNIFICANCE OF POSTULATES AND AXIOMS IN TEACHING OF MATHEMATICS

We have defined *postulates* as self-evident truths which are taken for granted without any necessity of proof or explanation. These are the first principles from which we deduce mathematical conclusions or inferences through a process of reasoning. To prove a theorem, we base our arguments on the previously proved statements. If we go back in this chain, we arrive at the earliest statements, prior to which no proved statements are available. For proving these initial statements, we have to depend upon our postulates, the self-evident truths. *Postulates* are suppositions, without proof. Some of the postulates are as follows:

(*i*) A straight line can be drawn from any point to any other point.

(*ii*) A finite straight line can be produced to any length in the line.

(*iii*) A straight line has one and only one middle point.

(*iv*) Two straight lines cannot intersect in more than one point.

(*v*) Any angle can be bisected by one and only one line.

(*vi*) We can draw a circle with given centre and passing through a point.

(*vii*) All right angles are equal.

(*viii*) Any geometric figure can be moved without changing its shape and size.

(*ix*) A triangle has interior and exterior angles.

(*x*) Two circles intersect at two points.

(*xi*) There is one and only one straight line through a point parallel to given line.

Axioms. Euclid regarded most other initial assumptions as axioms and called them common notion. They were accepted as true because of their conformity with common experience and sound judgment. The important notions are given below:

(i) Things equal to the same thing, are equal to one another.

(*ii*) The whole is equal to the sum of its parts and is greater than part.

(*iii*) If $a > b$, $b > c$, then $a > c$.

(*iv*) Magnitudes of figures which can be made to coincide with one another are equal.

1.3 MATHEMATICAL LANGUAGE AND SYMBOLISM

In mathematics we express lengthy statements in a very brief form by using various symbols. Thus mathematics has a peculiar language in which symbols occupy a most important position. According to Lindsay, "Mathematics is the language of physical sciences and certainly no more marvellous language was ever created by the mind of man."

Mathematical symbols can put the lengthy statements, accurately and in exact form, in a very brief description. For example, if we wish to say that the sum of the squares of two sides of a right angle triangle is equal to the square of the hypotenuse, then we can write it in mathematical language or symbolic form as $c^2 = a^2 + b^2$.

The symbols are used to make the mathematical results exact and readily useful. The skill in using mathematical symbol comes handy in solving many a complicated problems. It is a must for learning of higher mathematics. These days it is also essential for study of various branches of sciences because most of the results of scientific inventions and discoveries are stated through mathematical language making use of symbols.

Some of the important and familiar symbols used in mathematics are given below:

The symbol II stands for parallel lines

> for greater than

< for less than

≡ for congruency

√ for square root

∠ for angle

Σ for summation etc.

Truly speaking a comprehensive list of all the mathematical symbols is very difficult to prepare. Whenever we use any mathematical symbol an effort be made to clearly explain it to the students. Generally students fail to understand some mathematical procedure or process simply because of their inability to understand the symbols used. In the absence of any clear understanding they try to cram the statements and try to use these symbols mechanically, without much understanding. They begin to lose interest in the subject which appears to them, dull and boring. So teachers should train the pupils in the use of mathematical language and symbols. They should learn to appreciate the beauty, precision and exactness of mathematical language and symbolism.

1.4 PURE AND APPLIED MATHEMATICS

Pure Mathematics

Pure mathematics involves systematics and deductive reasoning, pure mathematics deals with exact statements, concepts and theories which are disconnected from perception. Of course, starting is made with perceptual concepts. These are so mathematised that these cease to be perceptual. It treats only theories and principles without regard to their application to concrete things. It consists of all those assertions as that, if such and such proposition is true of anything, then such and such another proposition is true of that thing. It is developed on an abstract, self-contained basis without any consideration of its possible application if any.

Applied Mathematics. Is the application of pure Mathematics in the real world. Applied mathematics considers those parts of mathematical theories that have certain direct or practical application to objects or actions in the material world. Principles of Applied Mathematics have been used to investigate phenomenon such as heat, sound, light, mechanics, astronomy, navigation etc.

Making use of only pen and paper, we can weigh the earth, prepare for any space flight, determine the paths of planets, solve complicated problems of business in the international world. Applied Mathematics thus helps in solving the intricate problems of the physical world.

In the beginning, man studied only those mathematical structures which were isomorphic to the structures of relationships in Nature and soon turned into abstraction. According to Dantzigs, "Applied Mathematics is like wine which becomes pure in course of time."

The relationship is beautifully illustrated by Synge as follows:

(*i*) A dive from the world of reality into the world of Mathematics.

(*ii*) A swim in the world of Mathematics.

(*iii*) A climb from the world of Mathematics back into the world of reality carrying the prediction in teeth.

Thus applied mathematics acts as a bridge to link pure mathematics with physical, biological, social sciences etc.

Applied Mathematics acts and reacts not only on science, technology but also on pure mathematics e.g. space dynamics, mathematical biology, mathematical economics, ballastics, fluid dynamics etc.

Relation between Pure and Applied Mathematics

We have already learnt that pure mathematics involves systematic and deductive reasoning. Quite often certain structures are discovered in social and physical sciences and a pure mathematicians makes an effort to develop some parallel structures in mathematics. Many a theories and structures of pure mathematics later on find many an applications which were not known at the time of their invention. Taking the example of *Complex numbers* we find that these numbers were developed for the point of view of pure mathematics but now complex numbers are widely used and they find intensive application in electricity, radio etc.

1.5 MODERN MATHEMATICS

In modern times many a new ideas, terms, topics have been developed in various branches of mathematics. Here we take up some of these concepts and topics for discussion.

Sets

Set theory is an important aspect of modern mathematics and its study rather mastery is essential to understand higher mathematics. The idea of set theory is basic to all mathematics.

A set is a collection of objects, also known as aggregate, e.g. set of instruments in a geometry box, tea-set etc. If we know the definite number of objects in any set it is called a defined set e.g.

(*i*) The set of integers 1, 2, 3 or A = (1, 2, 3)

(*ii*) Set of all positive integers or

B = (1, 2, 3, 4, 5,.....)

(*iii*) Set of all vowels or

C = (*a*, *e*, *i*, *o*, *u*)

(*iv*) Set of prime numbers, or

D = (2, 3, 5, 7, 11, 13,.....)

(*v*) Set of all rational numbers etc.

Empty, Null Set, or Void Set

A set which contains no element is known as a *void* or *empty* or *null set* it is denoted by the symbol; i.e.; Φ = ( )

Finite and Infinite Sets

A *Finite Set* is that which *contains* only a *finite number of terms* e.g. the set (1, 2, 3, 4, 5).

An *Infinite Set* is that set which is not a finite e.g. the set of all natural numbers (1, 2, 3, 4....).

Similarly various other terms such as *equal sets, equivalent sets, sub-sets, universal set, power set* etc. are in common use in modern mathematics.

Topology

It is derived from a Greek word which means *place*. In earlier days topology was defined as the study of a situation or position. Nowadays topology is considered a *qualitative mathematics* dealing with intrinsic qualitative properties of objects or figures. These properties do not depend on size, location or shape. These properties do not change even when the object under consideration is subjected to stretching or bending *without tearing*. The word without tearing is emphasised because the points originally close together remains close throughout the process of stretching.

Some times *Topology* is called *rubber sheet geometry* because if certain figures are drawn on a rubber sheet and the sheet is then stretched, there occurs no change in the intrinsic properties of the figure on the rubber sheet. Thus we can say that the figure remains unaltered topologically.

Topology aims at studying the properties of figures i.e. connectivity, orientability etc. If a circle made of pliable object is subjected to continuous stretching and bending without being torn in the process, the circle remains topologically unaltered. Thus in topology all such figures, circles, triangles, ellipses, polygons are topologically equivalent, and are known by the same term 'simple closed curve!'

The transformation of a circle into a square or a triangle is a topological transformation, but the torus and sphere are topologically distinct because one cannot be transformed into the other without breaking or tearing. Topology is concerned with the study of (*i*) topological properties of figures; (*ii*) topological transformation; and (*iii*) arbitrary continuous transformation of geometrical figures.

In topology, set of points are considered. A point may represent an object, a figure, a book, a dog, or a point in the sense of Euclidean geometry. Topology deals with the study of intrinsic qualitative aspects of points. The kinds of sets are called spaces in topology.

Algebraic Systems

To understand algebraic systems, we must have knowledge of sets, mapping and compositions. When a set is equipped with a binary composition or compositions, it is called an algebraic system. Some of the algebraic systems are groups, rings, fields, vector spaces, etc. these particular systems will be considered one by one:

Group: A set with composition is known as a group, it satisfies the conditions given below (adopting multiplication):

(*i*) The composition is associative, i.e., $(ab)\ c = a\ (bc)$ for every a, b, c belonging to G.

(*ii*) There is an identity which belongs to G so that $ae = a = ea$.

(*iii*) Every element of G has its inverse in G. Hence for every a belonging to G, there corresponds an element b of G such that $ab = e = ba$.

The set of all integers under the composition addition '+' is a *group*. This set is made up of integers... –3, –2, –1, 0, 1, 2, 3...

Let us see if it satisfies the above conditions. First condition is self-evident because the relations of the form.

$(4 + 5) + 6 = 4 + (5 + 6)$ are known to use to be true.

Here + is the composition because this connects every ordered pair of numbers with another number of the same set e.g., $4 + 5 = 9$. Here + connects 4, 5 with 9.

As regards the second condition, see here 'O' is the identity $4 + 0 = 0 + 4$ or $5 + 0 = 0 + 5$

Also we know that $-9 + 9 = 0 = 9 - 9$

i.e. every element has the inverse. Hence the *set of all integers forms a group*.

The set of rational numbers with composition '+' also forms a group.

The set of all natural numbers with composition '+' is not a group as it does not satisfy the third condition.

Ring: A set R with two structures or binary compositions (adopting additive) and (multiplicative notation) is a ring when it satisfies the conditions given below:

(*i*) The set R is a commutative group for additive composition:

Commutative property $a + b = b + a$ for every a, b, belonging to R.

(*ii*) Multiplication is associative i.e.,

$(ab)\, c = a\, (bc)$ for a, b, c belonging to R.

(*iii*) Multiplication is right as well as left distributive i.e., $a\, (b + c) = ab + ac$ (Right distribution) $(b + c)\, a = ba + ca$ (Left distribution).

All integers form a ring, because it is commutative group with respect to addition (Zero being the identity). Also the rational numbers and complex numbers form rings.

Field: A ring is known as a field if it contains at least two elements and

(*i*) is commutative

(*ii*) has unity (identity for multiplication)

(*iii*) has inverse for every non-zero element.

All rational numbers, all real numbers, all complex numbers form fields.

1.6 EDUCATIONAL VALUES OF MATHEMATICS

In this section on educational values of mathematics we will try to answer many a queries such as what is the use of learning mathematics? What will be the advantage of learning mathematics? What is the importance of mathematics in every day life etc.?

Mathematics is a subject of great educational values and makes a major contribution in achieving the aims of education. The main aim of education is to develop the individual in such a way that he becomes a contributory member of society, the three main considerations for sending a child to school are as under:

(*i*) To acquire knowledge and skill.

(*ii*) To develop intellectual habits and power.

(*iii*) To develop desirable attitude and ideals.

These three are known as utilitarian, disciplinary and cultural values of education respectively.

To acquire knowledge and skill is the *Practical* or *Utilitarian* value.

Development of intellectual habits and power is the *disciplinary* **value**; and development of training in desirable attitudes and ideals is the cultural value.

(i) Practical or Utilitarian Value

We find a large number of practical applications of mathematics in life. The knowledge of mathematics is needed at every step or stage of life. It is possible to do without the knowledge of our mother tongue but the life becomes a hell without the knowledge of mathematical calculations. Everybody, irrespective of the fact to which class of society he belongs, makes use of mathematical knowledge in one way or the other. For example, a labourer uses mathematical knowledge to calculate wages, to make purchases from market etc. He adjusts his budget with the help of mathematics. Various fundamentals of mathematics such as addition subtraction, counting, numerals, measurements etc. are used by all of us in our daily life. A businessman uses his knowledge of percentage, average, stock and share to run his business efficiently. The knowledge of mathematics is used by engineers, doctors, industrialists, administrators and all others in one way or the other way and so the application of mathematics spread over to almost all academic fields and vocations.

In the present world it seems impossible to live without having a basic knowledge of mathematics. Truely speaking the ignorance of mathematics in the masses is a formidable obstacle in the way of country's progress.

Generally all of us suffer from a misconception because of the feeling that whatever is taught in mathematics in higher classes is of little or of no use to common man. Such as knowledge is seldom used by an individual in his later life. But the value of subject should not be measured only by the number of times one actually makes use of it but by the number of times it can be made use of, this misconception of non-utility of higher mathematics in actual life arises because of the fact that mathematics taught in the class room in generally divorced from the mathematics of real life.

Talking about mathematics Napoleon said, "The progress and the improvement of mathematics are linked to the prosperity of the state". Mathematics will continue to occupy a prominent place in man's life. In all major and minor activities of life, like making purchases in the market, arranging a party, admitting the child to a particular class, joining a profession, purchasing or selling a property, celebrating a marriage, mathematical considerations are foremost in a human mind. To create system in life, we have to fix timings, prices, wages, rates, rations, fares percentages, targets, exchanges, commission, discounts, lengths, breadths, areas, volumes etc. In the absence of these fixations, life in the present day society will be full of confusion and chaos. The number imparts system to our life. In many types of our practical difficulties, number of measurements help us to solve the problem.

In the present day world we are likely to feel more and more about the practical value of mathematics in our life.

(ii) Disciplinary Value

The development of reasoning power and discipline are the two major aims of learning mathematics. According to Locke, "Mathematics is a way to settle in the mind a habit of reasoning." Reasoning in mathematics possesses the characteristics as outlined below:

(a) *Simplicity*. While reasoning in mathematics we proceed step by step from easy to difficult so reasoning in mathematics is simple.

(b) *Accuracy*. In mathematics teaching we are required to be accurate and precise. It thus leaves no scope for vagueness either in thought or in argument. Accuracy, exactness and precision form the beauty of mathematics. The student of mathematics adopts these in life and he learns to influence and command others by his accuracy.

(c) *Certainty of Results.* In mathematics the results are definite and exact and no difference of opinion is possible in mathematics. The mathematical answer is either wrong or right thus mathematics learning inculcates the habit of being certain in a child.

(d) *Originality.* Majority of work in mathematics is characterised by originality in mathematical reasoning. In mathematics, cramming or reproduction of ideas have no scope. In mathematics before undertaking the solution by a problem the student is required to understand it and have a firm grip on the situation, thus crammers can not learn mathematics in its real sense. In mathematics each problem has to be dealt with differently and a student has to solve the problem in his own way and with his own efforts thus a student of mathematics has to be an original thinker. This habit of thinking gets transformed to the problems of daily life also.

(e) *Similarity to Reasoning in Life.* As in mathematics so also in every day life, clear and exact thinking is important. As in mathematics so also in everyday life, before taking up a task, we should have a firm grip on the situation. Thus we find a similarity to reasoning in life.

(f) *Verification of Results.* A student can verify the correctness of his results himself by undertaking the reverse calculations. This gives the child a sense of achievement and develops confidence in him. It also develops in the child a habit of self-criticism and self-evaluation.

(g) *Concentration of Mind.* Concentration is habit of mind which can be developed through persistent practice, concentration is the most important thing to find a solution to a problem and concentration is developed best by mathematics. According to Hamilton, "the study of mathematics cures the vice of mental distraction and cultivates the habit of continuous attention."

(iii) Cultural Values

Mathematics has great cultural values, it has helped in transmitting and enriching our culture. It has helped in the development of various subjects and occupations. It is mainly responsible for the progress of our civilisation. It has been rightly said, "Mathematics is the mirror of civilisation." It has helped man in bringing him to the advanced stage of development.

There is a considerable amount of dependence on mathematics in every field of technological development. Modern life makes use of scientific contributions in all walks of life. With the introduction of new mathematics, many new dimensions of practical value have been opened. The most modern inventions owe their origin to mathematics. Some famous scientists like James Watt, Galileo, Pascal, Newton etc. were mathematicians also.

In words of J.W.A. Young, "wherever we turn in these days of iron, steam and electricity we find that mathematics has been the pioneer. Were its backbone removed, our material civilisation would inevitable collapse? Modern thought and belief would have been altogether different, had mathematics not made the various sciences exact. Different laws of science and the scientific instruments are based on exact mathematical concepts. Astronomy and physics are the most exact sciences and the exactness is the result of the usefulness of mathematics".

Mathematics is a pivot for all arts. The symmetry of a picture or a portrait, the beauty of a geometric design, the metre of a poem and the rhythm of music are nothing but mathematics.

(iv) Vocational Values

Mathematics has great vocational values. It finds extensive application in all vocations like agriculture, accountancy, banking, business, engineering, tailoring, carpentry, surveying etc. Thus the study of mathematics prepares the students for a wide variety of vocations.

(v) Aesthetic Values

Mathematics posses immense aesthetic value. According to Thorndike, "Education as a whole should foster the higher, impersonal pleasures." There are many an interesting riddles and paradoxes in mathematics. Different symmetric designs by Ramanujan are a source of great pleasure e.g.

$$1 \times 9 + 2 = 11$$
$$12 \times 9 + 3 = 111$$
$$123 \times 9 + 4 = 1111$$
$$9 \times 9 + 7 = 88$$
$$98 \times 9 + 6 = 888$$
$$987 \times 9 + 5 = 8888$$

and so on.

(vi) Utility Values

(a) *Art of Economical Living*. Study of Mathematics makes a man very calculating and he can forsee various possible expenditures and thus adjust his budget accordingly, mathematics gives us a training in economising in matter of time, money, speech, thought etc. It helps us to avoid wasteful and futile pursuits. It also inculcates in us the habit of thrift, sound investment and elimination of superfluous and in this way it helps in the development of economical attitude.

(b) *Development of Will Power.* Mathematics teaches a student to pursue a task to its completion and inculcates in him a habit to work and make determined efforts to solve the problem in hand. Because of such an attitude he develops a strong will power, patience and self-reliance.

(c) *Attitude of Discovery.* A student has to make use of creative powers of his mind to find a correct solution to a mathematical problem. It requires original thinking and leaves no scope for cramming. Solving of mathematical problems is in no way less than making a discovery. Thus mathematical study trains the faculties of discovery and invention.

(d) *Power of Expression.* The power of expressing our self clearly and accurately is a great asset in practical life. Mathematics teaches us the habit of using only appropriate words and terms. It also inculcates in us the habit of clearness, brevity, accuracy, precision and certainty in expression. The concepts and symbols of mathematics provide a means of concise expression.

(e) *Understanding of Popular Literature.* In modern times newspapers, magazines, journals, bulletins etc. all are full of mathematical symbols and terms and to properly understand these the knowledge of mathematics is essential. Even for pleasure reading such a knowledge is a must if you are interested in understanding the literature in your hand.

Chapter—2

Aims and Objectives of Teaching Mathematics

2.1 INTRODUCTION

No subject can be taught without having aims and objectives of teaching of that subject clearly before the eyes. These aims and objectives are the guiding stars. They provide proper direction to the teacher and the students. These aims and objectives are in conformity with the aims and objectives of society. The main educational aim is to provide the knowledge to the pupil so that he can become a useful citizen in the society. The aims and objectives of any subject should thus be guided by this very consideration. This is true in case of mathematics teaching as well.

2.2 AIMS OF TEACHING MATHEMATICS

Aims (or the goals or the values) are kept in mind while accomplishing a particular task, objectives are the means to achieve those aims. So it is the objectives which help in determining the values and aims of teaching of mathematics.

The important aims of teaching of mathematics are as under:

(*i*) Cultural and moral aim.

(*ii*) Disciplinary aim.

(*iii*) Practical or utilitarian aim.

(i) Cultural Aim of Teaching of Mathematics

Mathematics has a lot of cultural values. It helps in the formation of certain habits in the students and helps them to grow as cultured citizens. For any cultured person the development of power of reasoning and judgement is the basic requirement and mathematics develops these qualities in a student. In addition to development of power of reasoning and judgement mathematics also helps to develop in the child the qualities of concentration, thinking, precision, accuracy, self-confidence, expression etc. Thus mathematics teaching develops all those qualities in a student so that he becomes a useful member of the society.

(ii) Disciplinary Aim

The chief characteristics of the discipline are simplicity, accuracy, certainty of results, originality, reasoning and correlation of the teaching of the subject with the problems of life. All these characteristics are developed to a large extent by the teaching of mathematics so teaching of mathematics fulfils this aim of education.

According to Schultze: "Mathematics is primarily taught on account of mental training it affords, and only secondarily on account of knowledge of facts it imparts."

According to Locke: "Mathematics is a way to settle in the mind a habit of reasoning." Knowledge follows as a consequence of reasoning power.

(iii) Practical and Utilitarian Aim

Mathematics, apart from the value of bread and butter, has a value of wider practical applications. Principles and theories of mathematics are applied in different aspects of life. Thinking and reasoning are very much guided by mathematics.

Mathematics is helpful in other branches of science, such as Engineering, Physics, Economics etc. According to Roger Bacon, "Mathematics is the gate and key to all sciences".

According to Kent, "A science is exact only in so far as it used mathematics". According to J.W.A Young, "If its backbone (mathematics) is removed, the whole of material civilisation would inevitably collapse."

There is considerable amount of dependence on mathematics in every field of technological development. Modern life makes use of the scientific contributions in all walks of life. With the introduction of new mathematics, many new dimensions of political value have been opened.

The gist of above aims of mathematics can be given as under:

(*i*) It aims to enable the child to solve mathematical problems of his everyday life.

(*ii*) Its aims to develop in the child and acquaintance with his culture.

(*iii*) Its aims at providing a suitable type of discipline to the mind of the pupil.

(*iv*) It aims at preparing the child for technical professions like accountants, auditors, engineers, cashiers, scientists, statisticians etc.

(*v*) It aims to prepare the child for economic, purposeful, productive, creative and constructive living.

(*vi*) It develops in pupil a sense of appreciation of cultural arts.

(*vii*) It prepares him for elementary as also higher education in science, economics, engineering psychology etc.

(*viii*) It develops in the pupils such habits as concentration self-confidence and discovery.

(*ix*) It helps the child to follow the maxim, "Work is Worship".

(*x*) It develops in child the powers of thinking and reasoning.

(*xi*) To develop the learner's power of expression.

(*xii*) To enable him to understand and enjoy popular literature.

(*xiii*) To develop in him a scientific and realistic attitude towards life.

(*xiv*) To bring about all-round, harmonious development of the personality of the child.

2.3 AIMS OF TEACHING MATHEMATICS AT THE ELEMENTARY LEVEL

In the previous section we have discussed the aims of teaching mathematics in general. In this section an attempt will be made to discuss the aims of teaching mathematics at the elementary school level. Thus we have to think in a different way and our emphasis and priorities will vary. These aims can be enlisted as under:

1. To provide a good start to the student in learning mathematics.
2. To provide pupil a clarity about fundamental concepts and processes of mathematics.
3. To create in pupils an enduring interest on the subject and to develop a love for it.
4. To introduce pupils to mathematical games, puzzles, recreations, hobbies and activities and to unfold before them the mysteries of the subject.
5. To develop in pupils a taste for and confidence in mathematics.
6. To develop in pupils accuracy and efficiency in fundamental processes.
7. To acquaint pupils with the relation of mathematics with their present as also with their future life.
8. To develop in them the habits such as regularity, practice, patience, self-reliance and hard work.

9. To prepare pupils for the learning of those subjects which are intimately related with mathematics.
10. To acquaint pupils with mathematical language and symbolism.
11. To prepare pupils for the learning of mathematics of higher classes.
12. To initiate and develop required discipline in the learner's mind.

2.4 OBJECTIVES OF TEACHING MATHEMATICS

Objectives are the specific and precise behavioural outcome of teaching a particular topic in mathematics. The objectives of a topic in mathematics help in realising some general aim of teaching mathematics. The characteristics of a good objective are as under:

(*i*) It should be specific and precise.

(*ii*) It should be attainable.

Bloom's Taxonomy of Objectives

Bloom's taxonomy of objectives is a classification of instructional objectives in a hierarchy. According to it the specific objectives have been classified into the following three categories:

(*i*) Cognitive domain objectives.

(*ii*) Affective domain objectives.

(*iii*) Psychomotor domain objectives.

The cognitive domain objectives include knowledge, understanding, applications, analysis, synthesis and evaluation.

The affective domain objectives include the appreciations, values, attitudes; interests and feelings.

The Psychomotor domain objectives include skills.

Now an attempt will be made to briefly discuss these objectives.

1. Knowledge Objectives

To impart knowledge is the basic aim of education and so it naturally is the basic aim of teaching of any subject including mathematics. By imparting knowledge of mathematics to the students it is expected that he acquires a knowledge of the following:

(*i*) Knowledge of mathematical language e.g. symbols, formulae, figures, diagrams, definitions etc.

(*ii*) Knowledge of various mathematical concepts such as area, percentage, volume, locus, similarity, congruency etc.

(*iii*) Gets acquainted with the contributions of great mathematicians and also with the historical background of the development of the subject.

(*iv*) To understand inter-relationship between various topics and branches of mathematics.

(*v*) To acquaint the pupil with mathematical ideas, facts, principles, processes and relationships.

(*vi*) To make pupil realise the significance of units of measurement.

(*vii*) To acquaint the pupil with certain short cuts in mathematics e.g. multiplication in one line or two lines, logarithms, etc.

Knowledge objectives is considered to have been achieved if the student is able to recall and recognise scientific terms, facts, symbols, concepts etc.

2. Skill or Ability Objectives

These objectives aim at development of certain skills and abilities in the student. The following skills and abilities are intended to be developed:

(*i*) To develop the ability to express thought clearly and accurately.

(*ii*) To develop the ability to systematically organise and interpret the data.

(*iii*) To develop the skill to use mathematical language and knowledge so as to enable the child to tackle mathematical problems of everyday life.

(*iv*) To develop in child the habit of original thinking and investigation.

(*v*) To enable the child to generalise concepts.

(*vi*) To enable the child to perform calculations orally or mentally.

(*vii*) To develop the skill of drawing geometrical figures.

(*viii*) To develop the ability, in the child, to draw, read and interpret graphs and statistical tables.

(*ix*) To develop, in the child, the ability to estimate and verify results.

3. Appreciation Objectives

In regard to the objectives of the development of appreciation of the subject, the following things are kept in mind:

(*i*) To develop appreciation of the cultural values of Mathematics.

(*ii*) To develop appreciation of its contribution of physical and natural sciences.

(*iii*) To acquaint the child with the contributions of Mathematics in human progress and modern civilization.

(*iv*) To acquaint the pupil with the vocational values of Mathematics in modern business and industrial activities.

(*v*) To develop appreciation of rigour and power of mathematical processes, of the accuracy and precision of the result attained.

(*vi*) To appreciate the study of Mathematics for its aesthetic value.

(*vii*) To appreciate mathematical type of thought.

4. Attitude Objectives

Attitude objectives consist in the formation of certain attitudes and habits. In this regard the following are aimed at:

(*i*) To develop the habit of completing a task systematically and logically.

(*ii*) To develop the power of concentration and habit of self-study.

(*iii*) To develop clear expression.

(*iv*) To develop initiative and self-confidence.

(*v*) To develop rational outlook i.e. to express opinion precisely systematically and logically without any bias or prejudices.

(*vi*) To develop heuristic attitude.

(*vii*) To develop the habit of verification.

(*viii*) To develop the capacity of utilising the subject in day-to-day life—Mathematics has a value in our day-to-day life. Pupils should be taught to utilise the subject properly and this can be achieved by imparting them training to measure length, weight, capacity, etc.

(*ix*) To develop the capacity of analysing a problem—Pupils be taught to develop the capacity of successful analysis of the problem that confronts them. This helps the child in life.

(*x*) Formation of behaviour pattern—Formation of behaviour pattern or change in the behaviour pattern is another objective of the teaching of Mathematics. Through behaviour pattern, it is possible for a student to understand a problem and to know the subject through which he can arrive at the result.

(*xi*) Application of knowledge—We have already talked about the objectives of the application of Mathematics in day-to-day life. Objective of the application of knowledge is nothing but the application of the subject to day-to-day life.

(*xii*) *Knowledge of assumption*. In mathematics, we make certain assumptions to solve a problem. These assumption are generally not clear to the students, so we aim at making these assumptions clear to students by teaching of mathematics.

(*xiii*) *Generalisations*. The students be taught to proceed from particular to general.

(*xiv*) *Knowledge of Technical Terms*. In mathematics we come across a number of technical terms. The meaning of these terms and their connotations be made clear to the students.

2.5 OBJECTIVES OF TEACHING MATHEMATICS AT THE PRIMARY STAGE

A. Knowledge Objectives

(*i*) The concepts of number zero, units of measurements, size and shape, fractions, order, direction etc.

(*ii*) Mathematical facts and processes such as the place value of numbers, four fundamental relations, unitary method, percentage, simple interest, areas, profit and loss, geometrical solids, income and expenditure, decimal notation.

(*iii*) Arithmetical terms and symbols such as digits, numbers, symbols for operations, fractions, percentage etc.

B. Ability Objectives

(*i*) Ability to read, write and count different numbers.

(*ii*) Ability to use four fundamental operations of addition, subtraction, multiplication and division.

(*iii*) Ability to make use of mathematical skills in everyday life.

(*iv*) Ability to use multiplications tables.

(*v*) Ability to develop speed and accuracy in solving oral and written problems in mathematics.

C. Appreciation Objectives

To achieve this objective the teaching of mathematics has to be done in an evolutionary way. For this curriculum should include such topics where it is possible to reveal stirring biographical anecdotes, some stories having incidents of adventure, charm and romance. It is possible to achieve this objective by teaching history of mathematics including life stories of some mathematicians. This objective can be achieved by telling the impact of mathematics on modern life.

This objective of teaching of mathematics is considered to have been achieved if the pupil—

(*i*) appreciates the contributions of various mathematicians to human progress.

(*ii*) appreciates the history of mathematical development.

(*iii*) realises the importance of mathematics in modern civilisation.

(*iv*) takes pleasure in understanding the progress made by mathematics.

(*v*) appreciates the value of numbers in individual and social situations.

(*vi*) Appreciate the power of computational skills.

(*vii*) appreciates the recreational value of the subject.

D. Attitude Objectives

Development of mathematical attitude is one of the major objectives of teaching mathematics. It develops in the child a habit of critical observation, intellectual honesty, impartial thinking etc.

This objective is considered to have been achieved if a pupil—

(*i*) develops the habit of critical thinking.

(*ii*) develops confidence in solving elementary problems.

(*iii*) develops the habit of neat, accurate and systematic work.

(*iv*) develops an attitude of independent work.

2.6 CONCLUSION

The teacher is required to choose some of these objectives according to his topic or students. He is to try suitable methods of teaching as well. These objectives are also to be kept in mind while framing a curriculum.

However, neither the curriculum framers nor the teachers keep in mind these objectives. The curriculum is framed in accordance with the changing needs of the society and the developments in the subjects. The child's level is seldom kept in mind. On the other hand teachers try to concentrate on the subject-matter on the one hand and pupils on the other. They want to rush through the course and ask the students to cram up certain facts/formulae etc. Thus we find that objectives of teaching mathematics are generally neglected, however, certain knowledge objectives are unintentionally followed by the teachers.

Chapter—3

Correlation in Mathematics

3.1 INTRODUCTION

The major aim of education is the unification of knowledge existing in different branches of learning. To achieve such a unification a concious effort has to be made by teachers teaching various subjects. It is only by such a joint venture that we will be able to achieve the goal of unification of knowledge and bridge the gap that separates them.

3.2 IMPORTANCE OF CORRELATION

No subject can be taught in isolation particularly 'mathematics'. To take the learning process to its desire end we have to take full advantage of various correlations and applications of mathematics. Just for our convenience we have divided mathematics in different branches of study. However a concious effort is made now-a-days to integrate various branches of mathematics and to treat the subject as a synthetic whole. Teaching of mathematics is done keeping in view its correlation with other subjects. It helps in understanding of subject-matter by the students. It is possible to correlate different experiences and at the same time, allow different aptitudes and inclinations to work with coordination and correlation. The mind of the students works in such manner that he can understand a subject that is being taught, keeping in view its correlation with other subjects. Such a teaching brings about a healthy development of personality.

3.3 TYPES OF CORRELATION

The three important types of correlations are:

(*i*) Correlation of different branches of mathematics.

(*ii*) Correlation of mathematics with other subjects.

(*iii*) Correlation of mathematics with daily life.

1. Correlation Between Different Branches of Mathematics

Mathematics is not one subject. It is actually combination of many a subjects, such as, Arithmetic, Algebra etc. Apart from the branches of Mathematics, there is—Higher Mathematics, which includes Statistics, Hydro-dynamic, Mechanics etc. Truely speaking all these branches of Mathematics are correlated. In a simple manner, it can be stated that several difficult questions of Arithmetic can be solved through the equations and principles of Algebra. On the other hand L.C.M., G.C.M., Fractions, Square-root etc., in Algebra are based upon the rules of Arithmetic. That is also true about Algebra. While finding out the area of a particular triangle or a quadrangle, the principles of Arithmetic can be applied. The basic rules of Arithmetic like addition, subtraction, square-root etc. are found in all branches of Arithmetic.

Higher mathematics has a lot of bearing upon the elementary rules and regulations of mathematics. If a student of a higher mathematics is not well aware of the rules and regulations of Mathematics, he shall not be able to solve the problems of higher Mathematics. Thus, it may be said that different branches of mathematics like Geometry, Algebra, Hydro-dynamics, Statistics and Dynamics etc., are very much correlated. While teaching Mathematics, it is desirable to make it clear to the students that this correlation shall be helpful in their future study. Correlation with the topic in hand should also be made clear to them. If this correlation is made clear, they shall be benefitted by it at future stages besides the present.

Correlation Between Different Topics of a Particular Chapter or Branch of Mathematics.

What is true about different branches of Mathematics is also true about different topics of a chapter of Mathematics. A specific chapter of Mathematics, say L.C.M. has the relationship with the rules of addition and subtraction. Likewise in Algebra, to solve an equation we make use of the principle of simplification. During teaching of mathematics, an attempt be made by the teacher to make clear such a correlation between different topics of a particular chapter. This facilitates the study and helps the students in understanding the subject.

2. Correlation of Mathematics with Other Subjects and Aspects of Life

The correlation of one subject with other is of two types:

(*i*) Direct, and

(*ii*) Indirect.

(a) Indirect Correlation of Mathematics with Other Subjects and Aspects of Life

This is considered to be more physical and interesting method. In this, an attempt is made to give reference of certain other subjects while teaching a particular topic or subject of mathematics. It helps to make subject more interesting. An attempt be made to make references only to such things which are known to the students. It serves a dual purpose. Firstly it helps the students in understanding the topic in hand and secondly, it helps the students to acquire a broad and comprehensive outlook.

(b) Correlation of Mathematics with Other Subjects

Mathematics has a direct bearing on subjects of pure sciences such as physics, chemistry etc. It has a bearing on social sciences as well. Now an attempt will be made to study the correlation of mathematics with different subjects.

3.4 CORRELATION OF MATHEMATICS WITH PHYSICAL AND BIOLOGICAL SCIENCES

Some Quotes are given below which give an idea of correlation of mathematics with Physical and Biological sciences.

"All scientific education which does not commence with mathematics is, of necessity, defective at its foundation".

—Comte

"A natural science is a science only in so far as it is mathematical."

—Kant

"Mathematics is the indispensable instrument of all physical research."

—Berthelot

"Mathematics is the gate and key of sciences."

—Roger Bacon

(i) Correlation Between Mathematics and Physics

There is a close relationship between mathematics and physics. For higher education in physics, a good knowledge of mathematics is quite helpful. All the laws of physics are expressed in mathematical language. To solve numerical problems in physics we need a good knowledge of mathematics. In physics we have to be mathematically accurate e.g., launching of satelites on the moon required right amount of thrust in rockets, accuracy in time and speed, angle of launching, shape to provide minimum friction and so many other calculations. Working of a machine is possible when there is proper adjustment of its components. Principles of Physics are presented in a workable form. Some more examples are as under:

$S = ut + ½ft^2$

$V = u + ft$

Where the symbols have their usual meanings

$$G = K\frac{mm^1}{r^2}$$

The law of lever is based on the simple mathematical principle of balance of the sides of an equation. The units of measurement are frequently used in physics. Tables of specific heat, latent heat and melting points are prepared with the help of mathematics.

(ii) Correlation Between Mathematics and Chemistry

According to J.W. Mellor, "It is almost impossible to follow the later developments of physical or general chemistry without a working knowledge of higher mathematics".

All chemical combinations are governed by certain mathematical laws. All chemical compounds have their constituent elements in a definite ratio, e.g. in synthesis of water we take two atoms of hydrogen and one atom of oxygen under suitable chemical conditions. Chemical equations are balanced by counting the number of atoms on either side.

In the structure of atom, there are some set relations concerning electrons, protons etc. Valencies of elements have a mathematical base. Molecular weights of organic compounds are calculated mathematically.

(iii) Correlation Between Mathematics and Biology

"In Mathematics we find the primitive source of rationality and to mathematics must the biologist resort for means to carry on their researches."

—A. Comet.

Mathematical principles find many applications in observing and interpreting certain phenomena. The phenomena are described, classified and compared for generalising and deriving a biological law. Life processes are the most intricate of all natural phenomena e.g. composition of animal and plant cells is studied and expressed clearly and concisely in a simple intelligible language. Mathematics provides brief and precise expression of ideas.

Moreover, study of biology depends upon its branches–Biophysics and Biochemistry. Both these branches use mathematics on a wide scale. Recently Biomathematics has also started to grow and this is an important field of study for Biologists.

Various experiments in biology also need analysis. For many a complex problems the solutions can be found only be use of methods of statistics. Gestalt used this method for measurement of inheritance of stature of children and stature of their parents. He found this coefficient to be 2/3.

The Schultz-Borissoff Law of the Action of Enzymes such as pepsin and rennin is expressed by the formula

$$x - K\sqrt{F}.gt$$

Where x = amount of substance transferred.

t = time of transformation

f = concentration of enzyme.

g = initial concentration of substrate (e.g. albumin of milk) and K is a constant.

(iv) Correlation Between Mathematics and Engineering

Mathematics is considered to be the foundation of Engineering. Engineering has been defined as, "The art of directing the great sources of power in nature for the use and convenience of man".

For admission to any engineering course only those students are eligible who have offered mathematics course at the qualifying class. In various Engineering Courses we deal with surveying, levelling, designing, estimating construction etc. and for all these the knowledge of mathematics is essential. In all the branches of engineering such as civil, mechanical, electrical etc. mathematical principles are directly involved. It is possible to increase the durability of a product by the application of geometrical principles. Mathematical knowledge can also be used in verification of results in engineering.

All this is enough to bring to fore the close correlation between mathematics and engineering.

(v) Correlation Between Mathematics and Agriculture

Agriculture as a science is highly dependent on mathematics. We can attain desirable targets only if we have a calculating attitude. It is the need of the times that a common agriculturist should be so calculative as to be able to compare the amount of return he is likely to get by putting in his labour and money.

In agriculture we have to make various land measurements and for this purpose a knowledge of mathematics is essential.

Thus we find a lot of correlation between mathematics and agriculture.

(vi) Correlation Between Mathematics and Other Sciences

We have discussed correlation between certain branches of science and mathematics in the proceeding paragraphs but science is a very wide subject and it includes many a subjects. Mathematics has played a very important role in building our civilisation by perfecting all sciences. Mathematics is the science of all sciences and art of all arts. Almost all branches of science have a great deal to do with mathematics. Graphs and charts, curves etc. all are based on principles of mathematics. In *Astronomy* and *Hydromechanics* it is the principle of mathematics that works. Thus we can say that there is a lot of correlation between science and mathematics.

(vii) Correlation Between Mathematics and Social Science

Though the relationship between mathematics and social science is not very strong yet it is quite strong. In social sciences we come across graphs, charts, curves etc., thus we can say that social sciences draw a lot from mathematics.

The views of some thinkers on this relationship are quoted below:

"The social sciences mathematically developed are to be the controlling factors in civilisation".

—W.F. White.

"All great scientific discoveries are but the reward of patient, pains taking shifting of numerical data".

—Lord Kelvin.

"Analytical and graphical treatment of statistics is employed by the economist, the philanthropist, the business expert, the actuary and even the physician, with the most surprisingly valuable results, while symbolic language involving mathematical methods has become a part of well-nigh in every large business".

—L. Karpinsky.

Today collection of statistics is very important for Social Sciences. Without these statistics it is not possible to have a correct study of any subject. It is Mathematics that provides these statistics. In fact, statistics is nothing but an integral part of Mathematics. In the following lines we shall try to assess the correlation between different Social Sciences and Mathematics.

(viii) Correlation Between Mathematics and Economics

In economics, mathematical principles and language is freely used to describe and interpret social phenomena.

According to Marshall, "The direct application of mathematical reasoning to the discovery of economic truths has recently rendered great services in the hands of master mathematicians".

In economic we study the earning and spending factors of a society, population, production etc. In economics statistics plays an important role. The application of statistical methods is most helpful in economic forecasts. Trade cycles, trends of exports and imports, volume of trade etc. all are represented statistically.

The theory of probability applied to assurance is simply a mathematisation of economic problems. The word 'constant', 'average', 'ratio', 'variable' etc. are used by every magazine, periodical that deals with economic problems. All these are actually mathematical terms which are used in mathematics.

The businessman who is a leader in the field of economics, has to face problems involving simple and compound interest, instalment payments and accounting. He makes use of statistical methods for making economic forecasts.

The correlation between mathematics and economics is so vast that now-a-days in many a universities, a course in advanced mathematics is included as a part of degree course in economics. This is because of the fact that mathematics plays an important part in Economics.

(ix) Correlation Between Mathematics and Psychology

Without using mathematics psychology is only a flight of imagination.

In the works of Herbert, "It is not only possible but necessary that mathematics be applied to psychology".

Utility of psychology has increased tremendously in the modern world because of application of mathematics in the study of psychology. Various statistical methods are being used to interpret psychological data and experimental psychology has become highly mathematical as it deals with intelligence quotient, standard deviation, mean, mode, coefficient of correlation etc.

For example,

$$I.Q. = \frac{M.A.}{C.A.} \times 100$$

Where Abbreviations have their usual meanings.

(x) Correlation Between Mathematics and Logic

Logic is the scientific study of the conditions of accurate thinking and valid influence. All laws of logic are based on experiments and verification. D'Alombert says, "Geometry is a practical logic, because in it rules of reasoning are applied in the most simple and sensible manner." Mathematics is the only field of knowledge where the logical laws can be applied and results verified without any personal bias.

W.C.D. Whetham—"Mathematics is but the higher development of Symbolic Logic."

C.J. Keyser—"Symbolic Logic is Mathematics; Mathematics is Symbolic Logic."

Pascal says, "Logic has borrowed the rules of geometry. The method of avoiding error is sought by everyone. The logicians profess to lead the way, the geometers alone reach it, and aside from their science there is no true demonstration."

Logic makes us exact and systematic in use of our language while mathematics makes us exact and systematic when we translate these thoughts into action. A person having a sound knowledge of logic can not be led astray by any jugglery of facts in mathematics and vice-versa.

It can be easily said that geometry a branch of mathematics is a practical logic.

(xi) Correlation Between Mathematics and Philosophy

According to Herbert, "The real finisher of our education is philosophy but it is the office of mathematics to ward off the dangers of philosophy." Philosophy deals with abstract ideas. Mathematics tries to draw attention on the ideas that are practicable and worth while. According to A.N. Whitehead, "Philosophers when they have possessed a thorough knowledge of Mathematics, have been among those who have enriched the science with some of its best ideas." Mathematics helps the philosophers in sifting truth from falsehood, attainable from the unattainable, facts from fiction and so on.

According to J.S. Mill— "Mathematics will ever remain the most perfect type of Deductive Method in general; and the applications of mathematics to the simpler branches of physics, furnish the only school in which philosophers can effectively learn the most difficult and important portion of their art, the employment of the laws of the simpler phenomena for explaining and predicting those of the more complex."

Though to a common man it appears that there can't be any relationship between such widely different branches of knowledge, but the fact is that mathematics occupies a central place between natural philosophy and mental philosophy. Philosophers find orderly and systematic achievements of unambiguous truths. The philosopher can rely on mathematics. Truely speaking, it is the mathematical development of sciences that saved philosophy from degenerating into pure sensationalism and imagination.

(xii) Correlation Between Mathematics and Fine Arts

Mathematics is the pivot of all arts. An object is beautiful when depicted in correct geometrical proportions. That is why the Greeks, the greatest geometers of the age, were also successful in art sculpture. Mathematics itself is a great art of study of harmony and symmetry. The following views express the relationship between Mathematics and Fine Arts.

Leibnitz said, "Music is a hidden exercise in arithmetic of a mind unconscious of dealing with numbers."

Pythagoras said, "Where harmony is, there are numbers."

John Arbuthnot said, "Truth is the same thing to the understanding as music to the ear and beauty to the eye."

(xiii) Correlation Between Mathematics and Geography

Geography deals with the study of physical conditions of a particular country or society. It deals with the study of rivers, canals, mountains, population etc. In this we also try to measure heights and draw charts and graphs. In all these, mathematics plays a prominent role. Thus there is a great application of mathematics in geography. The areas of the earth's longitudes and latitudes, calculation of time at various places, rotation of the earth leading to formation of days and nights and seasons, moment of winds, falling of rains, factors influencing climate of a region etc. all depend upon mathematical calculations. Mathematics helps in drawing and understanding of maps. Graphs of various kinds are frequently used in geography.

Relief maps are based purely on mathematics. Geology though considered as a separate branch of science influences geography to a very large extent. The geological studies are not possible without the proper use of mathematical knowledge.

(xiv) Correlation Between Mathematics and History

The relationship between mathematics and history is reciprocal. History helps mathematics to know about various mathematicians who were pioneers in their field and enriched mathematics by their contributions. History also provides the information about the origin and development of mathematics.

Mathematics helps History in regards to calculation of dates and days etc. of various historical events. Thus there is a close correlation between Mathematics and History.

(xv) Correlation Between Mathematics and Drawing

In Drawing we come across many a branches such as geometrical drawing, memory drawing, figure drawing etc. In geometrical drawing various principles of geometry and frequently used thus we find a close correlation between drawing and mathematics. If we consider it the other way round we find that a good drawing is needed to draw good geometrical figures in the study of mathematics. The exactness of a figure can be measured only with the help of mathematics.

(xvi) Correlation Between Mathematics and Languages

No subject can be taught without the help of language. This is also true of Mathematics. The principles of Mathematics are expressed through the medium of language. Thus, it is the language that helps Mathematics. If the language that is spoken in a Mathematics class or written in a book is not correct, the exact idea of the subject-matter shall not be conveyed. This shall have a wrong impression on the mind of students.

Just as language helps Mathematics, also there is the story of Mathematics helping the language. Teaching of Mathematics develops an attitude of exactness in the students. This exactitude helps them to write the language correctly. Thus, it may be said that the relationship between the two is quite significant.

3.5 CORRELATION TEACHING OF MATHEMATICS WITH OTHER ASPECTS OF LIFE

Mathematics cannot be taught in isolation. The utility of this subject is no confined to the classroom or the school only. It has an important bearing on various aspects of life. As far as possible, while teaching Mathematics, a reference should be made to its use in actual life. Whenever we go out for shopping and purchase certain things, we get them measured and weighted. In this activity, it is the Mathematics that plays its role. The students should, therefore, be explained the utility of Mathematics in practical life.

The teacher of Mathematics should also try to explain to the students the practical application of the principles of Mathematics. He may also show the big electrical installations and bridges etc., and explain to the students that all this has been made possible only with the help of mathematics. This would impress upon them the utility of the subject-matter of life and the correlation between actual life and Mathematics. This would be scientific as well as an interesting method.

3.6 CONCLUSION

From the above discussion, it follows that Mathematics is intimately related with all physical and social sciences. It has helped a lost in perfecting all the sciences. It has been and is the science of all sciences and art of all arts. It may be a back-stage performer, but is a very powerful one.

The relation of Mathematics with various sciences can be beautifully illustrated with the Tree of Mathematics.

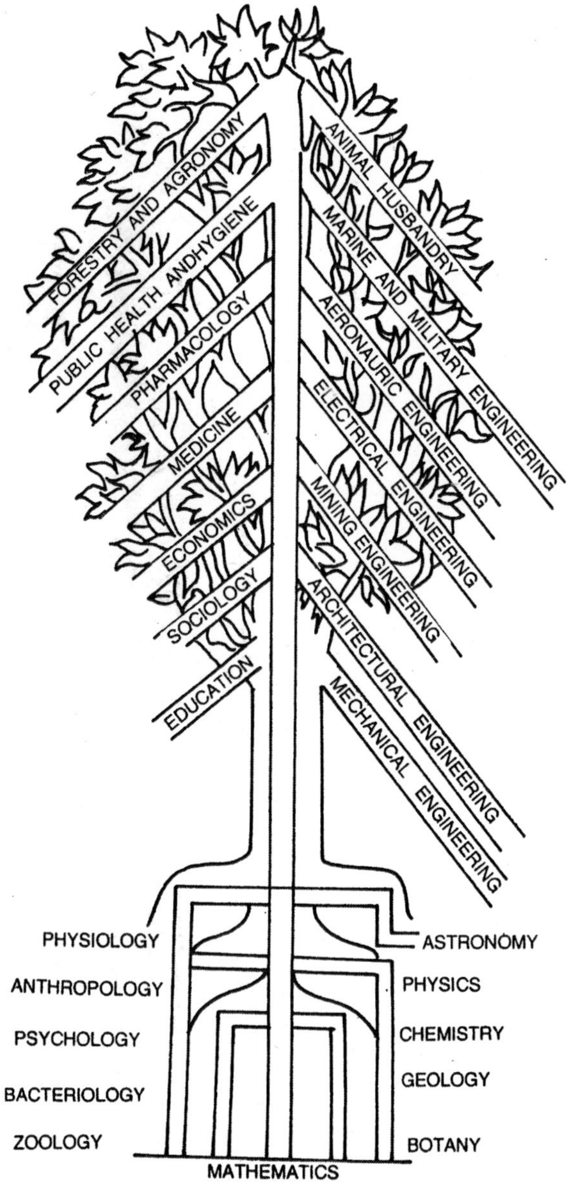

Tree of Mathematics

Chapter—4

Curriculum in Mathematics

4.1 INTRODUCTION

If instruction in Mathematics is to be worthwhile it must be planned with the idea of achieving certain aims which represent values attained from its study. Selection of material should be made with a purpose, that is to be served by Mathematics in the general scheme of education. In recent times, we find rapid, social, technological· and scientific changes. We also find significant changes in man's outlook on life.

4.2 NEED FOR THE PLANNING OF CURRICULUM

The word *'curriculum'* is derived from the Latin word *'curresre'* which means to *run*. So 'curriculum' is a course or path which one runs to reach a goal. Thus curriculum includes the subject-matter and all learning experiences arranged by the school for a particular subject.

The needs of life to on changing, so is education, hence we cannot go on with a static curriculum. The content has to be selected according to the changing needs of the society in general and the subject in particular. The curriculum has to be planned and organised in a scientific manner keeping in view the psychophysical requirements of the students. If the curriculum is properly organised, it enables the students to know the subject-matter which they have to study. On the other hand it also makes clear to the teacher, the material that they have to teach to the students. It also provides the same facility to the examiner.

4.3 CONSTRUCTION OF THE CURRICULUM

The following two stages are important in the construction of curriculum:

(*i*) Selection of the curriculum, and

(*ii*) Organisation of the curriculum material.

(i) Principles of Selection of Curriculum

Tradition is not going to be our guiding principle in the selection and arrangement of the subject-matter. It is not possible or advisable to carry out the selection of a curriculum in a haphazard manner. Curriculum has to be properly planned and to be based on certain principles. These principles will be discussed now.

(ii) Principles of the Selection of Curriculum or Subject Material

(a) Principle of Utility (or Use)

Knowledge for the sake of knowledge is a good aim but in the existing circumstances it is to a successful aim. At present we have to keep in mind the utilitarian aspect of every subject-matter. If the subject-matter is not of any use the students will not feel interested in it for a long time. Thus, the curriculum material should include only those topics which are useful for a particular grade in many ways. Firstly an attempt be made to include those topics which are useful in day to day life e.g. the four fundamental operations, tables, percentages, profit and loss, area, taxes, simpler notions of statistics, house-hold accounts, graphs etc. The curriculum material of the subject should have the following ingredients in it:

(*i*) It should be useful in everyday life.

(*ii*) It should be useful in the study of other subjects.

(*iii*) It should have some vocational utility.

(*iv*) It should enable students to understand and appreciate the role played by Mathematics in the development of civilisation and other branches of knowledge.

(b) Principle of Disciplinary Value

Teaching of Mathematics disciplines the mind. Previously this was the sole criterion to select the subject-matter. This brought into syllabus much useless material. The students used to study certain puzzles and riddles which had no practical utility. For disciplining the mind, one topic is as good as another. Unless and until a topic has some other values, it should not be included in the curriculum simply for its disciplinary value. Real useful problems train the mind better than unreal formal problems. When the students can get both useful knowledge and mental training from the same set of facts, it is not wise to make pupils learn one set of facts for mental exercise and another for the acquisition of knowledge. In the words of Thorndike, "Teach nothing merely because of its disciplinary value but teach everything so as to get, what disciplinary value it does have."

(c) Principle of Cultural Value

Mathematics has played an important role in the advancement of culture and civilisation. There may be certain ideas that were pursued by the students of Mathematics which may not be of any use now. But there are certain ideas and facts of Mathematics that form an integral part of modern culture and society. Such facts or ideas should be included in the curriculum. Their study will be a source of inspiration to the students.

(d) Principle of Preparatory Value

The material of the curriculum should be so selected that it should be preparatory as well as terminus. On the one hand it should train the students for life and on the other it should also prepare them for higher education. The content should include the topics which prepare the child (i) for university education, (ii) for life. Only a small percentage of the students go up to the university stage and for most of them school is a terminal stage. Hence the requirements of college course need not dominate the school curriculum. After every stage of education some students enter life while others go in for higher education. The curriculum should be such as to be able to provide satisfactory education to both these categories of students.

(e) Principle of Child Centredness

Mathematics is a very vast subject so it becomes difficult to make a selection of the things which are useful to the students. For taking a decision about usefulness of the content material we should always keep in mind the child for whom it is meant. Do not forget that curriculum is for the child and the child is not for the curriculum. While making a selection of useful topics for inclusion in curriculum child's interests, abilities, age levels etc. should be kept in mind. The duration of the course should also be given due consideration while making the selection of topics for inclusion in the curriculum. An attempt be made to provide in the curriculum topics for various categories of students.

(f) Principle of Community Centredness

Since every child has to live in and for the community, it would be desirable that he is able to live well in society. In the curriculum of Mathematics all such topics be included which cater to the needs of the society. Thus an attempt be made to shape the curriculum according to the needs of the society.

(g) Principle of Flexibility

The aim of education as also the aims of teaching a subject go on changing because they depend on the needs of every changing society. The developments in the subject also necessitate a change in curriculum. Thus it is not possible for us to follow any rigid curriculum forever. The curriculum has to be modified and reviewed quite frequently so as to shape it according to the latest developments of the subject. It is essential if we have to keep pace with the modern world. In this regards the views be sought from subject specialists.

(h) Teachers' Point of Views

While framing or revising the curriculum, the views of teachers, who are the real workers, should also be sought. They know the levels of students and the things which should be taught to the students. At present, the curriculum is imposed on the teacher and as such, they do not realise the significance of changes in the curriculum if any. The new trend expects participation and contribution from the teachers side.

So we see while constructing curriculum for a grade, various considerations are to be kept in mind. Nothing should be included simply because of disciplinary value. Utility should provide the chief criterion of curriculum construction. Of course, the latest trends in the subject, the needs of community, the needs of students and above all, the views of the teachers should be given due weight in any scheme of curriculum construction.

Views of J.W.A. Young in regard to Selection of the Subject-matter of Curriculum—According to Young, selection of the subject-matter of curriculum should be guided by the following considerations (or principles):

(1) To exhibit most clearly and to the best advantages the mathematical type of thought.

(2) To help to a better understanding of the laws of nature.

(3) To bring out clearly the mathematical relationships that exist in the social organism and in the activities of modern life, and to exhibit how mathematics helps in solving their problems.

(4) To give sufficient skill in the actual performance of mathematical processes so as to meet the future needs of the student.

(5) To allow the organisation of the material into a homogeneous whole, meeting the demands of the pedagogy.

4.4 ORGANISATION OF CURRICULUM

Curriculum has to be organised on the basis of certain principles. It is these principles that help the scientific planning of the curriculum. Organisation of curriculum lies in the distribution of subject-matter of the curriculum in different classes. It is quite essential that it is planned in a scientific way. The teacher should have a say in the selection as well as arrangement of the course content. His experience is of practical nature so it must count in this respect. Teachers should be actively associated with the organisation of the subject-matter of curriculum.

Good arrangement requires that,

(*i*) every topic should be divided into parts,

(*ii*) those parts should be graded according to difficulty, and

(*iii*) each part should be introduced at a proper stage.

Curriculum has so far been organised mostly for class teaching. The principles which are generally kept in mind while organising the curriculum are discussed in the following paragraphs.

1. Psychological and Logical Arrangement

Logical arrangement leads to the rigorous treatment of the subject-matter which is based on logical reasoning whereas psychological arrangement is from the point of view of the students. It seems that both the approaches are different but these can be easily merged. The organisation can both be psychological and logical. All thinking is psychological. Psychology throws light on the power of understanding of students at a particular stage. We can be logical in various ways. Psychology should decide which logical approach will suit for a particular topic. Logic will help in maintaining proper sequence of topics, so we should organise the topics in such a way that we may follow Psychology and Logic at the same time. The happy combination of the two is always desirable.

The nature of the subject 'Mathematics' is mostly logical and the subject-matter requires rigorous treatment. The subject grows on definitions, rules and reasoning processes. If we decide to deliver the content to the child it is merely subject centred approach which is not advocated in the interest of the learner.

Psychology throws light on the use of a topic for the pupil from the academic as well as practical point of view. It takes into consideration the power of grasping and understanding of pupils in a particular age group. The order in which topics are to be taken up will largely depend on its findings. Similarly logic must be there. Psychology should decide what kind of logic is appropriate for the pupil of a certain age and what type of topics will be most suitable for the development of such logical thinking. Logic will help in maintaining the link and sequence of topics found useful and meaningful for the child.

Logical organisation of the subject-matter deals with the vigorous logical reasoning associated with the subjects. Algebra or geometry, the mathematician is chiefly concerned with the logical arrangement of the content whereas the teacher who teaches the subjects needs to use the psychological approach. In logical approach the various abilities to be developed in the child are as under:

(*i*) Logical reasoning involved in solving problems based on factorisation of polynomials of second and third order, solving riders, proving a theorem or a mathematical proposition;

(*ii*) Intuitive thinking in hypothesising a result based on an axiom or a postulate; and

(*iii*) Inference based on mathematical induction.

2. Topical and Spiral Arrangement

Topical arrangement means that a topic should be finished entirely at one stage. It takes the topics as a unit. Spiral arrangement implies that a topic should be split up into different portions and these portions should be spread over different grades. Easier portions should be dealt with in the lower grades and the difficult portions should be gradually introduced in the next grade. The later is definitely a good arrangement. Topical arrangement requires that easy and difficult portions of a topic should be dealt with at one stage which is unpsychological.

However simple or easy topics may be finished at one stage, while spiral arrangement is good, long grinding at all grades is undesirable. The selection of a particular approach will depend on the topic.

3. From Easy to Difficult

Organisation of the content material of the curriculum be done keeping in view the mental development and the capacities of the students. The easier topics should come first and difficult ones later on. However we should bear in mind that what appears easy to the teacher, may not be easy to the student, so this is to be seen from the point of view of the student. For this we have to keep in mind the mental level, capacities and age level of the students.

The order in which the human race developed Mathematics can be used as a guideline to decide the difficulty level. For any particular class only those topics be included in syllabus which are within the comprehension of the students.

4. Principle of Activity

The child likes activity and these days activity plays an important part in teaching of a subject-matter. Organisation of curriculum should not fail to suggest some practical work where ever it is possible. In lower classes those topics be included which put more emphasis on practical work. It help in making clear various concepts in mathematics and thus help in developing a love for the subject. In lower classes we should take up handling of concrete objects like weighing, counting, measuring etc. Practical work should give place to abstract principles of mathematics in successive higher classes.

Following activities be kept in mind while organising the subject-matter of curriculum:

(*i*) Personal and home activities.

(*ii*) Recreational activities.

(*iii*) Vocational activities.

(*iv*) Community, civic and social activities.

(*v*) National activities.

5. Principle of Correlation

While organising the content in Mathematics the principle of correlation should always be given due weightage. Correlation may be of different varieties. The following types of correlation must be kept in mind while organising curriculum in Mathematics:

(*i*) Correlation of Mathematics with the problems of everyday life.

(*ii*) Correlation of Mathematics with other subjects.

(*iii*) Correlation between different branches of Mathematics.

(*iv*) Correlation between different topics of a particular branch of Mathematics.

(*v*) Correlation with craft or work experience.

For correlating subject-matter we must know the following:

(*i*) Day to day life activities of the students.

(*ii*) The nature of topics included in other subjects at the same stage.

(*iii*) The topics included in different branches of the subject e.g., Arithmetic, Algebra, Geometry etc.

(*iv*) The sequence of topics of the same branch of the subject.

(*v*) The nature of work experience or projects undertaken by the students.

6. Scope of Individual Teaching

Psychology shows that no two children are alike. There are individual differences in students. The same type or rigid syllabus may not suit all the students. There may be ability grouping of students i.e. the students of almost the same intelligence and achievement may be put in one group. Accordingly there should be grouping of topics in the curriculum. There should be differentiated assignments for bright and dull students.

The most prevalent view at present is that the requirements of the group as a whole should have priority over individual requirements. However Educationist differ in this regard and some of them emphasise that the subject-matter of the curriculum should be so arranged that the difference in the abilities of students are not neglected.

7. Voice of the Teacher

The teacher must have definite say in the selection and organisation of the curriculum in Mathematics. The teacher is the real field worker, who knows what is most suitable and where. At present, the teacher is not consulted at all. The curriculum is laid down for him. He is to faithfully go through it, without any alteration or modification.

8. Some other Requirements

(*a*) *Child centred Syllabus*—The curriculum should be child centred and not subject or topic-centred.

Unless the requirements of the child are kept in view, the curriculum shall not be useful.

(*b*) *From Impirical to Rational*—The curriculum should be so organised that the students are able to acquire facts through experience, intuition and induction. They should also be gradually made to feel the need for and appreciate the usefulness of deduction system of education. This method is known as the method of proceeding from impirical to rational. In other words, it means that the students should be made to proceed from known to unknown or from particular to general.

(*c*) *From Concrete to Abstract*—The curriculum should provide for the teaching of the subject on the principle of proceeding from concrete to abstract.

4.5 PLACE OF PROBLEMS IN TEACHING OF MATHEMATICS

While organising curriculum, due place should be given to the problems. Problems be linked with every topic and subject. These problems should have bearing not only on the subject but also on life. The practice in solving problems helps in developing speed, accuracy and ability to apply mathematical facts in different solutions. Problem solving trains the pupil in attacking and solving problems.

Selection of Problems

Selection of problems is quite important because all types of problems do not help in development of problem-solving skills. Broadly speaking following four types of problems are found in Mathematics:

(*i*) *Puzzle problems* are those problems which may puzzle the minds of the pupil. This type of problems are generally used as a sort of pastime.

(*ii*) *Catch Problems* are those which catch on trick and they involve jugglery of words. Such problems are quite useful to test mental alertness of the students.

(*iii*) *Unreal Problems* which have no relationship to real life situations. They give a false idea of what happens in life e.g. an aeroplane is flying at the speed of 5 km/hour.

(*iv*) *Real Problems* which are taken from life. The solving of real problems helps in training the child to grapple with new situations in his real life.

Real problems occupy an important place in Mathematics. This type of problems help in the achievement of the aims of subject and they should form an integral part of Mathematics curriculum.

The following points should be kept in view while selecting problems of Mathematics.

(*i*) It should have some practical and social value.

(*ii*) It should be in accordance with the level of pupils.

(*iii*) It should be related to the general interests and achievements of pupils.

(*iv*) It should be selected from common life situations.

(*v*) It should be worked in simple and understandable language.

(*vi*) The problems from other school subjects at a particular stage, may also be included in the curriculum.

(*vii*) The problem should pose a challenge to the intellect of student but it should be capable of being solved with reasonable amount of effort.

(*viii*) The problems that develop skills and attitudes required for preparing a sound base for higher studies and for vocations in life, should also be included.

4.6 PLACE OF LEARNING EXPERIENCES IN THE MATHEMATICS CURRICULUM

We have already emphasised the fact that learning experience (activity) occupies an important place in the Mathematics curriculum. Suggesting appropriate learning experiences wherever possible is very important in the formulation of curriculum of Mathematics. For this, we have to think about the types of learning experiences to be provided to the students in order to bring about the desirable behavioural changes.

The enlisting of learning experiences must be based upon a number of factors like needs of a particular community, abilities and interests of the students and facilities available in the school. First of all, a general view of the general standard and aptitudes of the students should be taken by estimating the above mentioned attributes. Then, in the light of this estimate, a few suggestions for the induction of suitable learning experiences may be incorporated.

The suggestions for learning experiences should not be very exhaustive, rather they should indicate only a few simple activities, that are likely to cause effective learning and help in achieving the set objectives. The validity and suitability of learning experiences selected in the curriculum of mathematics should be judged on the following basis:

(*i*) Learning experiences should be appropriate to the desired behavioural changes, defined under objectives of curriculum construction.

(*ii*) They should be suitable for the relevant topics of the concerned content areas of the curriculum.

(*iii*) They should be feasible.

(*iv*) They should be adequate and effective.

It should be kept in mind that we are to suggest suitable learning experiences so that the proposed objectives of curriculum are fully achieved. Hence the suggested learning experiences should be closely connected with the objectives of teaching Mathematics.

It should also be kept in mind that we are to suggest suitable learning experience in order to make the students practical in nature, so that they learn to apply their Mathematical knowledge in day-to-day life.

4.7 PLACE OF MATHEMATICS IN CURRICULUM

Important Place of Mathematics in the Curriculum

Mathematics occupies an important place in the curriculum. This has been there since ages. In Plato's view, "Those persons who are not able to study Mathematics and understand its problems should not be allowed to enter an institution." Majority of eminent educationists of past as well as of present, including Herbert, Froebel, Pestalozzi, Dr. Maria Montessori, Sir. T.P. Nunn etc. have advocated the importance of Mathematics. In their opinion, the intellectual and cultural development of a person is not possible without the study of Mathematics. In opinion of Napoleon the Great, without development of Mathematics, no nation can develop.

According to a survey conducted on behalf of UNESCO in 1981 the place of Mathematics in various regions of the world was as under:

Africa

Mathematics is a strong feature of the curriculum at all levels in all countries of the region.

Europe

In this region, Mathematics is found in the curriculum of all countries at all levels.

Latin America and the Caribbean

In this region, Mathematics is taught at all levels in all countries of the region. It is taught as an optional subject in

Saint Lucia during the final 4 years, in Jamaica during final 3 years and in Guyana in all secondary classes.

Asia and Pacific

Mathematics forms part of the curriculum of all the grades in every country, and its profile in most systems is high.

Here we take up the *Place of Mathematics in India.*

In most of the *Indian States,* Mathematics is taught as a compulsory subject upto the higher secondary or secondary stage. It has been suggested that the curriculum at the secondary stage should be terminus as well as preparatory. In those States where the students go to technical education after Middle School Education or Junior High School Education, Mathematics is a compulsory subject upto Junior High School or Middle School standard.

Mathematics as a Compulsory Subject for Boys. Generally, Mathematics is taught as a compulsory subject for boys. Girls have the option to leave this subject after Junior High School Education or Middle School Education. Because Mathematics taught at higher secondary stage finds no application in their daily work. Knowledge of Mathematics or Arithmetic up to Junior High School is sufficient for household work which majority of girls in our country do in life and that is why it is considered sufficient for them to get education in Mathematics only upto Middle standard.

Mathematics as an Optional Subject in Higher Education. In higher education, Mathematics is not a compulsory subject. Only those students have to study Mathematics who have a desire to pursue some specialised vocation or profession. This is correct in the sense that everybody is not expected to apply Higher Mathematics in everyday life.

4.8 CRITICAL EXAMINATION OF MATHEMATICS SYLLABUS IN OUR COUNTRY (INDIA)

In Indian school, the present syllabus of the school Mathematics has been modified in the light of changes suggested by Kothari Commission, guidelines suggested by N.C.E.R.T.

The Commission has suggested that at the primary level, the courses in Arithmetic and Algebra be integrated and the emphasis be laid on the laws and principles of Mathematics and logical thinking. The syllabus should include the development of number system, systems of numeration and notation, equations, groups and functions. The Geometry course should be reorganised in a more rational manner.

At the high, and higher secondary level, the Mathematics syllabus which at present is divided in the traditional manner into Arithmetic, Geometry and Algebra. Trigonometry, Statistics, Calculus and Coordinate Geometry, need to be revitalised and brought up-to-date. The whole of Arithmetic course and also the basic operations in Algebra can be so arranged as to be completed by the end of primary stage. There is a considerable room for eliminating out-dated material from the syllabus like simplification, factorisation, H.C.F., L.C.M., etc. Trigonometry should be related to Algebra and then there will be no need to treat it as a separate subject. Much of the work on identities, solution of triangles, height and distances can be cut down. The emphasis on memorising of theorems and exercises in Geometry should be given up. The approach to the teaching of Geometry should be changed and for it an axiomatic and systematic treatment be adopted.

'Set' language may be used in designing the basic terms in Geometry, the difficult portions should be gradually taken up in the next grades. The latter is certainly a good arrangement. Topical arrangement needs that easy and difficult portions of a topic be dealt with at one stage only which is unpsychological.

4.9 PROBLEM-SOLVING IN MATHEMATICS

Mathematics is a subject which is full of problems. There is no topic which does not require solving of problems of different types. It is practice in solving problems which develops speed, accuracy and ability to apply mathematical facts in different solutions. Problem solving trains the pupils in attacking and solving problems. Training children to solve problems is the essence training them to meet and surmount difficulties for themselves.

With the increasing availability of battery-powered calculators and micro-computers in schools, the opportunities to teach problem solving, the essential aim of teaching of Mathematics are becoming vastly greater than ever before in the history of mathematical education. Whether these opportunities are being seized by teachers remains largely unknown. At the same time the growing needs of the industry for technologists, and of commerce for statisticians, have implications for the content of Mathematics courses in school.

Chapter—5

Methods of Teaching Mathematics

5.1 INTRODUCTION

For teacher of every subject method is important. **Method** is nothing but *a scientific way of presenting the subject, keeping in mind the psychological and physical requirements of the children.*

For effective learning of Mathematics the method has to be as good as the content. It is through method only that is possible to make a subject interesting and useful. Without a method, teaching would be hard. The arrangement of the subject and its presentation is very important for successful teaching.

Method of teaching Mathematics differs from stage to stage and from age group to age group. The method to be adopted depends upon many factors which include the environment and the familiar situations or experiences that are to be correlated effectively. While teaching a set of pupils with varying interests, aptitudes and attitudes one has got to be aware of the psychological basis of teaching-learning process.

The term 'method' can be thought of as the most effective and economic way of learning to take place among students. Communication of ideas and development of concepts in a precise manner based on a logical development of subject is the most important prerequisite in teaching a subject like Mathematics.

Generally, students are afraid of studying Mathematics. There are various reasons for this, method being one of them. Pupils tend to learn Mathematics through a meaningful approach to Mathematics rather than by a mechanical process.

Teaching is thus the most difficult task and every body is not fit to be a teacher. Some persons may have a 'flair' for teaching and such persons have the ability to awaken interest and arrest the attentions of the students. Some others who are not so fortunate can improve their teaching through practice if they are fully acquainted with various methods of Teaching. In order to make children learn effectively the teacher has to adopt the right method of Teaching. For choosing right method for a given situation, the teacher must be familiar with different methods of Teaching. In this chapter an effort will be made to discuss some common methods used for teaching of Mathematics.

5.2 VARIOUS METHODS OF TEACHING OF MATHEMATICS

Some of the important methods of teaching Mathematics are as under:

(*i*) Analytical and synthetic method.

(*ii*) Inductive and deductive method.

(*iii*) Lecture method.

(*iv*) Heuristic method.

(*v*) Psychological method.

(*vi*) Dogmatic method.

(*vii*) Laboratory method.

(*viii*) Problem-solving method.

(*ix*) Project method.

(*x*) Concentric method.

(*xi*) Topical method.

(*xii*) Some other methods.

These methods will now be taken up for discussion one by one.

(i) Inductive Method

Inductive method is based on the process of induction. It leads from concrete to abstract, particular to general and from examples to general rules. In this, we first take a few examples and them generalise. Thus it is a method of constructing a formula with the help of a sufficient number of concrete examples. **Induction** means to provide a universal truth by showing that if it is true for a particular case, it is true for all such cases. A formula or a generalisation is thus arrived at through a convincing process of reasoning and solving problems.

For example, if we wish to frame the formula $(a-b)^2 = a^2 - 2ab + b^2$. Let the students actually multiply $(a - b) \times (a - b)$ and find out the product. They may then be asked to find the answers for $(p - q)^2$, $(l - m)^2$ etc., by actual multiplication. After this they be asked to observe results and be helped to make generalisation to get the required formula.

Many other examples can be quoted in support of inductive method.

$$\text{Simple Interest} = \frac{\text{principal} \times \text{rate} \times \text{time}}{100}$$

$$\text{Average} = \frac{\text{Sum of terms}}{\text{Number of terms}}$$

Merits of Inductive Method

(*i*) It is psychological method and in this method the interest of the student is sustained till the end.

(*ii*) It helps in understanding because the students know how a particular formula has been framed.

(*iii*) It is a natural method of making discoveries. Majority of discoveries have been made inductively.

(*iv*) Since it is a logical method so it suits teaching of Mathematics.

(*v*) It encourages active participation of students and thus stimulates self effort on their part.

(*vi*) It discourages cramming and also reduces home work.

(*vii*) It does not burden the mind. Formula becomes easy to remember.

(*viii*) It is based on actual observation, thinking and experimentation.

(*ix*) This method is found to be suitable in the beginning stages. All teaching in Mathematics is inductive in the beginning.

(*x*) It helps in increasing the pupil-teacher contact.

Demerits of Inductive Method

(*i*) This method is limited in range and is not suitable for all topics. Certain complex and complicated formula can not be generalised in this manner.

(*ii*) It is time consuming and laborious method.

(*iii*) Inductive reasoning is not absolutely conclusive because the generalisation made with the help of a few specific examples may not hold good in all cases.

(*iv*) We don't complete the study of a topic simply by discovering a formula but a lot of supplementary work and practice is required for fixing the topic in learner's mind.

Application of Inductive Method

Its application has to be restricted and confined the understanding of rules in the early stages. This method is quite useful in lower classes where certain simple generalisation are to be made. At the advanced stage it is not so useful. This method is psychological and gives very good results if followed by **deductive method.**

(ii) Deductive Method

Deductive method is the opposite of the inductive method. It is based on deduction. In this method we proceed from general to particular and from abstract to concrete. In this method the rules are given at the very outset. The students are asked to apply these rules to solve more problems. In this method the formula is accepted by the students as pre-established and well established truth, e.g. the formula.

$$\text{Simple Interest} = \frac{\text{principal} \times \text{rate} \times \text{time}}{100}$$

can be used by the students to solve problems.

Merits of Deductive Method

(*i*) It is short and time saving method.

(*ii*) This method suits all types of students.

(*iii*) This method is suitable for all topics.

(*iv*) This method provides sufficient practice in the application of various mathematical formulae and rules.

(*v*) The speed and efficiency increases by use of this method.

(*vi*) It completes the process of induction. Probability in induction gets converted into certainty by this method.

Demerits of Deductive Method

(*i*) It is not a psychological method.

(*ii*) It encourages cramming.

(*iii*) It taxes the pupils' mind.

(*iv*) Students get disinterested as they are only passive listeners.

(*v*) It puts more empasis on memory.

(*vi*) It is not found quite suitable for the development of thinking, reasoning and discovery.

Place of Deductive Method

It is a method of work and practice. While applying deduction, great care should be exercised so that no wrong creeps in. This method works well with average students and teachers. This method provides skill, speed and efficiency in solving problems. Most teachers follow this method and even text books are written according to this method. However this method gives good results if it is preceded by inductive method.

Thus we find that **induction** and *deduction* are complementary so beginning should be made with the inductive method which should then be followed by a sufficient **drill work** by deductive method. This promotes speed, accuracy and command of the subject. So understand Mathematics inductively and apply deductively. Best results are given by induction-deduction combination.

(iii) Lecture Method

The 'lecture method' is otherwise known as 'the chalk and the talk method' where in verbal explanation is given for facts. It is not all a method to be used in Mathematics teaching. Yet it becomes appropriate under certain conditions such as:

(*i*) While introducing a new subject.

(*ii*) For explaining abstract concepts.

(*iii*) For giving demonstration.

(*iv*) For preparing pupils for practical works.

(*v*) For summing up and reviewing certain concepts.

(*vi*) For initiating a discussion.

Merits of Lecture Method

Lecture method commands certain merits. They are:

(*i*) It is less expensive.

(*ii*) It is time saving.

(*iii*) It is effective in providing information.

(*iv*) It is much inspiring.

(*v*) It is best tool for motivation.

(*vi*) It gives a sense of satisfaction to the students as well as the teacher. It gives them a feeling that they have learnt something.

Demerits of Lecture Method

Lecture method suffers from the following defects:

(*i*) It is teacher centred and not a student centred method.

(*ii*) It is oral and verbal.

(*iii*) It ignores the basic principle of learning by doing.

(*iv*) It does not develop scientific attitude and skill.

(*v*) There is no built in feed-back.

(*vi*) It does not fulfil the needs and abilities of the individual students.

(*vii*) In this method ideas follow each other very rapidly and so it is not easy for students to comprehend the chain of the ideas properly, if their attention is diverted a little and if they miss one idea, they may not understand the whole topic at all.

(*viii*) This method does not keep teacher in contact with the students. There is no room for individual attention.

(*ix*) In this method the experimental side is totally neglected by the teacher.

(*x*) It is a kind of spoon-feeding and several facilities of students such as observation, independent thinking etc., get a little or no opportunity to grow.

(*xi*) This method is not at all helpful for the teaching of Mathematics, where a good deal of figure work has to be done.

(*xii*) Students, due to insufficient preparation, lack of maturity and several psychological drawbacks, do not get very much benefit by this method.

(iv) Heuristic Method

This method involves finding out by the pupil, instead of merely telling of every thing by the teacher. This method demands complete self-activity or self-education on the part of the learner. By this method students' learn to reason for themselves.

The word 'Heuristic' has been derived from the Greek word "Heuresco" which means 'I find'. This method implies that the attitude of student shall be that of the discovers and not of passive recipients of knowledge.

This method was originally introduced by Armstrong for learning of sciences. This method exphasises experimentation. In this method the teacher becomes on looker and the child tries to move ahead independently without any help or guidance. This method makes the student self-reliant and independent. It imparts a sound training in the education of self. The teacher's job is not to solve problems for the pupil, but to enable the student to solve problems for himself. It aims at developing a scientific or

Heuristic attitude in the pupil. It aims at training in the method of learning self-confidence, originality, independence of judgment and thinking power are to be developed in the individual to make him an ever successful pupil. The teacher and the student should not feel discouraged by the slow progress made by using this method.

Pre-requisites or Requisites of the Heuristic Method

Heuristic method cannot be used without certain prerequisites. The teacher has to keep followings things in mind before using this method. The pre-requisites of this method are:

(*a*) The teacher should develop the heuristic attitude and make a lot of preparation for it.

(*b*) The question should be so planned that it may be possible for the students to find the solution independently by proceeding in the proper direction. It is required because in this method the pupil is not told anything but he is led to see the solution through carefully planned and well-directed questions.

(*c*) This method is not suitable for the beginners because in the early stages, students need a good deal of guidance. This guidance should be planned in a scientific way.

(*d*) This method requires a lot of planning. Several precautions have to be observed so that thing may be planned properly and the lesson may be effective.

(*e*) The teacher and the student should not be discouraged by the slow progress that is made in this method. This method proceeds very slowly and the progress is not very marked.

(*f*) The teacher should realise his responsibility properly. He should know that in Heuristic method, the students are not to be left alone without any support. Their difficulty should be properly solved and they should be given a proper guidance.

Procedure

There are no definite steps to be followed in this method. The teacher gives a problem to the students, creates a learning situation and asks the pupil to solve the problem with their own efforts. The teacher puts thought-provoking questions and stimulates pupil effort.

Merits of Heuristic Method

(*i*) This method makes the students active participants in the process of learning and allows them to have independent thinking.

(*ii*) He learns by doing so there is a little scope of forgetting.

(*iii*) It is a psychologically sound method as the student learns by self-practice.

(*iv*) It inculcates in the students the interest for the subject and also develops willingness in them.

(*v*) It gives the students a sense of confidence and achievement.

(*vi*) It develops the powers of original thinking and reasoning in the pupil thus it develops scientific attitude.

(*vii*) The teacher is in contact with the whole of the class and there is very little of home-work for the students.

(*viii*) It promotes self-discipline in the students as they feel responsible for their work.

(*ix*) The students acquire command of the subject. He has a clear understanding and notion of the subject.

Demerits of Heuristic Method

Some of the demerits of this method are as under:

(*i*) This method is un-suitable for certain types of students, because all the students cannot become independent thinkers. Discovery of a thing needs hard work, patience, concentration, reasoning and thinking powers and creative abilities.

(*ii*) This method suits only hardworking and original thinking teachers. An average teacher cannot frame true heuristic questions and stimulate pupils' thinking.

(*iii*) This method does not suit larger classes. If the number of students is larger, individual attention by the teacher becomes impossible.

(*iv*) The method is slow. The student has to spend a lot of time to find out minor results. The teacher may find it difficult to finish the syllabus in time.

(*v*) It is not desirable to discover everything. Mathematics is a vast subject. There are so many things that have to be accepted as such. Moreover, the things discovered once, need not be rediscovered again and again.

(*vi*) The success of method depends upon well-equipped libraries, laboratories, and good text-books written on heuristic lines but such facilities are lacking in our schools.

(*vii*) The results found out by the student may not be correct. In the absence of individual checking, all the mistakes may not be rectified.

(*viii*) If the teacher is not able to distinguish between false and true heuristic questions, he may do more harm than good.

Conclusion

The success of this method depends upon a number of factors which may be mentioned below:

(*i*) The teacher must cultivate heuristic spirit in himself. This will require hard work on the part of the teacher.

(*ii*) The questions should be well thought of and these should be of true Heuristic type and the questions should not be leading ones, e.g. it would be wrong to ask a question like do you remember that the area of rectangle is equal to the product of length and breadth, rather the question be frame like, how to calculate the area of a rectangle.

(*iii*) The work to be carried out by a student should be in accordance with his level and ability.

(*iv*) Teacher should provide only the minimum and necessary guidance.

(*v*) The teacher should plan his lesson in such a way that copying from the text-books is not possible.

(*vi*) This method must be supplemented by other methods of teaching. Facts may not always be discovered.

(v) Psychological Method

In this method more emphasis is put on the psychology of the student. There aptitudes and facilities are kept in mind while teaching them the subject-matter. This method attaches a little importance to the teaching of subject-matter and lays more stress on the development of psychology and facilities of the child. Thus it is a more scientific and so a useful method of teaching.

This method makes the teaching of subject-matter interesting because here the faculties of the students and their psycho-physical requirements are kept in mind. While using this method following precautions be observed:

(*i*) The teacher should exercise certain limits and restrictions.

(*ii*) It should not be used in such a way that it leads to a total loss of the purpose of teaching and its only aim becomes the teaching method.

(*iii*) It should be used only as means and not as an end.

(iv) Dogmatic Method of the Teaching of Mathematics

Dogmatic method has a bearing on the attitude of the teacher as well as the mode of the presentation of the subject-matter. In this method, teaching of Mathematics is carried out by rigorous. Students are made to practise things rigorously. Believers in this method are of the view that once the rigour is given up, the purpose of the entire method is defeated. In this method, the pupil required to memorize formulae and cram up the rules and definitions.

Advantages or Merits of the Dogmatic Method

(*i*) This method saves time, energy and does not allow students to get involved in unnecessary thinking.

(*ii*) It gives exercise to memory and thus helps its growth. Moreover, rigour is quite useful for the development of the mathematical aptitude of the students.

Disadvantages or Demerits of the Dogmatic Method

(i) This method is unscientific and unpsychological.

(ii) This method kills the insitiative in the students and makes them a memoring machine.

(iii) This method is unpsychological, since it puts more stress on the subject-matter are not on the students who are to be taught.

(iv) The main object of teaching is to develop certain qualities in the students. The method fails to achieve that object and so it is not of much use in practical life.

(v) If this method is applied and the students forget the rules they cannot solve a problem.

(vi) The method provides only information and does not allow students to do things independently.

(vii) The method makes the teaching uninteresting and dull and converts the whole atmosphere of the class into a mechanical atmosphere.

(viii) Through this method, only students with a good memory can make progress. Such of the students who do not have a very strong memory shall not be able to use this method properly as they would not cram up the rules and memorize the problems.

Importance of this Method

In spite of all the drawbacks, this method cannot be condemned wholly. It has its own utility, but at a proper stage. Given proper circumstances and situations this method can help the teacher to cover a good deal of syllabus in a short time.

(vii) Laboratory Method

This is a method that is used in teaching almost all the science subjects. In this method the students are required to do some experiments and practical work and verify certain mathematical truths. In this method an attempt is made to stimulate the activities of the students and to encourage them to make discoveries. Here we proceed from concrete to abstract. In the words of J.W.A. Young, "The laboratory method aims to arouse teachers to a belief, not only theoretical but practical and effective as well, that mathematical dishes must be made appetizing and palatable. They are to be accepted with pleasure and digested with ease." In a sense, it is only experimental portion of inductive method or heuristic method in the practical form. Students not only listen certain information but also do something practically. It shall be wise if this method is used as a complementary part of lecture method. Really, speaking this method has the elements of lecture method as also of Heuristic method in it.

Pre-Requisites for Success of Method

The success of the method depends upon a well-equipped Mathematics laboratory which should be equipped with mathematical instruments and other teaching aids. It should have geometrical instruments, mathematical models of geometrical solids such as cuboid, sphere, cube, prism etc. It should also have charts, balance, weights, pendulum, pulley, lever, wedge, screen, angle mirror, dividers, calculating machines etc. Various items of apparatus, instruments and teaching aids be properly arranged and organised. Such an arrangement is essential for employing the laboratory method, of teaching of Mathematics, successfully.

Illustration of the Method

Following examples illustrate the method:

Example 1. To find the ratio between the circumference and diameter of a circle.

The students may be given a number of circular discs of different diameters, say 5 cm, 2.5 cm, 10 cm, 20 cm etc.

Let them measure the circumference and diameter of each disc using a measuring tape.

Let them find the ratio of circumference to the diameter. They will find that in each case, the ratio comes out to be same about 22/7 or 3.14159.

Example 2. Area of Circle. A circular disc may be cut into 8 equal parts. The 8th part may further be split into two. The student may adjust these parts as under:

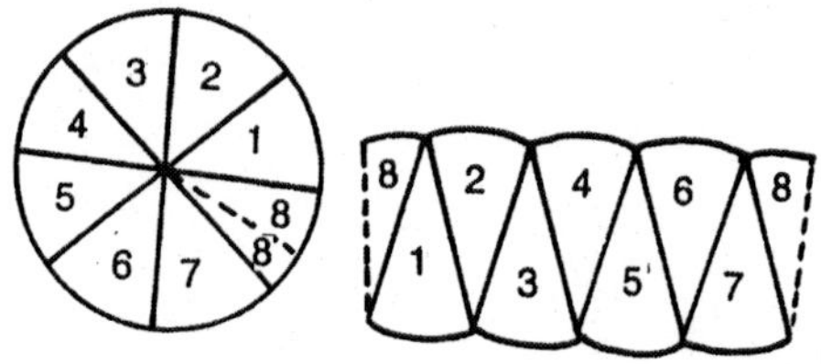

Then the students will be made to understand that if the parts of the circle are increased indefinitely, and adjusted, the figure will be reduced to a rectangle. So

$$\begin{aligned}\text{Area of the Circle} &= \text{Area of the rectangle so formed}\\ &= \text{Its length} \times \text{breadth}\\ &= \frac{1}{2}(\text{circumference}) \times \text{radius}\\ &= \frac{1}{2}.2\pi r.r\\ &= \pi r^2\end{aligned}$$

Example 3. Area of Rectangle. The students will be asked to draw a number of rectangles of dimensions, say 6 cm × 3 cm, 4 cm × 2 cm, 4 cm × 4 cm etc. Let them divide each rectangle into unit squares as shown.

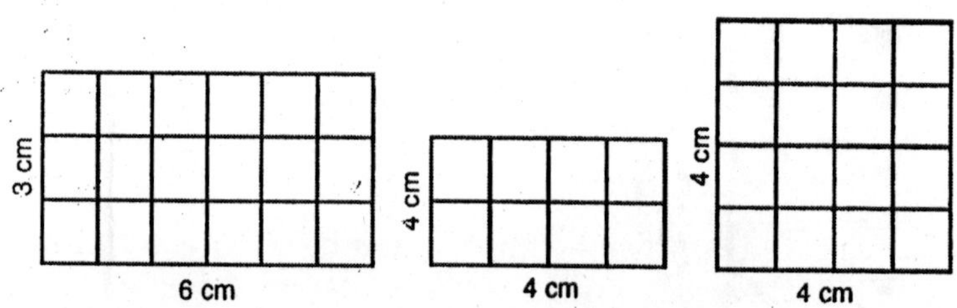

Let them count the number of unit squares in each rectangle. This will lead then to the conclusion that

Area of rectangle = length × breadth

Merits of the Laboratory Method

This method has following merits:

(*i*) This method is psychologically more sound as in it we proceed from known to unknown.

(*ii*) This method is based on the principle of learning by doing.

(*iii*) It is in accordance with the nature of children who are active by nature. They have a liking to observe, to handle and to work with concrete material.

(*iv*) This method helps in making clear certain fundamental concepts, ideas etc. to the student.

(*v*) It is a scientific method and helps to develop in the pupil a habit of accepting results only after verification. It develops in the child a habit of scientific enquiry and investigation.

(*vi*) In this method the rules of Mathematics are given in a practical form. Students get an opportunity to apply the mathematical principles in practical and actual life.

(*vii*) The things learnt experimentally can be used by the pupil in many situations.

(*viii*) This method suits the average and below average students and to such student who can not understand things at the abstract level.

(*ix*) In this method there is a close relationship between the teacher and the taught because the teacher is required to supervise the work of all pupils.

(*x*) It develops in students the self-confidence and teaches them the dignity of labour. It also makes them self-reliant.

(*xi*) This method develops group feeling amongst the students as they get opportunities of working in groups.

(*xii*) In this method the students get an opportunity to establish correlation of one subject with other allied subjects. While learning Mathematics through this method, the students also come to learn about physics, chemistry and other sciences.

Demerits of Laboratory Method

Inspite of so many advantages this method also have certain demerits. Some of these are as under:

(*i*) It is a complicated method that requires a lot of planing and organisation. If it is not done, the purpose shall be defeated.

(*ii*) It is not a teaching method for Mathematics unless preparation for it is made, because through experiments, it is not possible to find out mathematical fact easily and quickly.

(*iii*) Through this method it is not possible to make progress quickly. The results are sometimes discouraging to the students as well as to the teacher.

(*iv*) This method has very little of theoretical part in it. Due to this drawback, sometimes it becomes difficult for the students to know about the reasoning part of the Mathematics which is the real pleasure-giving aspect of this subject-matter.

(*v*) Development of the power of reasoning is one of the objects of teaching Mathematics. Through this method, it is difficult to develop this particular power.

(*vi*) This method is suitable only for certain topics.

(*vii*) This method is not useful for large classes.

(*viii*) This method requires well equipped Mathematics laboratory which is not generally available in most of the schools.

(*ix*) Text-books in use do not indicate the practical work that can be done by the students.

(*x*) In higher classes this method is not suitable. In these classes students are expected to grasp abstract ideas and concepts.

(*xi*) This method tends to become an end in itself, rather than a means to an end. The students may remain at the concept stage only and never proceed to the abstract stage which is the ultimate goal of Mathematics.

Application

This method can be used only as a complementary method to complement lecture method. The method should be applied in lower classes where we have to make clear certain mathematical concepts and ideas. When the students begin to understand at abstract level this method should be dispensed with.

(viii) Problem-Solving Method

This method generally referred to as **Problem Method** consists in training the pupils to solve problems. This method is based upon the process of finding out the results by attacking a problem in a number of definite steps. In this method the student is involved in finding out the answer to a given problem and thus actually it is a discovery method. In the words of Yoakan and Simpson, "a problem occurs in a situation in which a felt-difficulty to act is realised. It is a difficulty that is clearly present and recognised by the thinker. It may be purely mental difficulty or it may be physical and involve the manipulation of data. The distinguishing thing about a problem however, is that it impresses the individual who meets it as needing a solution."

Procedure

The method proceeds in various steps discussed in the following lines:

1. **Recognising the problem**. First of all, we sense the presence of a problem and then identify the problem.

2. **Defining the problem**. The problem is then defined very precisely and accurately.

3. **Collecting relevant data**. Then all sorts of relevant data, which can be helpful in solving the problem, and collected and arranged in proper order.
4. **Organising the data**. The data is then organised in such a way that it can lead to the solution of the problem.
5. **Formulating the tentative solution**. On the basis of the organised data, the student formulates tentative solutions of the problem.
6. **Arriving at the correct solution**. Out of the tentative solutions a correct solution is found out by a process of reasoning.
7. **Verifying the results**. In Mathematics, we do not accept a conclusion without proper verification. The students are required to verify the conclusion by reversing the process of reasoning.

To illustrate the method let us assume the problem as the one of finding the area of four walls of a room. In this, we recall the previous knowledge about area of rectangle because the total area is equal to the sum of area of four rectangular walls. This can be verified by actual calculations and the formula so derived may be used in future.

Merits of Problem-Solving Method

(*i*) It prepares the students in problem-solving. This training in solving-problems is quite useful in solving problems in actual life.

(*ii*) It stimulates, thinking, reasoning and imagination of the students.

(*iii*) It develops, a habit of doing work independently, in the students.

(*iv*) This method of teaching is quite suitable for Mathematics as Mathematics is full of problems.

(*v*) It stimulates intellectual curiosity and motivates the students to exert further.

(*vi*) In this method there is ample scope for individual work as a student is free to solve as many problems as he likes.

(*vii*) It develops in the student a habit of self study.

(*viii*) While learning by this method the student learn by doing and so the information is retained by him for a longer period of time.

(*ix*) There is a close teacher-pupil contact.

(*x*) It develops qualities such a patience, cooperation, self-confidence etc.

(*xi*) It provides to students a training in technique of information processing.

(*xii*) It helps to develop intellectual honesty in students.

(*xiii*) In helps the students to learn relationship pattern among things and variables.

(*xiv*) It provides the students a training in the methods and skills of discovering new knowledge in Mathematics.

Demerits of the Problem-Solving Method

(*i*) It is a long drawn out and time consuming method.

(*ii*) It is not suitable for all topics in Mathematics.

(*iii*) This method is suitable only for bright and creative students.

(*iv*) This method is not suitable for students in lower classes.

(*v*) This method requires special preparation on the part of the teacher. An average teacher may find it difficult to adopt this method.

(*vi*) The content of Mathematics can not be organised according to requirements of this method.

(*vii*) Suitable text-books for use of this method are not available.

Application

This method trains the pupils in problem-solving. They learn to sense, analyse, reflect, organise and solve the problems. It helps us at every step in our teaching-learning process. The teacher should carefully select the problems which are real and have definite educational values. The teacher should also prepare himself well for the success of the problem-solving method.

(ix) Project Method

This method was given by Dewey—the American philosopher, psychologist and practical teacher. The project method is a direct outcome of his philosophy. According to Dr. Kilpatrick, "A project is a unit of whole hearted purposeful activity carried on preferably, in its natural setting". According to Stevenson, "A project is a problematic act carried to its completion in its natural setting". According to Ballard, "A project is a bit of real life that has been incorporated into the school".

The project method is not totally new. Project equivalents are advocated for the adolescent period by Rousseau in Emile (BK-III). A project plan is modified form of an old method called "concentration-of-studies". The main features of "concentration-of-studies plan" is that some subject is taken as the core or centre and all other school subjects as they arise are studied in connection with it.

Project method is based on the following principles:

(*i*) Learning by doing.

(*ii*) Learning by living.

(*iii*) Children learn better through association, cooperation and activity.

In this method, a project is taken, which is then completed in a natural and social setting. As the project is carried to completion, the students learn so many things.

Procedure

Project method generally involves the following steps:

(*i*) **Providing a situation.** The teacher provides a situation wherein the students feel like working on certain projects.

(*ii*) **Choosing.** Then the pupils are helped to choose a project linked to their need.

(*iii*) **Planning.** Pupils then discuss how that project is to be executed? Steps of the procedure are planned and noted down.

(*iv*) **Executing.** The project is then executed as planned. Every body contributes his share of work.

(*v*) **Evaluating.** The project is then evaluated and the possible knowledge is reviewed.

(*vi*) **Recording.** The knowledge gained is then recorded for future reference.

The following examples Illustrate the Method:

Example: Problem. *Opening a Cooperative Store:*

While opening and managing the store the pupils learn the elements of shopping such as buying, selling, weighing, measuring and preparing bills, preparing budgets, different ways of saving leading to the learning of topics like simple interest, stocks and shares insurance etc.

Example: Problem. *Celebration of Republic Day*:

In addition to the knowledge of other subjects, the students may learn the following facts of Mathematics:

(*i*) Calculating the estimated expenditure.

(*ii*) Tapping various resources of expenditure.

(*iii*) Make the adjustments in expenditure while preparing the budget.

(*iv*) Keeping an account of receipts and expenses.

(*v*) Making purchases.

Merits of Project Method

(*i*) It arouses interest of the pupils.

(*ii*) It provides knowledge in the integrated form.

(*iii*) The facts learnt are easily remembered.

(*iv*) There is an opportunity for mutual exchange of views.

(*v*) In this method the student is free to work according to his capacity.

(*vi*) It reaches the student the dignity of labour.

(*vii*) It helps in developing self-confidence and self-discipline in the student.

(*viii*) The project is not forced on the student rather it is chosen by him so they are motivated to learn.

Demerits of the Project Method

(*i*) It provides the knowledge of Mathematics in a very haphazard way but since Mathematics is a sequence subject so its teaching must be systematic. Thus this method is not quite suitable for teaching of Mathematics.

(*ii*) It does not provide the necessary drill work which is essential to have mastery of the topic.

(*iii*) It does not suit the fixed curriculum.

(*iv*) It is quite lengthy, time consuming and expensive method.

(*v*) In this method there is a chance that some students may shirk work.

(*vi*) Since each student has to perform certain specified duties for the completion of the project, the learning will not be uniform.

Place of Project Method in Mathematics

This method is not suitable for teaching of Mathematics and so must not be used as a regular method of teaching. The subject is learnt only incidently and there is no sufficient drill work which is essential for mastery of a topic in Mathematics. Mathematics being a sequence subject can not be taught by this method. Moreover, it is not possible to cover all the topics through this method.

However, the projects are useful to arouse interest, to encourage initiative and to provide a sense of achievement to the students. These integrate the knowledge of Mathematics with other subjects. These also provide real life situations to apply the learnt facts of Mathematics.

Some small projects can be occasionally undertaken to provide necessary supplements to regular teaching. Costly projects should be avoided. The teacher should select certain projects which can be undertaken in the school, without upsetting regular teaching of the subject.

(x) Concentric Method

This is a system of organising a course rather than a method of teaching. It is therefore better to call it *concentric system or approach*. It implies widening of knowledge just as concentric circles go on extending and widening. It is a system of arrangement of subject-matter. In this method the study of the topic is spread over a number of years. It is based on the principle that subject cannot be given an exhaustive treatment at the first stage. To begin with, a simple presentation of the subject is given and further knowledge is imparted in following years. Thus beginning from a nucleus the circles of knowledge go on widening year after year and hence the name concentric method.

Procedure

A topic is divided into a number of portions which are then allotted to different classes. The criterion for allotment of a particular portion of the course to a particular class are the difficulty of portion and power of comprehension of students in that age group. Thus it is mainly concerned with year to year teaching but its influence can also be exercised in day-to-day teaching. Knowledge being given today should follow from knowledge given yesterday and should lead to teaching on following day.

Merits of Concentric Method

(*i*) This method of organisation of subject-matter is decidely superior to that in which one topic is taken up in particular class and an effort is made to deal with all aspects of the topic in that particular class.

(*ii*) It provides a frame work from science course which is of real value to students.

(*iii*) The system is most successful when the teaching is in hands of one teacher because then he can preserve continuity in the teaching and keeps his expanding circle concentric.

(*iv*) It provides opportunity for revision of work already covered in a previous class and carrying out new work.

(*v*) It enables the teacher to cover a portion according to receptivity of learner.

(*vi*) Since the same topic is learnt over many years so its impressions are more lasting.

(*vii*) It does not allow teaching to become dull because every year a new interest can be given to the topic. Every year there are new problems to solve and new difficulties to overcome.

Drawbacks

For the success of this approach we require really capable teacher. If a teacher becomes over ambitions and exhausts all the possible interesting illustrations in the introductory year then the subject loses its power of freshness and appeal and nothing is left to create interest in the topic in subsequent years.

In case the topic is too short or too long then also the method is not found to be useful. A too long portion makes the topic dull and a too short portion fails to leave any permanent and lasting impression on the mind of the pupil.

Conclusion

It is a good method for being adopted for arranging the subject-matter. It should be kept in mind, by the organisers, while organising the subject-matter that no portion is too long or too short. It would also be much useful if the teacher teaches the same class year after year so that he can reserve some illustrative examples for each year and thus can maintain the interest of the students in the topics.

(xi) Topical Method

In this method a particular topic is started in a particular class and finished over there, however, this method has failed to get approval from a majority of education thinkers. In their opinion if this method is used, many irrelevant things may creep in and many relevant things may be left out. The students may be forced to study such things which are of no immediate importance to them. Moreover, if this method is adopted only a few topics will find a place in any particular class, because all types of problems on that topics shall have to be solved by the students in one class. In the opinion of such Educationist the **Spiral Method** of organisation of curriculum is preferable. In the Spiral Method a topic is divided into a number of small independent units to be dealt with different classes that suit the mental capacities of the pupils. In their opinion such a method is more natural and less tiring to the students. To support it they argue that in such a method student loses nothing in accuracy and gains a lot in power of application of the general rules to particular problems.

The criterion of difficulty lays more emphasis on the fact that topics should be arranged in order of difficulty. But to take the topic as a unit is not a good arrangement. Topical arrangement is based on the unity of the topic i.e. exhaustion of the topic at the same time or at a stretch. However, it is unnatural and also impracticable to take a topic and exhaust all its possible portions and problems, simple as also complex, in the same class. For a good arrangement the following be kept in view:

(*i*) Every topic should be divided into parts.

(*ii*) These parts should be graded according to difficulty.

(*iii*) Each part should be introduced at a proper stage.

These different portions be allotted to be taught in different classes according to their difficulty and maturity of minds of pupils. Such an approach is called a **Spiral Approach**.

A portion is introduced when a sufficient back ground has been prepared for it. The remaining more tedious portions are left, for being taken up later on. Every thing is taken up at its proper stage and there is enough opportunity for revision. The precaution to be observed is that the portion should neither be too long not too short.

Presently "Topical Method" is more a system of arrangement of subject-matter than a method of teaching. The topic is to be taught at a stretch, without a break or gap, continues teaching of topic not only will save the students from divided attention and will also ensure their full and whole hearted concentration on the topic in hand. Thus a natural link will exist in the day-to-day work in the class room.

(xii) Some Other Methods

Some other methods used in teaching of Mathematics are:

(*a*) Genetic Method.

(*b*) Play way Method.

(*c*) Montessori Method.

(*d*) Text-book Method.

The out lines of all these methods are given here:—

Genetic Method. This method is nothing but an improved form of Heuristic Method. In this method attempt is made to retain the spirit of the Heuristic Method and do away with its limitations. Here the whole class is treated as a co-operating group rather than as a separate individual. This method is also a combination of several procedures that include questioning, providing information, explaining, guiding etc.

Play Way Method. It is a method where teaching is carried out in play. While teaching Mathematics, several games and plays are restored to. This method may be useful for the teaching of Mathematics, because it would facilitate the learning.

Montessori Method. Montessori Method is a well-known method on which certain apparatuses are applied for the teaching of the subject-matter. This method has also been applied for the teaching of Mathematics to the students of younger age-group. This method is not useful for the students of the grown-up-age.

Text-book Method. It is a method in which Mathematics is taught with the help of text-books. It is not a fit method for teaching of Mathematics. Here students cannot be asked to read books or learn the doing of sums. In the teaching of Mathematics text-books serve only as aids for providing standard sums and problems.

(xiii) Analytical Method

In this method we proceed from known to unknown. The word 'Analytic' is derived from the word 'Analysis' which means to break up or to resolve a thing into its constituent elements. Thus in this method we break up the unknown problem into simpler parts and then see how these can be recombined to find the solution. Therefore it is the process of unfolding of the problem or of conducting its operation to know its hidden aspects. In this process we start with what is to be found out and then think of further steps or possibilities that may connect the unknown with the known and find out the desired result. It is believed that all the highest intellectual performance of the mind is analysis.

This method can be illustrated by following examples:

Example 1. x is true if y is true

y is true if z is true.

But z is true if x is true.

Example 2. Prove that the diagonals of a parallelogram bisect each other.

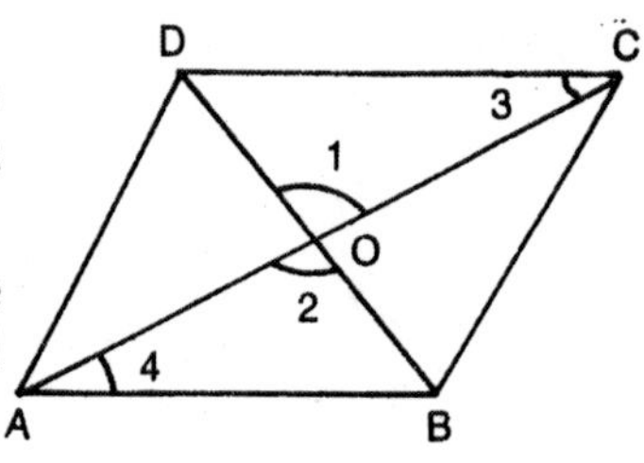

To prove it analyticaly, we will start with question and answers as follows:

What is given?

A parallelogram ABCD, the diagonals AC and BD intersect at O.

What is to be proved?

The diagonals AC and BD bisect each other.

To prove the above which parts of the given figure are to be proved equal?

We should prove $OA = OC$

and $OB = OD$

How can we prove that $OA = OC$?

How can we prove that $OB = OD$?

OA and OC will be equal if they are the corresponding sides of two congruent triangles.

Similarly OB and OD will be equal if they are the corresponding sides of two congruent triangles.

Thus we have to prove that triangles AOB and COD are congruent.

Are there any equal elements in these triangles?

Yes, $\angle 1 = \angle 2$ (vertically opposite angles)

$\angle 3 = \angle 4$ (corresponding angles)

AB = CD (Sides of a $||$gm)

Thus Δ AOB = Δ COD

or AO = OC, OB = OD

Thus, diagonals bisect each other.

Example 3. If $\frac{x}{y} = \frac{p}{q}$, prove that

$$\frac{xp + 2y^2}{yp} = \frac{p^2 + 2ya}{pq}$$

Now $\frac{xp + 2y^2}{yp} = \frac{p^2 + 2ya}{pq}$ is true

if $$\frac{xp}{yp} + \frac{2y^2}{yp} = \frac{p^2}{pq} + \frac{2yq}{pq}$$

if $$\frac{x}{y} + \frac{2y}{p} = \frac{p}{q} + \frac{2y}{p}$$

if $$\frac{x}{y} = \frac{p}{q}$$

but this is true, hence proved

Merits of Analytical Method

(*i*) It helps in developing reasoning power of the students.

(*ii*) It helps in a clear understanding of the subject because the students have to go through the whole process themselves.

(*iii*) In this method students participation is encouraged.

(*iv*) It is a psychological method.

(*v*) No craming is required in this method.

(*vi*) This method has little rather no scope for forgetting.

(*vii*) Teaching by this method, teacher carries the class with him.

(*viii*) It helps in developing spirit of discovery amongst the students.

(*ix*) It develops self-confidence in the pupil.

Demerits of Analytical Method

(*i*) It is a time consuming and lengthy method, so it is uneconomical.

(*ii*) In this method facts are not presented in a neat and systematic order.

(*iii*) This method is not suitable for all the topics in Mathematics.

(*iv*) This method does not find favour with all the students because below average students fail to follow this method.

Applicability

In Mathematics teaching this method is suitable for complicated problems. It analyses the problem into sub-parts and various parts are reorganised and the already learnt facts are used to connect the known with unknown. This method is particularly suitable for teaching of Arithmetic, Algebra and Geometry. It puts more stress on reasoning and development of power of reasoning is one of the major aims of teaching of Mathematics.

(xiv) Synthetic Method

In this method we proceed from known to unknown. Actually synthesis is the complement to analysis. The word 'Synthetic' is derived from the word 'synthesis' which means to combine together. In this method we combine together a number of facts, perform certain mathematical operations and arrive at the solution. In this method we start with the known data and connect it with the unknown part. It is the process of putting together known bits of information to reach the point where unknown information becomes obvious and true. Thus in this method we proceed from hypothesis to conclusion.

Following examples illustrate the method:

Example 1. A is true because B and C are equal to A.

$\therefore$ B is true; and $\therefore$ C is true.

Example 2. If $\frac{a}{b} = \frac{c}{b}$, prove that $\frac{a+b}{a-b} = \frac{c+d}{c-d}$

Let $\frac{a}{b} = \frac{c}{b}$ = k (why?)

Then $a = bk$, $c = dk$

Now $$\frac{a+b}{a-b} = \frac{bk+b}{bk-b} = \frac{k+1}{k-1} \quad \text{...(i)}$$

and $$\frac{c+d}{c-d} = \frac{dk+d}{dk-d} = \frac{k+1}{k-1} \quad \text{...(ii)}$$

Since (i) and (ii) are equal, thus

$\frac{a+b}{a-b} = \frac{c+d}{c-d}$ (Proved).

Example 3. Prove that: The Median to the base of an isosceles triangle is $\perp$ to base.

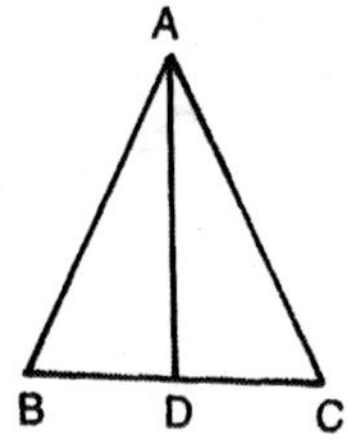

Given: An isosceles triangle ABC in which AB = AC

AD is median to BC

Such that BD = DC

To prove: AD ⊥ BC

Proof: In Δ ABD and ACD

We have, AB = AC (given)

AD = AD (common)

BD = DC (given)

Hence Δ ADB = Δ ADC

∴ ∠ ADB = ∠ ADC

But these are supplementary angles so each is equal to 90°.

Hence AD ⊥ BC.

Merits of Synthetic Method

(*i*) It saves time and labour.

(*ii*) It is a neat method in which we present that facts in a systematic way.

(*iii*) It suits majority of students.

(*iv*) It can be applied to major·ty of topics in teaching of Mathematics.

Demerits of Synthetic Method

(*i*) It makes the students passive listners and encourages cramming.

(*ii*) While teaching by this method, teacher does not carry the class with him.

(*iii*) This is an unpsychological method.

(*iv*) In this method there is a scope for forgetting.

(*v*) In this method, confidence is generally lacking in the students.

Application

This method suits the average teacher and the average student. It is a time saving and neat method so teachers usually prefer this method. However, if it follows the analytical method then it gives the best results.

Combination of Analytical and Synthetic Method

Analytical and synthetic methods are inter-dependent or complementary. One is incomplete without the other. Analytical method is a logical way to develop a solution as it accounts for each and every step. But if we follow only analytical method we fail to present the facts in a systematic way.

The analytical proof is lengthy but it is based on a sound footing and if forgetting it would be much easier for the pupil to recall and reconstruct the proof for himself.

In synthetic method we proceed from known to unknown and it is a neat and concise method. The synthetic proof is shorter but it has no sound footing. Once forgotten it can not be reconstructed. Synthetic method shows that every step is true but does not reveal the process adopted and the reason for selecting a particular sequence for reasoning.

Therefore to make the teaching effective both the methods should be applied together. The students should be encouraged through Analytical Method to cooperate with the teacher and then teacher may use Synthetic Method to provide knowledge, Synthetic Method helps the student to learn the subject-matter. If we use a combination of both the method the teaching becomes interesting as well as complete. We quote here the words of Arthur Schultze to justify it, "Analysis is the method of discovery, Synthesis is the method of concise and elegant presentation."

Chapter—6

Techniques of Teaching

6.1 INTRODUCTION

There are many a techniques which can be effectively used for the teaching of Mathematics. Some of these are oral work, home work, assignments, self study, group work, review and supervised study etc.

In this chapter an attempt will be made to discuss these techniques of teaching.

6.2 ORAL WORK

Oral work is done orally (mentally) without the help of pen and paper. Oral work occupies a special place in life and in Mathematics. Mathematics is science of figures and written work. Major part of Mathematics has to be covered in written form, but its application lies in oral form. If the principle of Mathematics can be discussed orally it is more helpful. The importance of oral work in Mathematics is discussed below:

Importance of Oral Work in Teaching of Mathematics

In teaching of Mathematics oral work plays an important part. Oral work keeps the mind alert, oral work also helps in the development of the habit of accuracy and speed. Oral Mathematics saves a lot of time and cuts short the process that would have to be done unnecessarily in written Mathematics.

The importance of oral work in Mathematics may be summarised as under:

(*i*) It trains the pupils in solving day-to-day problem of life. Oral calculation have to be done in life at many a occasions because we are not expected to carry pen and paper all the times with us.

(*ii*) It develops mental alertness and quick thinking.

(*iii*) It develops speed in solving problems.

(*iv*) It has been found to be an effective way to introduce a lesson. Previous knowledge of the student can be tested orally.

(*v*) Oral questions help in making a lesson easily comprehensible and clear.

(*vi*) Oral questions, are helpful in developing a lesson. It ensures brisk style and is stimulating for the students.

(*vii*) Oral questions provide a convenient way to test the comprehension of the students.

(*viii*) It helps the quicken wits and sharpen intelligence.

(*ix*) It brings variety in the monotonous process of teaching of Mathematics.

(*x*) It helps in learning the written work in Mathematics. Once a student has become well at oral Mathematics, he enters the field of written Mathematics with confidence and is likely to succeed in that field.

(*xi*) It helps in diagnosing the difficulties or doubts of individual students.

(*xii*) It helps in maintenance of discipline in the class.

(*xiii*) Since it appeals to the eyes, and ear so it is likely by the pupils.

From the above discussion it becomes clear that oral work occupies an important place in teaching of Mathematics. All new facts can be fixed in student's mind orally. Oral mastery of every new idea must be the first concern of every Mathematics teacher. Every new concept must be given a sufficient oral drill.

However oral work has its limitations too. Some of the demerits of oral work are as under:

(*i*) It develops a hasty attitude in the students.

(*ii*) It gives an unsystematic and haphazard out look. In written Mathematics work has to be done systematically step by step but in oral Mathematics no such thing is required. The students are left free to arrive at the results. If not handled properly such a thing is likely to develop a haphazard and unsystematic out look in the pupils.

(*iii*) In oral Mathematics there is likelihood of inaccuracy. If oral Mathematics is not conducted properly the mistakes are likely to be caused because of the speed and haste and lack of any systematic work.

(*iv*) *Waste of Time and Energy*. If the work in oral Mathematics is not conducted properly, it is likely to cause mistake which accompany the haste and so it would be a waste of time and energy.

Precautions to be Observed in Regard to Oral Mathematics

After going through the merits and demerits of oral Mathematics, we list the precautions which should be observed in the use of oral Mathematics. Without these precautions, the demerits and dis-advantages are likely to have sway:

(1) **Oral Work be based on the Previous Knowledge of the Students.** As far as possible, the oral Mathematics should be based on the previous

knowledge of the students. Unless it is done, it is not likely to yield proper results.

(2) **Oral Work be used as a Means of Revision and Test.** As far as possible, oral Mathematics should be used only as a means of revision and testing the knowledge imparted.

(3) **Proper Gradation of the Oral Work.** Oral Mathematics should be properly graded. It should start from simple to complex. While doing this gradation, the psychophysical needs of the students must be kept in mind.

(4) The Mathematics teacher while using oral Mathematics, should try to create an atmosphere that is conducive for sharp mental working. It should not be done in an atmosphere that is full of dullness and melancholy.

(5) As far as possible this method should not be used in fractional and decimal work and such other works.

(6) The teacher should not reach to any conclusion about students on the basis of the oral Mathematics. He should try to give some practice of this form of Mathematics every day in the class.

Question to be used in Oral Mathematics. The questions that may be used in oral Mathematics should be such as to fulfil one or more of the following objectives:

(1) They should help recall of the past knowledge.

(2) They should help in comparison of the present with some other aspect of knowledge.

(3) They should show contrast with certain other things.

(4) They should explain the cause and effect.

(5) They should be helpful in evaluation of certain things or illustration of certain points.

(6) They should help in classification and definition of figures and other subject-material.

(7) They should help in proof and plan of the subject-matter.

(8) They should help in analysis and synthesis of the subject-matter and problems.

Though oral work in Mathematics is very important but all the work cannot be done orally. There are certain steps and processes which are to be written down so written work has to be done and thus written work also occupies an important place in Teaching of Mathematics. In fact, written work is only an extension of oral work. Written work in our ultimate aim, it ensures, exactitude, precision and accuracy. It is an admitted fact, "Reading maketh a full man, conference a ready man and writing an exact man."

6.3 WRITTEN WORK IN MATHEMATICS

It is most possible to completely isolate oral work from written work because when we do written work, we carry out certain calculations orally. Written work leads to accurate, neat and systematic work. Thus we see that oral and written drills supplement each other, one without the other is vague, and purposeless. If both are used then the process of instructions become complete. Both yield best results in combination and partnership.

Written Mathematics and Its Importance

Most of the Mathematics has to be in the written form because Mathematics is a science of figures and written work. Written Mathematics is some what different from oral Mathematics. The figures and other things put into black and white and most of these have to be done on the paper.

Psychologically speaking written work has an important place in Mathematics and it is only in written work that the concentration of attention can be determined.

Purpose of Written Work in Mathematics

In Mathematics the written work has the following purposes:

(*i*) It enables the teacher to know the amount of work done by the students.

(*ii*) Written work helps in testing the knowledge imparted orally.

(*iii*) In written work we can make the students to work in accordance with proper rules and processes.

(*iv*) Written work helps in conduct of bigger classes.

Merits of Written Work

(*i*) Written work helps to make clear the thoughts and proper reasoning. It is quite helpful in mental development of the student.

(*ii*) Written work is quite helpful in solving lengthy problems and complicated sums which are a bit difficult to be solved orally.

(*iii*) Using written Mathematics we solve the problems correctly without any fault and flaw.

(*iv*) The chances of mistakes are diminished to the minimum in written Mathematics.

(*v*) Since written work is of permanent nature so we can judge the performance of the student in a better way.

(*vi*) In future life we have to make use of written Mathematics.

(*vii*) Written work provides an opportunity to the teacher to carry out the inspection work and see the students while they are busy in written work.

Precautions about Written Work

To achieve the real objective the following precautions be observed while using the written work. In these precautions are not observed there are chances of mistakes creeping in, which may spoil the entire work.

(1) **Instructions about the Process of Actual Work.** The teacher should give proper instructions to the students about the work, time limit etc.

(2) **Written Work must keep in Mind the Mental Needs of the Students.** Written work should not be beyond the psychological limits of the students.

(3) Written work should be such that it keeps the entire class busy.

(4) The questions and the sums which are given should be clear and definite and, as far as possible, have bearing on the life of the students.

(5) The written work should be examined thoroughly and properly. As far as possible, the examination should be done in the classroom and in the presence of the students. It should be done in such a manner that other students may also be benefited by it.

(6) **Verification of the Written Work.** As far as possible, the written work should be verified to ensure the correctness of the results. If verification is not done, the purpose of the written work gets defeated. While doing the verification, the following points be kept in mind:

(*a*) No work should be left unexamined or uncorrected. The students should not be given much of the opportunity to correct their mistakes. There should be a little gap between the actual work of the students and the examination by the teacher.

(*b*) The students should be asked to go through the corrections and re-write them. This would help them to avoid mistakes in future.

(*c*) The teacher should make frequent use of the blackboard in the correction work. This would help the students to correct their mistakes and know them fully.

(*d*) The students should be habituated of getting their work corrected by the teacher. The teacher should try to encourage the students to do things correctly and write such remarks that shall encourage even those students who correct their mistakes. This would enable students to correct their mistakes and do things correctly in future.

(*e*) While verifying the written work, the teacher should also have a look at the corrected work. If he does so, then students shall try to do the written work correctly.

6.4 DRILL IN MATHEMATICS

Drill is a way to revise a lesson that has already been taught. Thus it is a means to strengthen the knowledge already acquired. Drill work is based on the principle of learning by doing and on the law of exercises. It is an admitted fact that practice makes a man perfect. Psychologically it has been found that learning is followed by forgetting.

Functions or Importance of Drill

Drill is an important device to fix an impression in the minds of the pupils. Making use of drill we can expect speed and accuracy in solving mathematical problems. Through drill it is possible to test the knowledge and strengthen the knowledge acquired by the students. Its importance is felt and realised in the teaching of Arithmetic. Arithmetic requires more of practice and exercise. Rewriting tables makes the knowledge perfect in lower classes.

The importance of drill can be summarised as under:

(*i*) It is the most effective means of fixing the impression of learned facts in mind.

(*ii*) It helps in development of communicational skills. Such skills are quite helpful in learning of Algebra, Arithmetic and Geometry.

(*iii*) It gives a sense of achievement and confidence and so it proves a positive stimulus for further learning.

(*iv*) It helps in developing speed and accuracy in learning of Mathematics.

(*v*) It helps in clarifying even the minutest details of the topics.

(*vi*) It has been found quite useful particularly in case of average or below average students.

(*vii*) Drill is quite helpful in revision and interview work.

(*viii*) Drill provides an opportunity to the student to work independently.

Advantages of the Drill

Merits of the Drill. Drill has the following merits:

(1) It keeps the teacher conscious of his responsibilities. It does not allow him to sleep over the matter for the year because he shall have to teach the students in the next class.

(2) It keeps the students awake. They have to work regularly, so as not fail in the examination.

(3) It helps the school authorities to know about the work that has been done in the class.

(4) It is helpful in strengthening the knowledge of the students. It gives an opportunity to the teacher and the authorities to award proper position to the students in the class.

(5) Through this method, it becomes possible to distinguish between the dull and the bright

students. Bright students shall be able to solve the exercises rapidly.

(6) It helps the teacher to know the weakness of the students and provide individual attention to them.

Demerits of the Drill or Exercise. In spite of the various advantages enumerated above, this method has certain drawbacks.

These are as under:

(1) It provides an opportunity to the teacher to sit at ease in the class and ask the students to solves exercises or do the drill.

(2) If exercises are not properly given to the students, it is likely to jeopardise the interest of the students in subject.

(3) If not properly handled, it is possible that the students may ask some one else to help them in their work. This would make them dependent upon others. Thus the very object of teaching of Mathematics i.e., creation of the feeling of self-dependence, shall be done away with.

Importance of Drill and Exercises in the Teaching of Arithmetic

Although drill and exercises occupy an important place in the teaching of the Mathematics as a subject, yet its importance is more felt and realised in the teaching of Arithmetic. Arithmetic needs more of practice and exercise. The teachers know very well that rewriting of charts and tables makes the knowledge perfect in lower classes. The teacher of Arithmetic should try to give the exercises that are psychological and proper. He should try to give the exercises based on the subject or topic already taught. After examining the achievements of the students and correcting their mistakes he should proceed further. The teacher should try not only to encourage the students to do exercises accurately, but also try not to discourage the students who commit mistakes.

Precautions in Regard to Drills and Exercises

This method should be employed with proper care and precaution. If the following precautions are not taken, the purpose is likely to be defeated.

The following points be kept in mind to make drill work more effective and useful:

(*i*) Drill work should be properly planned. The teacher should be clear about the timing of drill work and the quantum of drill work needed at a particular stage.

(*ii*) Drill work should follow understanding. The teacher should make sure that the students have understood the facts or rules. Only then, drill work is useful. In the absence of understanding, they may repeat a number of wrong things.

(*iii*) It should be an interesting affair, and not become boring or unpleasant. The teacher may use teaching aids and also introduce play spirit in drill work.

(*iv*) It should be meaningful. The students must know why they are having drill in a particular topic and the purpose behind it.

(*v*) The drill work should be individualised to the maximum possible extent. All the students do not have the same level of learning and intelligence. The consideration of individual differences should always be kept in mind.

(*vi*) The drill work should always be based on the facts taught. New facts or rules should not be given in drill work.

(*vii*) The drill work should be moderate and should not be continued for a long time otherwise it is likely to create distaste and boredom.

(*viii*) It should be properly supervised. The students may commit certain mistakes. These should be immediately identified and corrected.

(*ix*) Drill work should be varied. It should not always be of the same type otherwise it will become monotonous.

(*x*) For success in drill, the drill work should be graded properly.

(*xi*) Drill work should never be given as punishment. Drill assignments should not be made tasks.

(*xii*) The achievements of learners should be evaluated frequently.

(*xiii*) The teacher should provide proper environment for drill work.

Thus the effective drill requires proper planning and careful supervision. Only then it leads to perfecting skills and maintenance of good results.

6.5 SUPERVISED STUDY

By Supervised study we mean to study under the supervision of the teacher. The students are asked to solve problems or to do some practical work in the school hours or even in the afternoon if it is a residential school. The teacher gives guidance and direction on the spot. The study may be individual or collective. The students are free to work independently or to perform activities in consultations with their teacher. It is the responsibility of the teacher to see that the students make efforts in the right direction.

Importance of Supervised Study

Supervised study has been found to be helpful in a number of ways in the teaching of Mathematics. For example:

(*i*) It helps in creating a suitable atmosphere for the self study of the students.

(*ii*) It helps in providing on the spot help and guidance to the students.

(*iii*) It provides enough scope for mutual consultation amongst students as also amongst student and teacher whenever the need arises.

(*iv*) It helps the teacher in knowing about the doubts and difficulties of individual pupils. Such a knowledge is useful for teacher and he is then in a better position to understand and guide the students.

(*v*) The presence of the teacher makes the atmosphere of learning more congenial and the students have to complete the work given to them.

(*vi*) It is helpful in development of the habit of regularity, punctuality, and systematic work.

(*vii*) It helps to save time as also energy of students as they are guided in the right direction.

(*viii*) It helps in solving the problem of indiscipline because the students are kept busy in one or the other thing.

How to Make Supervised Study More Effective

Following points if kept in view will help to make supervised study more effective:

(*i*) It should be well planned after taking into consideration the work to be accomplished, the time that is available and the type of students etc.

(*ii*) For success of supervised study a congenial atmosphere, in the class-room, should be ensured.

(*iii*) The students be allowed sufficient freedom to work in their own way.

(*iv*) The teacher should provided only the minimum essential guidance.

(*v*) In case of larger classes, the students be asked to work in small groups. For supervision work the teacher may take the help of bright students or he may ask some other teachers for such a help.

(*vi*) All efforts be made to see that the work of students has began individualised because all the students do not have the same speed, interest and achievement level.

(*vii*) Efforts be made to pay individual attention to the student.

(*viii*) The period of supervised study should not be too long.

(*ix*) The teacher should supervise the work of students actively and he should not sit passively in a corner.

Drawbacks of Supervised Study

Some of the drawbacks of supervised study are as under:

(*i*) It overburdens the teacher because he has to plan, supervise and guide pupils individually. Thus it demands too much work from the teacher.

(*ii*) In supervised study the teacher is required to supervise and guide pupils individually. Such a supervision may not be possible in large classes.

(*iii*) The teacher may be tempted to provide too much guidance, which amounts to interference in the free work of pupils. Guidance should be neither too much nor too little.

(*iv*) The supervision may become purposeless, when it is done by the teacher merely to keep the students busy or to penalise them.

(*v*) The teacher should not be very strict, otherwise the students will be afraid to consult him.

Supervised study is a useful technique and it trains the students to work independently. They need guidance, the need of the teacher is desirable. As the students learn to work themselves, the amount of guidance should be decreased. The success of the technique depends upon teacher's devotion and hard work. A well organised and supervised study is quite helpful in learning Mathematics. The teacher should remember the goal of supervised study, the ultimate goal is self-learning.

6.6 SELF STUDY

Self study means independent work to be carried out by the students. In self-study, the individual studies and learns by himself. He attempts and solves every problem himself. So self-study is a habit of independent learning so that the students are able to solve problems acquire knowledge and skills of Mathematics with their own independent efforts.

Importance of Self-Study

(*i*) It prepares the students for real life where he can not depend on others.

(*ii*) By self-study the students learn to make use of their knowledge in tackling various problems.

(*iii*) Self-study is the best way to supplement class-teaching. Self-study is the best way to practice various things.

(*iv*) Self-study develops problem-solving and heuristic attitude in the students. It also develops initiative and independent thinking in the students.

(*v*) It helps in widening the mental horizon of the students.

(*vi*) It discourages cramming.

(*vii*) It builds up self-confidence in the students and they do not hesitate in tackling problems.

(*viii*) It helps in proper utilisation of leisure time.

(*ix*) It helps in developing the interest of the students in the learning of Mathematics.

Suggestion for Encouraging Self-Study

To encourage self-study the following points are quite useful:

(*i*) An effort be made to convince the students about the fact that Mathematics is best learnt through self-effort.

(*ii*) An all out effort be made to inculcate the habit of self-study in the students at the earliest possible stage.

(*iii*) The teacher should adopt, Heuristic method of teaching, in the class-room. He should encourage independent work on the part of the students.

(*iv*) Teacher should properly grade the work that he wished to accomplish through self-study.

(*v*) Teacher should encourage the students to make proper and full use of library books. For this he may suggest them certain interesting readings.

(*vi*) The students be also trained to take notes in independent self-study.

(*vii*) The teacher should ask the students to read a topic in advance, before taking it up in the class.

(*viii*) The students who study independently should be praised publicly.

(*ix*) The cooperation of parents should be sought to ensure regular progress of a student in self-study.

(*x*) The work accomplished by the student in self-study should be checked, corrected and evaluated by the teacher.

Self-study is the most effective technique in teaching of Mathematics. The teacher must cultivate this habit in himself. As and when possible, he should encourage this habit in the students.

6.7 GROUP DISCUSSION

There is a number of techniques which can be effectively used for the teaching of Mathematics. *Group work* is one of them.

Group work is a via-media between class teaching and the individuals independent work, since individual methods of work are almost impossible under the present circumstances and class teaching does not fulfil the purpose of modern education. We have to strike a via media in the form of Group work. It is for these reason that we started to think of team teaching, tutorial seminars and symposium in Teaching of Mathematics.

Group work aims at securing the advantage of individualized instructions retaining at the same time the economic and socially advantageous way of teaching the students together. The large and unmanageable class is divided into small and mangeable groups. The groups are formed keeping in view the abilities, interest, achievements and speed of the pupils. The pupils in a group are almost of the same level. In such a smaller unit it is possible to pay individual attention. In such a group over individualism is also avoided. In such groups pupils work under group feeling and there is more cooperation, homogeneity and healthy competition.

The **Importance of Group Work** is summarised below:

(*i*) Group work is useful in large classes, where there are wide individual differences. The pupils of almost the same level are put in the same group.

(*ii*) Group work facilities mutual exchange of views. The students are able to consult the members of the group and the teacher. It develops in them social habits such as cooperation etc.

(*iii*) It solves the problem of paying individual attention.

(*iv*) It provides healthy change in the class-room atmosphere.

(*v*) For doing project work, group work is very useful. Group work provides opportunities for effective learning of Mathematics.

Scope of Group Work

In Mathematics there is ample scope for group work. The students may voluntarily engage in group work for doing their homework. They pool their resources and thus complete the assignment jointly which none of them may be capable to do single handed.

If a teacher chooses to do his teaching through activities, projects, assignment or practical work, the students find opportunity for group work. Preparation of a mathematical model or some other material will require a group of students to work in cooperation. If the Mathematics room is to be decorated and equipped for the subject, it will be a group work for the students.

Group work can thus be used when

(*i*) Home work is to be done.

(*ii*) Assignments are to be completed jointly.

(*iii*) Oral drill is conducted in the earlier stages.

(*iv*) Activities, practical work, project work, project work etc. are to be completed.

(*v*) Mathematics room is to be decorated etc. etc.

Suggestions for Effective Use of Group Work

Following points be kept in view:

(*i*) As far as possible, the group should be homogeneous in level of intelligence and level of achievement.

(*ii*) The group should neither be too large nor be too small. It should have members from 3 to 7 but there can not be any rigidity about it.

(*iii*) A single student should not be encouraged to monopolise the group work. Teacher should ensure that every member of the group share the work (activity).

(*iv*) The purpose of group work should be adequately clear.

(*v*) The teacher should actively guide the work of the pupils.

(*vi*) The teacher should encourage healthy group competition but should guard against mutual jealousies or differences.

Limitations of Group Work

As in every other technique of teaching so also in Group work there are certain limitations some of these are as under:

(*i*) It provides a scope to shrink work. In a group certain students simply do not work. They let others work.

(*ii*) Group work does not clearly indicate individual progress. It indicates the progress of the group only.

(*iii*) Various members of a particular group do not get all the knowledge from their own experiences. They perform only specific duties and activities, hence their knowledge may also be partial.

(*iv*) The working within the group some times lead to certain dissensions and differences. As a result the group work suffers seriously.

(*v*) The group work may not suit in higher classes. It may not suit all topics.

However, group work is quite useful when the teacher properly plans organises and supervises group work. He must know when and how group work should be used.

6.8 REVIEW—ITS PLACE IN MATHEMATICS

Review means to view again. It means going over the learnt materials. It is to view the learnt facts in wider perspective in order to have better understanding of the subject-matter. It is different from drill which means mere repetition of facts. Review always involves new relationships and reorganisation of old materials.

Purpose of review. Review in Mathematics can be used for the following purposes:

(*i*) *To have better understanding*: Review involves viewing again, of different facts. When we recall the facts even the minutest details become clear.

(*ii*) *To fix the knowledge*: Review helps in the fixation of knowledge. Review involves mental recall of learnt material which helps in the retention of knowledge.

(*iii*) *To discover relationships*: Review helps in discovering relationships between various topics. This facilities learning of the subject.

(*iv*) *To develop new interest in old materials*: When the previously learnt materials are reviewed, the pupils develop new interest in the old materials.

(*v*) *To link the new with the old*: The previously learnt facts are reviewed so as to prepare a background for the new lesson.

Review in Mathematics is helpful in remembering the facts and maintaining the sequence of topics. It is very useful to consolidate the learnt materials in the mind. Review in Mathematics may take any of the following forms:

(*i*) Before starting a new lesson, the previous lesson or lessons must be reviewed briefly. It may be in the form of a daily lesson review.

(*ii*) When a topic is finished an effort be made to correlate various sub-topics.

(*iii*) After finishing some topics, they may be reviewed in order to integrate the learning of the subject-material.

(*iv*) It is possible to do the review work by solving-problems. For this purpose exercise given at the end of chapter are quite useful.

(*v*) Review can also be done by drawing graphs, figure, charts, tables etc. provided such charts, figures etc. are based on learnt facts.

(*vi*) Some project activities can also serve the purpose of review.

Suggestion for Effective Review

Following suggestions are quite useful for effective review:

(*i*) It should not involve more repetition of facts.

(*ii*) It should lead to new learning.

(*iii*) It should lead to discovering of inter-relationship.

(*iv*) It should lead to continuity, coherence and unity of subject-matter.

(*v*) It should be directed at the weak points or doubts of the students.

(*vi*) In review avoid details and stress only the main points.

(*vii*) Review should be varied. It may some times be done by solving problems, sometimes by drawing graphs, charts etc., and so on.

(*viii*) Review should be taken up both at shorter and longer intervals.

Thus we conclude that review is an important teaching technique of fix the learnt material. The success of this technique depends on the method adopted to conduct review.

It requires planning, supervising and evaluating the facts to be reviewed.

6.9 ASSIGNMENT TECHNIQUE

Assignment is a work allotment. It is the work assigned to the student. It may be done by the student at home or at school. There may be a pre-lesson or post-lesson assignment. Assignment is a sort of undertaking or commitment on the part of the learner. He undertakes upon himself the responsibility of carrying out the work assigned. It may consist of solving a few Mathematical problems, undertaking a proposition, solving riders based on proposition, making many propositions of the same type, preparing illustrations for a topic, collecting mathematical data, finding out applications of mathematical knowledge, tracing out historical background of a mathematical concept. Formulating problem on a topic, carrying out a mathematical project and so on.

Assignment is a sort-study which supplements class-room teaching. In this technique, the teacher assigns work, provides guide lines and sets time limit for the completion of assignment. The teacher may write it on the black-board, dictate it or it may be given in the form of a cyclostyled or typed sheet.

Various Steps in the Assignment

In the assignment of work the following steps are involved:

(*i*) *Planning of the assignment work.* The teacher has to select work according to the level of the pupils and the time available.

(*ii*) *Providing guidelines.* Assignment is actually a directed study, merely dictating of questions or problems is not an assignment. Hints have to be given for the successful completion of assignment.

(*iii*) *Supervising the work assigned.* The work of the students should be supervised if it is to be done in the class-room.

(*iv*) *Evaluating the assignment work.* The assignment work be carefully checked and mistakes pointed out.

Characteristics of Assignment

The important characteristics of assignment are as under:

(*i*) It should have correlation with previous knowledge and experience of the pupil.

(*ii*) It should have clarity and definiteness.

(*iii*) It should help in removal of pupils difficulties.

(*iv*) It should be stimulating.

(*v*) It should take into consideration the individual differences.

Suggestions for Effective Assignment

(*i*) The purpose of assignment should be clear to the teacher as well as to the students.

(*ii*) The assignment should be properly planned, keeping in mind the level of students and the availability of time.

(*iii*) Assignment must have clear-cut hints. So that the pupils can do the work following these directions.

(*iv*) Assignment should be directed at the weak points of students. It should clarify their doubts or misunderstandings.

(*v*) The assignments should be given according to the individual differences in pupils. The bright and weak pupils should not be given the same type of assignment.

(*vi*) The teacher must put in hard work to devise suitable assignments and familiarise himself with the teaching learning material relevant to the assignment.

(*vii*) The assignment work should be a cooperative activity wherein the teacher and the pupils participate actively.

(*viii*) The assignment work should be properly checked and mistakes be pointed out.

The assignments if properly planned and evaluated, cultivates the habit of self-study in the pupils. Pupils learn to finish the work with their own efforts. It is a sort of self-study which supplements class teaching. The success or effectiveness of assignment depends on the amount of work done independently by the students.

6.10 HOME-TASK

It can not be expected that all learning could be done during school time. School time is not sufficient to exhaust everything meant to be taught during the course of the year. Since in Mathematics a lot of practice is needed in the application of rules so home-work has to be given regularly to provide for application and practice and to supplement class-room teaching. The home-work in Mathematics may consist of some problems based on facts taught in the class. Students may be asked to learn certain principles, facts, definitions etc. by heart, they may be asked to draw graphs, charts etc.

Perhaps if the school time is used sincerely and efficiently home-work may not be necessary. Under normal conditions, the child does a good amount of work in the school. Giving home-work means creating in the child a 'school feeling' at home also. Some teachers have a liking for home-work and they over burden the students with home-work. However, assigning of home-work has been criticised by many educationists. The criticism is based on the following grounds:

(*i*) It may adversely affect the health of the students.

(*ii*) It is educationally unsound to load the child with home-work.

(*iii*) It deprives the children of their leisure time.

(*iv*) A large amount of home-work may create a distaste for school in the child.

(*v*) In quite a few homes, the conditions may not be congenial for the child to do the home-work.

(*vi*) The constant anxiety of doing home-work may adversely affect the progress of studies.

(*vii*) Sometimes it may lead to a disgraceful reaction towards the subject which may be transferred onwards to the teacher.

Utility of Home-Work

The importance and need of home-work can not be minimised. The advantages of home-work may be summarised as under:

(*i*) It supplements class teaching.

(*ii*) It develops a habit of independent work in the students.

(*iii*) It develops a habit of regularity in the students.

(*iv*) It makes a proper utilisation of the leisure time of the students, which otherwise would have been wasted.

(*v*) It is a practical means to cover comfortably the lengthy and heavy syllabi.

(*vi*) It serves as a link for parent-teacher cooperation.

Suggestions for Making Home-Work More Useful

Home-work can become more useful if following suggestions are kept in mind while assigning home-work:

(*i*) Home-work should be well graded.

(*ii*) Its nature and amount must determined by the individual's capacity and interest and not be the whims of the teacher.

(*iii*) It should neither be too easy or too difficult.

(*iv*) It should not be assigned as a sort of punishment.

(*v*) Home-work should be based on the principle taught in the class.

(*vi*) While assigning home-work, home conditions of the individual children must be kept in mind.

(*vii*) Home-work time table should be prepared in advance in consultation with other subject teachers.

(*viii*) Home-work should be regularly corrected and checked. If the home-work is not checked, the students may fall into the bad habit of evading it or copying it.

(*ix*) Home-work may be of practical type. Making a model, collecting some data or solving a riddle etc.

(*x*) It should be assessed as a part of the over all assessment of a student.

(*xi*) Home-work should appear enjoyable, useful and attractive. It should suit the individual speed and interests.

(*xii*) It should be intelligently planned and selectively assigned.

Correction of Home-Work. In Mathematics teaching checking of home-work is must, otherwise many mistakes or faulty processes may become fixed in the minds of students. However, regular correction of home-work is also very difficult as the time-table period may be wholly consumed by the teacher for the purpose. To overcome this the teacher may divide the students into groups and brilliant students may be appointed group leaders for the purpose. Their help may be sought as and when required. The teacher may have some sample checking everyday and thorough checking occasionally. The teacher can also introduce cross checking or checking by mutual exchange of note-books. The teacher may indicate the correct solutions on the black-board.

The problem of correction work becomes light in case the pupils have thoroughly understood the subject. If the students have not understood it, they will commit more errors. The errors will be minimum when there is thorough understanding of the subject-matter and neat systematic work that should be insisted on by the teacher.

Home-work is very useful, rather indispensable in Mathematics. But it should be properly planned and regularly checked.

Chapter—7

Teaching Aids in Mathematics

7.1 INTRODUCTION

It is now a well recognised fact that to keep teaching interesting and make it effective we have to make use of certain material aids. The use of these material aids makes the teaching effective, simple and interesting. The use of sensory aids in teaching of Mathematics is of recent origin. We have been using text-books, writing materials, geometric instruments and the black-board since long as indispensable equipment for Mathematics classes. All these are now considered as sensory aids. For many years resourceful teachers have been using models, instruments, drawings and other devices for stimulating interest and to facilitate learning of Mathematics. Since Mathematics is considered as a dry subject so to create interest in learning Mathematics has been a constant problem for teacher. In Mathematics teaching we require one or the other aid at every step. In the following pages an attempt will be made to discuss various teaching aids that are used in the teaching of Mathematics.

7.2 PLACE OF TEACHING AIDS IN MATHEMATICS

There are so many abstractions in Mathematics which can not be easily followed by the students. To make such abstract or complex ideas less abstract, rather concrete, teacher takes help of various teaching aids. Thus teaching aids are, actually, aids to imagination of pupils. Since most of the learning in children takes place at the sensory level, so the senses are the gateways of knowledge. Teaching aids influence the minds of learners through their senses. The importance of teaching aids in teaching of Mathematics is justified on the following considerations:

(*i*) They help in clear understanding of the subject and clarifying the abstract ideas.

(*ii*) They appeal the senses of the pupuls and so they satisfy their innate tendencies and interests.

(*iii*) They stimulate pupil participation. They are based on the maxim, "learning by doing".

(*iv*) They make the teaching-learning process interesting.

(*v*) They help in saving time and energy because it takes a long time to clarify an abstract idea verbally but the point can be made clear at once by using some appropriate teaching aid.

(*vi*) The needs of individual students are met. Some pupil learn by listening but a majority of them learn by doing.

(*vii*) They facilitate the application of Mathematics in various situations. The students may be required to recall and apply the learnt facts in situations suggested by an aid.

(*viii*) They help in creating a lasting impression on the mind of the learner. Things are well retained in the mind since the sensory impression are more permanent.

7.3 SUGGESTION FOR EFFECTIVE USE OF TEACHING AIDS

These aids serve their purpose best only when these are highly used. Following suggestions be kept in mind while making use of these aids:

(*i*) The aids should serve some useful purpose. Aid should not be used just for the sake of using an aid. Rather it should help in teaching a particular lesson. The teacher should be clear about the purpose for which he is using the aid.

(*ii*) The aid should be selected according to the general interests, abilities of the pupils.

(*iii*) The size of the aid should be neither too large nor to small. It should be clearly visible to the students.

(*iv*) In Mathematics, the diagrams, concepts, figures, formulae etc. depicted through the aids must be accurate. Accuracy is very important.

(*v*) Aid should be used only at the right moment. If it is meant for introduction of the lesson, it should be shown at the proper time. Aid used at the wrong time may prove harmful.

(*vi*) If the number of aids are to be used, then every aid must be used at the proper time and not in a haphazard manner. The systematic display gives god results.

(*vii*) The aid should be kept before the students as long as it serves some purpose. It should be removed when it has served its purpose.

(*viii*) While using aids teacher should always bear in mind that teaching aids are only means and not an end.

7.4 VARIOUS AIDS IN TEACHING OF MATHEMATICS

Various Types of teaching aids are used in Mathematics. Some of these are as under:

(*i*) Real objects.

(*ii*) Models.

(*iii*) Charts.

(*iv*) Black-Board.

(*v*) Flannel-Board.

(*vi*) Projective aids such as Magic lanterns, Film strip projector, Epidiascope, Motion pictures etc.

(*vii*) Excursions.

(*viii*) Collections.

(*ix*) Text books and Work books etc.

(i) Real Objects

They are the most useful and most effective means of providing direct experiences to the pupils e.g. to teach the area of four walls of a room we can make use of the four walls of class-room. Similarly black-board can be used to teach the area of a rectangle.

There are various objects which can be used by Mathematics teacher for teaching various topics.

(ii) Models

In order to clarify and explain the abstract things, some thing concrete like models have to be presented to explain those abstract things. These models help the students to grasp the point, models also create interest in the students.

Models are the three dimensional representations of the real objects e.g.

(*i*) Models of geometrical solids such as cone, sphere, cylinder etc. These models may be made out of card-board or chart paper and may be used to teach topics such as area of a cone, area of a sphere, area of a cylinder etc.

Similarly a model of cuboid can be used while teaching the volume of a cuboid.

(*ii*) The concept of angles can be explained easily if two strips are hinged at one end.

(*iii*) To explain the concept of congruency of triangle models of triangles made out of card-board can be used, the congruency can be proved by superimposing them.

(*iv*) To prove that the sum of three angles of a triangle is 180° we can take a chart paper model of a triangle and fold it as under.

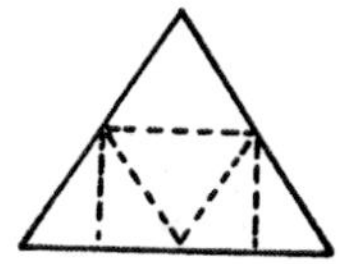

(*v*) To illustrate the area of a circle can be obtained by cutting a piece of cardboard. This circle is then cut into eight equal parts and these parts are then assembled as under.

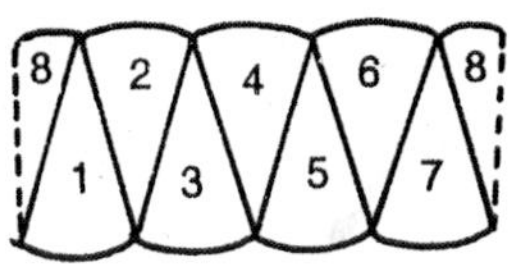

Many more examples of the use of models can be cited. Models are very useful as aids because they can be easily handled and manipulated. The pupils can be encouraged to make certain models themselves.

(iii) Charts

The charts are very useful teaching aids because they help the teacher to explain the point which otherwise would be difficult to explain. In teaching of Mathematics charts are an inevitable material aid, charts can be used almost in every topic. The charts helps in creating a suitable subject atmosphere in the class room and in elucidating various points. These charts can also pertain to the proofs of almost all the propositions and their exercises and corrolaries. Charts help in saving time because instead of drawing them on the black-board, the teacher can depend upon the pre-drawn diagrams. More over it is not always possible to draw a diagram on black-board with accuracy.

It is better if the charts of the topic, being dealt with in the class are living prominently in fairly good number. Charts should be changed with the topics.

Some examples of the use of charts are as under:

(*i*) Charts can be prepared for various units of weights and measures. Relationships among the various units of measurement can be easily illustrated with the help of a chart.

(*ii*) In Algebra, the charts can be effectively used in teaching of directed numbers, four fundamental rules and problems based on equations.

(*iii*) Various geometrical figures and shapes can be easily illustrated with the help of charts e.g. charts of triangles, squares, rectangles, circles polygon, cones, cylinders, spheres etc.

(*iv*) Charts can be used for depicting certain important formulae or results of Mathematics e.g.

$$S.I = \frac{P \times R \times T}{100}$$

Area of a rectangle = length × breadth and so on.

Various definitions or concepts can be written down on the charts.

(*v*) Various steps of a problem or proof can be systematically displayed on a chart.

(*vi*) Commercially prepared charts are also useful e.g. charts on sets, number systems, fractions, decimals, units of measurement etc.

Charts are very useful in the teaching of Mathematics.

Suggestions for Effective Use of Charts

Following points should be kept in mind while using charts as teaching aids.

(*i*) The chart should be neatly prepared. Important results or figures should be systematically drawn.

(*ii*) The size of a diagram, figure or shape should be appropriate. It should neither be too big no too small.

(*iii*) To draw attention to some specific points different colours can be used while making a chart.

(*iv*) Charts should be accurate.

(*v*) The chart or a portion of the chart be depicted only for a short duration whenever it is needed.

(*vi*) It is desirable that the students are encouraged to prepare simple charts.

(iv) Black-Board

Black-board is an integral part of the Mathematics classroom. The black-board should be well polished and smooth. It should be black in colour and fit for writing with a chalk. In some countries the colour of black-board has now been made green. This has been done because the green colour is useful for eye-sight. The use of coloured chalk can be made to draw geometrical figures, various ways in which a black-board is used in teaching in Mathematics are as under:

(*i*) It is used to develop various steps of the solution of a problem or proof of a theorem.

(*ii*) It is used for drawing important diagrams.

(*iii*) It is used to compare and contrast certain important results. Such are noted down on black-board.

(*iv*) Teacher can write down certain important points on the black-board to invite the attention of the students to such points.

(*v*) Black-board can also be used for writing down the problems for drill work or assignments etc.

(*vi*) Black-board can also be used to plot certain graphs or curves showing various inter-relationship, presenting statistical data etc.

Suggestions for Effective Use of Black-Board

For effective use of black-board following points be given due consideration:

(*i*) Active cooperative of the students be encouraged to develop the black-board work. If possible students be encouraged and given opportunity to write and draw on the black-board.

(*ii*) Coloured chalks may preferably be used.

(*iii*) The teacher should draw neat diagrams and write legibly on the black-board.

(*iv*) The teacher should speak while writing on the black-board.

(*v*) Teacher should take extra-precautions not to write any thing wrong on the black-board.

(*vi*) While writing on the black-board teacher should keep an eye on his students.

(*vii*) The black-board writing should always be in horizontal straight lines.

(*viii*) Only that portion of the black-board be used for writing which is visible to the students.

(v) Flannel-Board

Generally the teacher finds it convenient to depict items on the flannel-board. Various items are made out of chart paper. Pieces of sandpaper or cotton are pasted on the back side of each item. Instead of writing with a piece of chalk various items are stuck against the surface of flannel board.

Flannel-board is useful to depict certain diagrams results etc. Particularly when we have to make clear inter-relationships or continuity of various steps e.g. in finding the area of a circle, various parts of the circle can be divided into equal parts and depicted on the flannel-board. Flannel board introduces novelty changes in the class atmosphere.

(vi) Projective Aids

In this type of teaching aids are included aids such as filmstrips, opaque pictures, motion pictures etc.

Following advantages accrue in use of such aids:

(*i*) The filmstrips can give new colour and attraction to different ideas of Mathematics.

(*ii*) The image can be kept before the students as long as we desire. The diagrams of results etc. can be shown again and again.

(*iii*) These do not burden the minds of students and can be shown even in off hours.

(*iv*) There is an element of novelty and motivation in projective aids.

Slides are not convenient for use in Mathematics. Filmstrips can be used with good effect. A filmstrip contains a series of still pictures, about 24 to 48 frames arranged in a sequence.

Following film strips are available:

(*i*) What is a fraction?

(*ii*) Multiplying a fraction by a fraction e.g. $1/2 \times 1/2$, $1/2 \times 1/4$, $1/2 \times 1/3$ etc.

(*iii*) Use of graphs.

(*iv*) Percentage in everyday life.

(*v*) Drawing an angle.

(*vi*) Using a bank.

(*vii*) Measurements.

The film strips combine certain diagrams and situations in a proper sequence. The ideas are beautifully presented before the students. However, the teacher should plan the use of a filmstrip and see for himself before using them for the pupils. The teacher should know the details and other points that have to be emphasised.

Film may also explain the history of Mathematics.

In India, films are not much in use in the teaching of Mathematics, but in foreign countries they are much in use. Other audio-visual aids available are projectors, slides, gramophone etc.

Following projecting devices are used for this category of teaching aids:

(*a*) Magic Lantern

A magic lantern can be used to project different diagrams, results, picture etc. While projecting the slides the teacher also explains the related things.

(*b*) Film-Strips Projector

It is used to project film-strips on the screen. It is generally a hand operated device. It contains of pictures drawn on a 35 mm or 16 mm film.

(*c*) Epidiascope

This device can be used to project transparent as well as opaque pictures. It can be used to project slids, film-strips etc. It can also be used to project the contents, figures and diagrams of the printed or written pages. It is quite useful for depicting complicated figures.

(*d*) Motion Pictures

Motion pictures are useful if we are interested in showing some action or motion. Such pictures are used to stress the applications of Mathematics and development of concepts and generalisation. Such pictures are capable of introducing real life situation in the class-room.

(vii) Excursions

Excursions are helpful in providing the knowledge of Mathematics and in developing interest and understanding of the subject. For such excursions students may be taken to post-office, bank, market, insurance office etc.

(viii) Collections

The collections of data while on excursion or the collection of various mathematical data from other sources such as magazines, news papers etc. may be encouraged.

(ix) Radio and T.V.

These days we are having regular programmes on radio and T.V. intended for school and college students. Students can be benefited a lot if proper arrangements are made to show these programmes to the students.

(x) Text-Books

Text-books are standardized collection of the subject-matter that has to be taught to the students. They facilitate the teaching of new concepts and skills and maintain the knowledge already acquired and help the correlation of the theoretical knowledge with the practical aspects of life. There are three categories of the text-books:

(*a*) Reference books;

(*b*) Main text-books; and

(*c*) Supplementary books.

Value of a Good Text-book

The value of a good text-book of Mathematics is considered under various headings:

(*a*) Utility to the teacher.

(*b*) Utility to the student.

(*c*) Utility to maintain uniform standards.

(a) Utility to the Teacher

(*i*) It provides suitable subject-matter and guidelines regarding the syllabus of the subject. So the teacher neglects no portion of the syllabus and does not waste time on irrelevant details.

(*ii*) It helps the teacher to teach in an organised and systematic way, as it contains various topics in a proper sequence.

(*iii*) It is the most reliable source of information as it is generally written by experienced teachers. It serves as a reference book to the teacher.

(*iv*) A good text-book suggests the steps of planning, method of teaching and suitable illustrative materials to the teacher, regarding a particular topic.

(*v*) It provides certain well illustrated examples about a topic.

(*vi*) It provides the teacher with a number of well graded problems which he can give to the students.

(*vii*) Text-books help the teacher is assigning home-work to his students. They also help him to assign drill work.

(*viii*) It also suggests possibilities of correlation and related project activities.

(*b*) Utility to the Students

Text books are quite useful from the point of view of students as they save their time and they are saved from taking class notes.

Some other uses are:

(*i*) They provide the students with well graded exercises for drill, revision and review.

(*ii*) Text-books helps a student to understand the subject-matter as it makes the things clear.

(*iii*) Since every text-book contains some solved problems so the student can take help of these problems in solving other unsolved problems.

(*iv*) The student can learn a topic in advance with the help of text-book.

(*v*) Text-books are also quite useful in case a student has to remain absent from class due to one or the other reason.

(*c*) Utility to Maintain Uniform Standards

Text-books play an important role of maintaining a uniformity in standards. The text-books are quite helpful to examiners in their evaluation work because they come to know of the standards expected of a particular class.

Characteristics of a Good Text-Book

The text book helps the teacher to know what he has to teach. It helps the students to revise what has been taught to them in the class-room. Only a good text-book will help in this matter. The selection of a good text-book has to be done by the teacher. The teacher should keep the following points in minds while making such a selection:

(1) It presents the subject-matter strictly in accordance with the latest syllabus.

(2) It is written by experienced teachers.

(3) It is written according to the aims and objectives of teaching of Mathematics.

(4) It presents the subject-matter in a proper sequence. It may be so organised that it may be possible for the students to revise what they have learnt in the class. An effort be made to present the topic in a spiral form.

(5) It should contain well graded problems for revision.

(6) The books be so written that they awaken intellectual curiosity of the students and also keeps their interest alive.

(7) The language of the book should be in accordance with the age group of the students.

(8) The printing and get up of the book should be attractive.

(9) It should suggest the teaching method, the possible aids for teaching the topic, correlation of the topic and the activities or practical work connected with the topic.

(10) It should contain well illustrated material but not many solved problems. The answers given to problems should be correct.

(11) It must also contain objective type and short answer questions.

(12) Hints for difficult problems be provided.

(13) It should be moderately priced.

(14) It should give only upto-date material.

Thus to evaluate a Mathematics text-book, the criterion may be useful content material, proper organisation of subject-matter, proper gradation of the exercises, material aid devices for motivation, simple language, good number of illustrations, good printing and an impressive get up. It should be moderately priced and free from mistakes and errors. It should not contain too many solved problems and should be up-to-date in its contents.

(ix) Work Books

In addition to text-books, work books and exercise books are also used as teaching aids. The main aim of these is to provide proper exercises for the students. It would be better if the work book is viewed as a synthesis of a text-book and exercise book. Work books are different from text books as they help the students to learn the subject at their own rate of learning. They can cater to the needs of individual differences among pupils. They conserve the time of the teacher and increase the effectiveness of instructions particularly in junior classes.

The following are the needs and requirements of these books:

(*i*) The work book should be uniform.

(*ii*) The work book be so designed that there is a space for solving the exercises and also correcting them.

(*iii*) In a work book provision for evaluation be also made.

(*iv*) It is better if work books are accompanied by answers to the assignments given in the work book.

The concept of work book should not be mistaken to substitute a text book. They help in supplementing the text books. The best thing is the synthesis of text books and exercise books.

Conclusion

India is a country with limited resources. It is not expected to have large collection of such material aids. However, it cannot be denied that the material aids make the teaching interesting and lively.

The teacher has to employ these material aids with caution. He should keep in mind the psycho-requirements of the students. Material aids should be used sparingly, of course, keeping in view the requirements of the subject-matter. Thus we see material aids are very necessary for teaching Mathematics.

Chapter—8

Mathematics Laboratory

8.1 INTRODUCTION

Like any other subject room there should be a separate room for Mathematics. The setting and arrangement of this room should be such that it creates an atmosphere for the study and teaching of Mathematics. The students entering the room, would find themselves interested in the bearing of Mathematics.

Different charts and models depicting various applications of Mathematics can be displayed in this room. The black-board of Mathematics room be larger than the normal size. In schools it would be more appropriate to have a room to serve as a Mathematics museum-cum-Mathematics laboratory.

8.2 IMPORTANCE OF MATHEMATICS LABORATORY

In Mathematics laboratory all essential items (e.g. Set-square, Compass, Models etc.) concerning the learning activities in Mathematics are kept. It also provides facilities for laboratory work. The main aim of teaching of Mathematics is the development of power of abstract thinking and reasoning. For this we must start from concrete subjects. When the students handle, concrete objects, his learning is quicker and understanding is better. Use of geometrical models helps the student in grasping various geometrical facts. If mathematical facts are verified physically then they could be understood more easily and can be easily applied in new situations. Furthermore any practical work in Mathematics makes the subject interesting to the students.

Importance of Laboratory work in Mathematics can be summarised as follows:

(*i*) It helps in making clear and in understanding abstract concepts.

(*ii*) It saves teacher's time by cutting short certain lengthy explanations.

(*iii*) It helps in developing the habit of verification in the students. They accept Mathematical truths only after confirming their validity practically.

(*iv*) It enables the students to apply Mathematical facts and principles in a actual life.

(*v*) The pupils develop love for the subject and arousing their interest in Mathematics.

(*vi*) It enables the students to learn by doing. The things so learnt are retained in the mind for a longer time.

(*vii*) It is multi-sensory approach to learning.

In the lower classes, laboratory work helps the students in learning elementary Mathematics. Even the mentally deficient children can profit from practical work. Moreover, Mathematics laboratory in a rich repository of audio-visual aid that can be used in day to day teaching.

8.3 EQUIPMENT FOR MATHEMATICS LABORATORY

Mathematics laboratory serves not only as a laboratory but also as Mathematics room and Mathematics museum. Keeping in view the various purposes it should have the following equipment:

(*i*) **Concrete Materials**. It should be provided with concrete materials connected with simple arithmetical topics such as beads, sticks, pebbles, ball frames, number cards, seeds, balances, coins, weights, measuring tapes, didactic, apparatus which is used in Montessori Method, scissors, pins, card-board, chart paper, graphs, nails, hammers, ropes etc. It may also be provided with the following materials:

(*a*) *A Number Kit* consisting of a set of wooden blocks of different colours, labelling the digits from one to ten. Each block has the numeral and word representing the numeral.

(*b*) *Place value pockets* is a box having three or four portions labelled as Units, Tens, Hundreds, Thousands. This is used to teach place value of numbers, idea of carrying processes of addition and subtraction etc.

(*c*) *Fractional Parts* is a series that is divided into halves, thirds, fourths, fifths etc. These are quite useful to illustrate the concept of fractions, addition, multiplication etc.

(*d*) *Charts*. A number of Mathematical charts should be kept in the Mathematics laboratory. Charts can be used to explain certain points which otherwise would be difficult to explain. These charts are drawn on paper with the help of colour as well as pencil. These charts may be got prepared by the students on different topics such as %age, average, fractions, circles, cubes etc. Some set of charts are also available from the market.

The charts, as far as possible, should be accurate, interesting and good looking. If the charts do not fulfil these requirements, they shall not be useful for the class-room teachings. There may be charts and models of certain geometrical figures such as triangles, quadrangles, rectangles.

(*ii*) Pictures and Photographs

The pictures and photographs of various Mathematicians be prominently displayed in the Mathematics room. It would be much useful if the contributions of these Mathematicians are also indicated on such charts.

(*iii*) Models

Various Mathematical models such as those of triangles, squares, solids etc. be stored in a Mathematics laboratory. These help in understanding abstract Mathematical concepts. Now various models illustrating Mathematical proofs or principles or statements are available in the market.

(*iv*) Black-Board and Geometrical Instruments

As already pointed out the size of black-board provided in Mathematics room should be larger than ordinary size. Provision for coloured chalks may also be made in the laboratory. Coloured chalks are required for use in drawing various figures and diagrams. A set of geometrical instruments like protractors, compass, rulers etc. be kept in a Mathematics laboratory. Stencils for drawing geometrical figures are also important equipments for Mathematics laboratory.

(*v*) Bulletin Boards or Display Boards

Such boards are used to display various illustrations concerning Mathematics. The material for display on such boards e.g. Mathematical figures, rules, graphs etc. can be collected from various sources.

(*vi*) Equipments and Materials Concerning Other Subjects

Mathematical principles and procedures are used in other subjects and the materials, equipment illustrating the application of Mathematics (e.g. barometer, hydrometer, pendulum etc.) be also kept in Mathematics laboratory.

(*vii*) Proportional Dividers, Slide Rules, Calculating Machines etc.

These are quite useful in the study of similarity of geometrical figures and be kept in a Mathematics laboratory.

Making use of these instruments we can magnify or reduce figures, graphs, maps etc. Slide rules are quite useful in Mathematical calculations. A training in Mathematical calculations can be provided by using simple calculating machines.

(*viii*) Surveying Instruments

Various instruments used in surveying kept in a Mathematics laboratory because surveying is concerned with Mathematics. Some of these instruments are—

(*a*) *Angle Mirror* which is used for laying out right angles in the field.

(*b*) *Plane Table and Alidate* which are used for elementary mapping and surveying.

(*c*) *Hypsometer and Clinometer* are simple devices to measure angles of elevation and depression. These can be used to measure heights and distances of objects indirectly.

(*d*) *Level* which is an instrument used in finding differences in elevation.

(*e*) *Transit* which is an angle measurer and a levelling instrument.

(*ix*) Projective Aids

Various projective aids and projecting devices such as magic lantern, film-strip projector, epidiascope etc. should also be kept in Mathematics laboratory.

At present many film-strips on mathematical topics are available from various sources. Film showing the application of Mathematics may also be obtained.

(*x*) Collections

The students be encouraged to collect Mathematical data from different sources e.g. data on graphs, percentage, t-ratios, income, investments, budgets, insurance etc. in the form of cutting, pictures, charts, models etc. from various magazines, newspapers, books etc.

There can be so many other materials or instruments of Mathematical interest available from different sources. However, the teacher should bear in mind the needs and requirements of students and should encourage them for improvisation and self-collection. Students should be actively involved in the maintenance and organisation of Mathematics laboratory.

However, laboratory work should be properly planned. These should provide useful learning experiences to the students and should not degenerate into mere mechanical handling of materials or mere play. Laboratory experiences should be supplemented by regular teaching.

Chapter—9

Mathematics Library

9.1 IMPORTANCE OF LIBRARY

Mathematics is quite a vast subject. Even if a teacher is to restrict himself to a certain amount of subject-matter according to a particular class, that too can be done in so many ways. A Mathematics teacher should not follow only the text-book. The teacher must study some standard books from the library. This will provide him a deeper insight into the subject and thorough command of the same. The teacher will be able to plan and organise his teaching in a better way, better than that given in the text-book.

Mathematics library is quite useful to the students. When students read or consult some books from the library, their doubts become clear. Moreover, the study of library books acquaints them with new exercises or problems and prepares them better for the examination. A good Mathematics library also helps in inculcating proper attitudes, interests and appreciations in the students. It can acquaint them with the historical background of different topics and the contribution of various Mathematicians.

Library Facilities in the School

In our schools, there are two types of libraries:

(*a*) General School Library.

(*b*) Mathematics Department Library.

(*a*) *General School Library*. In most of our schools, there is a general school library which contain books and magazines on all subjects. Then there should be separate sections for Mathematical books. For the teachers, there should be good books on methodology of teaching, historical background of topics and the contributions of famous Mathematicians. Some literature of Mathematical teaching can be obtained from N.C.E.R.T.

For the students, there should be books on recreational activities in Mathematics, well selected text-books some reference books and works of Mathematicians.

(*b*) *Mathematics Department Library*. If resources permit there should be a separate Mathematics library. It may be housed in Mathematics laboratory. The librarian or the incharge of it must classify the books properly so that the students do not find any difficulty in getting the books issued. Mathematics teacher should keep himself in touch with the latest books or magazines on the subject and make additions in the library. A number of copies of a good book should be purchased. A few copies of the prescribed text-books may be purchased for the use of poor students.

9.2 IMPORTANCE AND NEED OF MATHEMATICS LIBRARY

Importance of Mathematics Library

Library has a key role in scheme of education. Class room teaching must be supplemented with the dissemination of knowledge through library. In Mathematics the students are required to do a lot of practice work which they can do so most efficiently in Mathematics library. Different types of books in Mathematics library can help the students to tackle all types of problems emerging from different topics prescribed in their syllabus. They are also acquainted with different types of approaches in solving the problems.

Class room teaching sometimes leaves many gaps and doubts. They can be removed if the students make use of good books available in the library. Mathematics teacher can help the students in the selection of good books in the library.

A Mathematics library, is not only a source of learning and inspiration for students but it also serves the need of the teachers. A teacher must keep his knowledge ever fresh and up to date, this is possible only by making a free use of Mathematics library. He can also learn the latest methods of teaching Mathematics from the new books available in the library. Thus, a good Mathematics library helps to keep the lamp of Mathematics knowledge burning so as to kindle light in the minds of the students as also the teachers.

Need of Separate Mathematics Library

In most schools, there is a general library in which all kinds of books related to different subject are kept. Such libraries serve purpose of encouraging the students to make use of library services, but the students cannot get proper guidance for removing their deficiency in a particular subject. For this a separate library of the subject concerned is essential. A separate library for Mathematics is a great necessity for rendering proper help to needy students. Such a library can be housed in Mathematics room and can be put under the charge of Mathematics teacher. There should be a period of library reading in the time-table so as to enable the students of every class to make use of the library. A separate Mathematics library is essential because of the following reasons:

(1) Separate arrangement of Mathematics library helps to bring efficiency in the organisation of library service.

(2) Mathematics teacher remains in constant touch with the latest books in Mathematics.

(3) It provides a sense of separate identity to Mathematics and helps to inculcate interest in the subject.

(4) The students get better library facilities.

(5) It helps the activities of Mathematics club.

(6) It can be of a help to gifted and bright students.

Thus, it is essential that all out efforts be made to establish a separate Mathematics library in every school.

Suggestion for Effective Use of Library

A well-equipped library is useful only when it is properly used by the teachers and the students. Suggestions given below will help in the proper use of Mathematics library:

(*i*) There should be an incharge of library books. Even if there is librarian, the Mathematics teacher should be actively associated with the functioning of Mathematics section of the library.

(*ii*) The Mathematics teacher should himself read library books, only then he can suggest books to the students.

(*iii*) While teaching in the class, the Mathematics teacher should make reference to related books or magazines in the library.

(*iv*) The teacher should give some assignments or work based on certain books in the library.

(*v*) The students should be involved in the maintenance and classification of library room.

(*vi*) There should be certain meeting of Mathematics club where the students have to study library books for active participation.

(*vii*) The Mathematics teacher should suggest Mathematical riddles and recreations from library books.

(*viii*) Library room should be made attractive by depicting pictures relating to the history, progress and application of Mathematics and portraits of eminent Mathematicians.

(*ix*) There should be proper display of the new books on the bulletin board, along with brief comments.

(*x*) There should be some provision in the time-table for library reading. Teacher should see that every student goes to the library and borrows books regularly, from the library.

(*xi*) There should be some sort of test based on suggested books from the library.

So we have seen that a good Mathematics library is quite useful for properly developing good study habits in students. Library also is quite useful to students for updating their knowledge and develop a taste for the subject. To achieve maximum benefits the Mathematics teacher shall have to take pains by putting in more efforts.

9.3 MATERIAL FOR MATHEMATICS LIBRARY

Mathematics library should contain useful visual aids in teaching Mathematics. The educational pictures, charts, maps and posters about Mathematics be displayed on walls of library.

In Mathematics library there should a good collection of useful books in Mathematics. The Mathematics teacher should be responsible for making a wise selection of books for the library. The books be kept in separate almirahas under the following heads:

(A) **The Prescribed Text-Books** of Mathematics for the different classes.

(B) **Books on Teaching of Mathematics** meant for teacher such books should be of high standard, published in India as well as in foreign countries.

(C) **Books of Recreational Activities.** There are very few good books of this type published in India. Hence good books published in foreign countries should be procured for this purpose. Following books are suggested:

(1) Puzzle Mathematics by Gamow published by Macmillan & Company.

(2) Amusement in Mathematics by Dudney published by Nelson & Company.

(3) Mathematics Recreation by Ball & Coxeter published by Macmillan & Company.

(4) Mathematical Recreation by Maurice published by Dover Publication, New York.

(5) Riddles in Mathematics by Northop published by Nelson & Company.

(6) Ganit Manoranjan by Kotharia & Om Prakash published by NCERT.

(D) Books on Biographies and History of Mathematics

A few of such books are given here:

(1) History of Mathematics by Boyer published by John Wiley & Sons.

(2) Men of Mathematics by Bell published by Simon & Co., New York.

(3) Hindu Ganit Ka Ithas by Dutt and Singh published by Govt. of U.P., Lucknow.

(4) World of Mathematics by Newman published by Simon & Co., New York.

(E) Books Showing Contribution of Mathematics to Other Fields

A few books in this area are:

(1) Mathematical Advantages in Social Science by Davis published by American Mathematical Magazine.

(2) Mathematics in Human affairs by Ko Komer published by Prentice Hall.

(3) Mathematics for the millions by Lance lot published by Norton & Co., New York.

(F) Mathematics Journals

(1) The Mathematics Teacher Journal, SITU Colony, Madras-28.

(2) The Mathematics Education Journal, P.O. Siwan, Distt. Saran (Bihar).

(3) NCERT and SCERT Mathematics periodicals and magazines.

Chapter—10

Mathematics Teacher

10.1 INTRODUCTION

The success or failure of a Mathematics course rests mainly with the teacher. He may be provided with all the possible facilities in terms of laboratory, apparatus and equipment. Given an ideal syllabus and a sufficient time for teaching of Mathematics but he is not likely to achieve success unless he is enthusiastic about his work, knows the subject and really knows how to teach Maths. On the other hand a keen and well informed teacher who loves his subject and believes in its value will succeed inspite of difficulties and handicaps.

In this regard the Kothari Commission Report (1966) says, "*of all the different factors which influence the quality of education and its contribution to national development, the quality, competence and character of teacher are undoubtedly the most significant.*"

Dr. S. Radhakrishnan emphasises the role of teacher in the following words, "*The teacher place in society is of vital importance. He acts as the pivot for transmission of intellectual traditions and technical skill from generation to generation, and helps to keep the lamp of civilisation burning. He not only guides the individual, but also, so to say, the destiny of nation. Teachers have therefore to realise their special responsibility to the society. On the other hand it is incumbent on the society to pay due regard to the teaching profession and to ensure that the teacher is kept above want and given the status which will command respect from his student."*

10.2 IMPORTANCE OF A TEACHER

"A teacher is more like a gardener who tends each plant, examines water and sees that the plant may take its own nourishment. The teacher should be a guide, helper and a friend. The teacher must study the child, must know the effect of environment on the child, and should know the laws of learning for which a study of psychology is necessary.

The teacher is an integral part of the process of education. He imparts education and teaches his students the subject-matter prescribed for them. He has to perform a difficult job. In addition to teaching in class room he has to look after various extra-curricular activities. Thus a teacher is expected to discharge varied functions.

10.3 FUNCTIONS OF A TEACHER

Some of the important functions to be discharged by a teacher are as under:

(1) He is expected to bring about the successful teaching and build up understanding and motivation among the students.

(2) He is expected to study and organise the learning plans of the students and distribute the load for each student in a proper and scientific manner.

(3) Teacher is also expected to give due regard to individual differences.

(4) The teacher is also expected to create in the students the interest for the subject through proper appreciation of the achievement of the students. Through personal contact and knowledge, he can create love for the subject.

10.4 QUALITIES OF A MATHEMATICS TEACHER

As in the case of other teachers, many things are expected of the teacher of Mathematics. Teaching is not an easy job. A teacher has to bear in mind many factors—the children with their individual differences and objectives of the subject, the selection of suitable subject-matter, method of teaching etc. His obligations are not only confined to the class room but also extend in many other directions.

No teacher can do a thorough good job of teaching Mathematics unless he is willing to make a careful analysis of his job and be guided by that analysis in making his preparations and in conducting the work of his class.

Following qualities are expected in a good Mathematics teacher:

(*i*) **Thorough Knowledge of the Subject.** If a teacher has a thorough knowledge of his subject it gives him confidence in his teaching. If a teacher is not clear about certain facts or rules. He will be afraid lest he should be caught somewhere. Suppose a pupil asks a question and the teacher is not able to give a satisfactory answer. He will fail to exercise his influence on the students. They will not longer listen to him attentively. He may have some problems of indiscipline as well.

(*ii*) **Knowledge of Methods.** Only having good knowledge of Mathematics is not sufficient. The teacher should be able to communicate his knowledge to the pupils. For that, the teacher must be well conversant with the various methods of teaching the subject. He should have professional training. He must know the latest methods and techniques of teaching. As far as possible, the teacher should be trained, particularly in case of secondary school teachers.

There are two equally important aspects of any true profession, viz, significant knowledge and effective technique. One can not be efficiently professional if there is any serious weakness in either of the two.

In the beginning of his carrier the teacher will need to spend most of his time in improving his knowledge of teaching field and his technique of teaching.

(iii) **Interest in the Subject**. The Mathematics teacher must have a love for his subject. Such a love and interest in subject would help him to create a similar love and interest for Mathematics in his students.

(iv) **Love for the Students**. A teacher must love his students. Unless the teacher likes them, they will not like him. Like or dislike is a reciprocal process. If the students do not like the teacher, the students will not like his subject. So the first essential before a teacher is to establish rapport with the students. He should understand them, their abilities, interests, achievements etc.

(v) **Impressive Personality.** The teacher should possess an impressive personality. He should have a thorough command on the subject and should be able to present it in such a manner that students grasp what he says or does in the class-room. Mathematics is a dry subject and so it would be preferable if the Mathematics teacher possesses a good sense of humour.

The teacher should keep himself properly dressed and should possess presentably physical features. There should be an aptitude of sobriety and seriousness in the teacher. This helps in discipline. The teacher should have healthy qualities. His behaviour should serve as an ideal to the students.

(vi) **Knowledge of Educational Psychology**. The teacher must have knowledge of child psychology. It is then possible for him to know the psycho-physical requirements of his students and organise his teaching accordingly. Mathematical facts are not be told, these are to be properly exposed and made understandable.

(vii) **Capacity to Inspire Confidence in His Students**. The teacher of Mathematics should have the capacity to inspire confidence in his students. This can be done only by example and devotion to duty and certain other qualities. If the teacher can inspire confidence in his students, he can very safely carry them along with himself.

(*viii*) **Proper Habits and Attitudes**. A good Mathematics teacher is expected to possess good habits like patience, confidence, hard work, initiative etc. He is expected to have rational and heuristic attitude. He is expected to possess a strong will power and a power of concentration. He is also expected to possess neat and systematic habit of work. He is expected to possess qualities of cooperation and sympathy.

(*ix*) **Awareness of Aims**. The teacher must be clear about the aims and objectives of teaching of Mathematics at various stages. Such a knowledge helps him in carrying out his job thoroughly.

(*x*) **Originality**. The quality of originality is a must for every teacher and so is the case with a Mathematics teacher. This helps the teacher to devise ways and means for imparting knowledge effectively and properly. His approach should be original and he should not depend on any particular book-text or help book.

(*xi*) **Knowledge of Application of Mathematics**. The teacher should have a good knowledge of the application of Mathematics in other subjects, vocations, real life etc. Such a knowledge is quite helpful in making the teaching meaningful and interesting.

(*xii*) **Organising Ability**. A good teacher is expected to be a good organiser. He is required to organise his teaching work and other co-curricular activities of Mathematics club, library etc. He has also to organise tests etc.

(*xiii*) **Capacity of Analysis and Comprehensive Description.** While teaching a subject a teacher is required to give even minute details to explain things to his students. For giving such details teacher should possess the capacity of analysis. A Mathematics teacher should also possess mathematical skills such as computational skill, drawing and sketching skill, problem solving skill etc.

(*xiv*) **Up-to-date Knowledge of the Subject**. A teacher must keep his knowledge up to date. He should study mathematical journals and other useful books on the subject.

He should attend refresher courses, work shops, seminars etc. on the subject. He may do professional research work. He may join various Mathematical Organisation, visit good schools and hold discussions with reputed teachers of the subject.

(*xv*) **Capacity to Prove Things More by Action than by Words.** "Practice is better than precept." This is true for a Mathematics teacher like any other teacher. The teacher has to prove things by example and not by words. If he can do that, he is sure to influence his students and so he will be able to make them interested in his subject.

(*xvi*) **Studiousness**. The teacher is expected to be studious. Studiousness is essential to keep ones knowledge up-to-date.

(*xvii*) **Presence of Mind**. Presence of mind is the basic requirement of any teacher. Unless he possess this quality he will not be able to solve the difficulties that beset his path in the teaching of his subject in the class-room.

(*xviii*) **Aesthetic and Artistic Outlook**. Such an outlook helps the teacher in presenting things in proper perspective in an attractive manner.

10.5 PROFESSIONAL QUALIFICATION OF A MATHEMATICS TEACHER

A mathematics teacher is expected to possess certain academic qualifications as also certain professional qualification.

As regards academic qualifications it is usually a pass in Matriculation/Senior Secondary Examination for becoming a Mathematics teacher in a primary school. A pass in B.A./B.Sc. examination for being a Mathematics teacher in a middle or high schools and a pass in M.A./M.Sc. examination for being a teacher in a senior secondary school (grade 11 and 12).

For a Mathematics teacher a teaching experience is a valuable asset and some of this experience should be acquired by him before he joins professional educational course. During his professional education period he should acquire a fair knowledge of the applications of Mathematics to various fields of life. During supervised teaching practice he should devote more attention to the preparation of his lesson plans.

In-service training has been introduced recently. Seminars and work shops are occasionally arranged for the subject teachers. A teacher must undergo such an inservice course during summer vacations. By attending such courses he can keep himself in touch with the latest knowledge in his subject.

The teacher should study Mathematical journals and modern books of professional interest. He may visit certain schools of outstanding merit into investigate the quality and nature of work done.

The teacher should study Mathematical research work and write professional articles or books for publication.

The teacher should participate enthusiastically in various school activities such as

(*i*) Faculty Meetings.

(*ii*) Students Projects.

(*iii*) Mathematics Club.

(*iv*) Social Events.

(*v*) School Publications.

(*vi*) Excursions.

(*vii*) Educational Fairs.

(*viii*) Educational Quiz etc.

For the development of Mathematics it is desirable if Mathematics teacher form some Mathematics teachers organisation at district, zone and state level. These organisations should take up only academic things and nothing else.

10.6 DUTIES OF A MATHEMATICS TEACHER

In addition to his teaching duties a Mathematics teacher is expected to help the school administration by performing various types of duties. A few commonly assigned duties are:

(*i*) Departmental Duties

A few common departmental duties are mentioned below:

(*i*) Participation in departmental meetings and discussions.

(*ii*) Selection of text books.

(*iii*) Acting as sponsor of Mathematics club.

(*iv*) Selection and ordering of library books and periodicals.

(*v*) Selection and ordering of class room equipment.

(*vi*) Taking charge of remedial class in Mathematics.

A Mathematics teacher should participate honestly and seriously in all these activities.

(*ii*) Administrative Duties

Mathematics teacher should try to serve on some administrative committee in the school. He should take upon himself the duty of supervising some important activities of the school.

(*iii*) Community Activities

School is, in fact, the centre of educational life for parents as also for children.

Mathematics teacher should co-operative with parents in improving school and community relations. He should actively participate in all meetings of social or civil groups. He should also actively participate in parents' associations and old students' organisations.

He should explain to parents and visitors the facilities offered by the school for teaching of various subjects, particularly the subject of Mathematics.

He should organise local fairs and exhibitions, and throw them open to students as also to public. He should try to see that some good items of mathematical skill and included in these fairs and exhibitions. He should try to see that some good items of mathematical skills, prepared by his students are shown in these fairs and exhibitions. He should explain to the visitors the important role played by the students of Mathematics in preparing those items.

He should direct every service undertaken by his students for the uplift of the community.

He should work for teaching duty in an evening school for adults. He should instil an interest for simple Mathematics in the minds of adults.

He should lend a helping hand to the farmers of the village, in which the school is situated. If his school is situated in a town or city, he should try to render some help to the farmers of a neighbouring village, especially during harvest time.

Mathematics teacher should realise that he is not an individual but an institution. His responsibility are great and he should try to carry out his responsibility honestly.

Chapter—11

Evaluation in Mathematics

11.1 INTRODUCTION

Once a teacher has a clear idea of what she will teach and how she will teach it, she is concerned with knowing to what extent children learn from her lessons. This chapter will deal with specific procedures for evaluating the effectiveness of Mathematics teaching-learning.

Evaluation is a continuous process which is an integral part of teaching. It is not merely a test at the end of Mathematics lesson or unit. Instead, evaluation goes on constantly during lessons and units and is clearly related to the teacher's goal and points of view on Mathematics teaching.

Besides being a continuous experience, evaluation is cumulative. A cumulative record should be kept for all children. If such a record is available then his Mathematics exposure can be quickly and easily seen.

The recent trends in learning and evaluation link them to behavioural objectives. According to a behaviourist psychology learning is defined as *a change in the behaviour of an individual that can be described in terms of observable and measurable performance*. The changes in behaviour are affected by providing experiences and thorough teaching.

The test efficiency of teaching, to judge the progress of students and to discover their achievements and evaluate the whole school system, we require some sort of measuring tools. These tools are tests or examinations. Tests are essential to grade and rank pupils, however, if evaluation is used merely to indicate areas of science to which children have been exposed or for classifying and categorizing students, a great value is lost. The same loss occurs if evaluation is interpreted only as arriving at numerical or alphabetical ratings for report cards. In this way much of the positive use of evaluation as a means of teaching and learning could be destroyed.

Effective instructional planning and evaluation of students performance have always stressed on the statement of instructional objectives so that they are of great help to the student. According to Muller, an instructionally usable objective must state the intended outcome in terms of the terminal behaviour of students. Terminal behaviour here means the behaviour of students after the class-room instruction and evaluation is possible if the learning outcomes are classified. By combining continuous evaluation with immediate application of what has been learned, the teacher can provide for:

(*i*) The stimulation of students who learn rapidly to greater growth toward goals by application of advanced works,

(*ii*) The identification of specific weaknesses and difficulties in functional understanding (concepts, principles, generalization) and the needed retreaching of varied activities skills or problem solving abilities, and

(*iii*) The clarification, modification or complete alternation of the goals as needed for the unit.

Evaluation, teaching and learning are the three corners of the education system. *Evaluation* is concerned with finding out how far students have learned as a consequence of teaching. There are two kinds of evaluation depending upon whether the comparison of student is made with some absolute performance standard or with other students of a given group. These are known as *criterion referenced evaluation and norm referenced evaluation*.

Criterion-Referenced Evaluation

It assesses the students performance in terms of a specified performance standard or criterion without any mention of the performance levels of the other students of the group. This evaluation methods is related to mastery an development test.

Norm-Referenced Evaluation

It assesses the students performance relative to other students of the group. Students are awarded marks and relative ranks in this method of evaluation.

11.2 PURPOSE OF EVALUATION

In Mathematics evaluation is needed for the purposes noted below:

(*i*) For determining the teaching learning process.

(*ii*) For revising curriculum.

(*iii*) To provide an objective basis for reporting progress of students.

(*iv*) For securing effective cooperation from the parents and the community.

(*v*) For determining the policies of promotion.

(*vi*) To provide suitable guidance to pupils, on the basis of their evaluation.

Thus we find that evaluation is an essential part of the educational process. It helps in realising the goals of instruction. It points out the defects in the teaching-learning process. It also helps in ascertaining the effectiveness of the curriculum, methods and devices of teaching etc.

11.3 CHARACTERISTICS OF A GOOD TEST IN MATHEMATICS

A good test in Mathematics should have the following characteristics:

(*i*) **Validity**: The test should be valid. It should fulfil the objectives for which it is meant. If our aim is to measure the ability to understand and application of mathematical facts then language difficulty and speed should not come in way. Thus it should be free from defects that are likely to affect the valid results.

(*ii*) **Reliability**. The test is considered to be reliable if it gives same results every time when it is used for testing the individual's abilities under same conditions. An objective test is bound to be reliable.

The reliability of a test is affected by the following factors, thus to be reliable it should be free from:

(*a*) The whims of an examiner.

(*b*) The physical and mental condition of the student.

(*c*) The language of the questions-lack of clearness or any ambiguities in statements.

(*d*) Lack of clear-cut instructions for marking.

(*e*) Inefficient methods of scoring.

A reliable test is not influenced by subjective conditions, it is objective.

(*iii*) **Comprehensiveness**. Any good test should be comprehensive i.e. it should assess knowledge, skills, abilities, attitudes etc. as adequately as possible. No aspect of the curriculum should be ignored while making evaluation.

(*iv*) **Administrability**. It should be easy to administer, economical in time and money, easy to score and interpret. The directions of the test should be clear-cut. There should be answer-keys for scoring.

(*v*) **Capable of Maintaining the Interest of the Students**. Any good test should be able to capture the interest of the students and maintain it. Thus it should be interesting for the students. A good test is motivating for the students and stimulates their best efforts. It should be neither too easy nor too difficult. It should never be used as a means of punishment.

(*vi*) **Diagnosticity**. A good test is diagnostic. The aim of diagnosis is to analyse the difficulties of a student in a particular phase of work. The aim is to reveal reliable information concerning his weaknesses in order to overcome them by concentrated action and for remedial teaching. In this way it would help the teacher to guide them properly and adopt remedial measures to eliminate their weak points.

(*vii*) **Utility**. A good test is useful in various way. For example, a test result may be used for improvement of teaching, may be useful to measure some desired quality/ability in the student, useful in finding out deficiencies in pupils so that remedial measures by taken up for their removal etc.

11.4 TYPES OF TESTS OR EXAMINATIONS

Generally, the test are of two types:

(1) Traditional or essay type examinations; and

(2) New type test or examination.

Traditional types of test or traditional type of examination consist of only one form of questions and that is essay type questions.

New type of Examination or Test. These tests are known as objective test. They consist of the following types of tests:

(1) Recall type of test.

(2) Alternate response type of test.

(3) Multiple choice type of test.

(4) Matching type of test.

(5) The completion type of test.

(6) Classification type of test.

Defects of Traditional Type of Tests or Examinations

At present new type of tests are taking the place of traditional or essay type of tests. This trend is gaining importance because traditional type of examinations suffer from following defects:

(*a*) Defects From the Point of View of Students

(*i*) The essay type tests are less objective and so they **lack validity**. This type of test can reveal child's cramming capacity only.

(*ii*) These tests **lack reliability**. A student is compelled to have a selective reading. He depends more on guess papers and so there is an element of chance.

(*iii*) It keeps the students busy and full of nervous tension. The study does not spread over the whole year and is limited to a short period just before the examinations. Thus a habit of irregular study is developed in the student.

(*b*) Defects of Essay Type Examination From the Point of View of the Teacher

(*i*) The teacher covers only a limited and important portion of course because his aim is to see that maximum number of his students pass the examination.

(*ii*) The teaching programme of the teacher is wholly examination oriented and the basic principle of teaching his students are given least consideration.

(*iii*) The teacher is compelled to encourage his students to cramming which is not a psychological method of teaching.

(*iv*) Since a teacher is judged by the results of his students so every thing becomes subservient to the examinations.

(*v*) To show good results some times the teacher devotes a good deal of his time to indulge in guess work which affects his teaching.

(*c*) Defects From the Point of View of Achievement

(*i*) Essay type tests are not comprehensive and some students may get good marks only because the questions have been set from the portion prepared by them.

(*ii*) These tests are not objective and the score of a student depends on various factors such as Examiner's mood and whims etc.

(*iii*) This type of tests are not useful from the point of view of improvement. They fail to throw light on the defects of teaching-learning process or the defects of the curriculum.

From the above it can be concluded that essay type examination is not a correct method of evaluation in Mathematics. The improvement in system of evaluation is possible if following suggestions are given due consideration.

(*a*) Improvement in Essay Type Examination

In essay type examination an improvement is possible if we set shorter questions spread over the whole course. The language of question should be clear and precise, clear out directions be given for scoring.

(*b*) The Use of Objective Tests

In addition to essay type tests, some objective type tests may also be used for evaluation. The objective type tests can be of the following types:

(*a*) True-false type.

(*b*) Completion type.

(*c*) Multiple choice type.

(*d*) Matching type.

(*e*) Short answer type.

(*c*) Use of Oral Tests

In such test oral questions are given and students are required to give answers after oral calculations. Such tests require quick recall and thinking. These test help in assisting the ability of the student to apply the knowledge of facts in different situations.

(*d*) Assessment of Regular Work

For such an assessment a record of child's developments should be kept. Such a record may be kept for his home-work practical work etc. and this should be taken into consideration while assessing a student.

Thus we find that no single device is enough and a judicious blend of various evaluation tools is the best approach.

11.5 OBJECTIVE TESTS

At present objective tests are used for evaluation. The objective tests consists of completion type test, matching type tests, True/false type tests etc. Such objective tests have following merits:

(*i*) The objective tests have little or no scope of subjectivity. The score does not depend on Examiner's mood or whims.

(*ii*) These tests are more reliable. The score does not depend on expression, speed, style etc.

(*iii*) These are comprehensive. This requires from the students, thorough study of the syllabus.

(*iv*) There is no chance element in this type of tests.

(*v*) These are easy to administer and easy to score.

(*vi*) These are economical in respect of time.

However they also suffer from certain drawbacks. Some of these are as under:

(*i*) The objective type tests fail to test the organising ability of the students.

(*ii*) These tests fail to develop thinking and reasoning powers of the students which is one of the main aims of teaching Mathematics.

(*iii*) These tests put more emphasis on factual knowledge and very little importance is given to processes, methods or originality of thought.

(*iv*) These tests encourage guess work.

(*v*) These tests are not diagnostic. Because they do not show the defects in the teaching learning process.

(*vi*) These tests may pose some administrative difficulties as there may be indiscipline in the students. They may use unfair means, wishper answers or make some gestures.

(*vii*) It needs a lot of time and labour for preparing such a test.

Different Types of Objective Test. We have already seen the various types of objective tests. Let us now describe each of them in some detail.

1. **Completion Type of Test or Memory Recall**. This type of test consists of questions that are either sentences or statements, in between the words a bland is left within the

body of the material. Sometimes the space is left in the margin which has to be filled in by the students. Given below are a few examples of this type of test:

(*a*) The interest or Rs. 2,000 at the rate of 5% per annum for four years is------.

(*b*) The sum of the two sides of a triangle is greater than the ------.

(*c*) 4 : 5 :: 8 :

(*d*) The square root of 625 is------.

(*e*) The sum of exterior angles of a polygon is ------.

In this type of tests words used are quite important and so the statement or the question should be worded carefully leaving no scope for ambiguity. If the student get confused the very purpose of such a test is lost.

2. **True and False Type.** In this type, a number of statements are given. Some of these are true and some are false. The students are required to tick or write 'yes' before a correct statement.

Examples

(*i*) $(a + b)^2 = a^2 + b^2 + 2ab$

(ii) $x^2 - y^2 = (x - y)^2$

(*iii*) The sum of the angles of a triangle is always equal to two right angles.

(*iv*) Intersecting circles are concentric circles.

These tests can cover a wide range of subject-matter and wide sampling of knowledge is possible. There is an objectivity in scoring. Such a test is not difficult to construct but while constructing such a test the care be taken not to put very deceptive statements before the students.

3. **Multiple Choice Tests.** The multiple choice test contains a number of items, each of which has two or three

responses. One of the responses in each item is correct. The students are required to tick the correct response.

Examples

(*i*) $a^2 \times a^3 =$ (*a*) a^5, (*b*) a^6, (*c*) a^7, (*d*) a^4.

(*ii*) The sum of the angles of a triangle is equal to (a) 90°, (b) 180°, (c) 120°, (d) 360°.

(*iii*) The length of a rectangle is 5 metres and breadth 2.5 metres. Its area is (a) 7.5 sqm, (b) 12.5 sqm. (c) 10.5 sqm, (d) 25 sqm.

(*iv*) Sin 60 =

(*a*) $\frac{1}{2}$, (*b*) $\frac{\sqrt{3}}{2}$, (*c*) 3, (*d*) $\sqrt{\frac{3}{2}}$.

$\sin^2\theta + \text{Cos}^2\theta =$
(*a*) $\sin\theta$, (*n*) $\cos\theta$, (*c*) $\tan\theta$, (*d*) 1

(*vi*) sin 60° =
(*a*) sin 30, (*b*) cos 30, (*c*) tan 30, (*d*) cos 60.

This type of test requires memory as also the correct knowledge and a good vocabulary.

4. **Matching Type Tests**. In these tests, in each item, there are two columns. Each item in the first column is to be matched with the relevant item of the second column, not given in the same order. To avoid guess work, the items in the second may be more or less in number than the items in the first column.

For Example

Column 1	*Column 2*
10 × 12	length × breadth
20 ÷ 5	120
100 + 50	150
Area of rectangle is equal to	4.

5. **Classification Type of Test**. In this type of test such

questions are set which contain certain groups of words. Every group contains about five words out of which one is the correct answer to the questions. The correct work has to be underlined.

In fact, it involves memory recognition as well as recall.

For example:

(1) Underline the word that does not belong to the group; rectangle, square, triangle, quadrilateral, rhombus.

(2) Underline the equation that does not belong to the groups. $x^2 - 7x + 12 = 0;$

$$x+3 = 7;$$

$$x^2 = 9;$$

$$(x+1)^2 = x^2 + 2x + 1;$$

$$x/5+2 = x-10$$

A thoughtful consideration of essay type and objective type tests reveals that we should use both type of tests for evaluation. Depending upon what teacher wants to assess he should decide which type of test will be more useful in assessing the same. For removal of any guess work in objective type tests the following formula is useful

$$\text{Score} = R - \frac{W}{N-1}$$

Where R = number of right responses

W = number of wrong responses

N = number of alternative responses.

Requirements of the New Type of Test. New type of tests have to be carefully constructed. The following precautions be taken otherwise, these tests are likely to lose the utility:

(1) Careful planning and construction.

(2) These tests should be carefully planned and

constructed only then they shall serve their purpose. For this the following things are needed:

(*a*) **Determination of the Purpose**. The basic purpose of the test must be decided first.

(*b*) **Selection of the Test in Accordance with the Purpose**. After the purpose has been decided, the test has to be found out which would suit the purpose.

(*c*) **Objective Questions**. The questions that are constructed should be objective.

(*d*) **Ability of the Students to be kept in Mind**. The individual differences and the mental ability of the students should be kept in mind, otherwise the purpose shall not be served.

(*e*) **Scoring Key to be Prepared**. The scoring key, that provides answers to the questions, must also be prepared. Unless it is done, the purpose shall not be served. Without this, it shall be difficult to award marks.

(*f*) **Standardization**. These tests need standardization. Then only it is possible to do away with the element of subjectivity.

(*g*) **Intelligent Planning**. It is not possible for all the teachers to plan these tests. These tests have to be planned and constructed by intelligent teachers as they require intelligent planning.

Other Types of Tests. In addition to the tests given above, the following types of tests are also used:

(*a*) **Intelligence Test**. The basic object of these tests is to ascertain the mental capacity or the psychological capacity of the students. These tests require such questions that would give an idea about the mental age of the students.

(*b*) **Recognition Test.** These tests have the element of the traditional examination as also the new system of examination. In these tests, a figure is drawn or a particular question is given and the students have to recognise it. It may be very easily applied to Geometry.

(*c*) **Logical Selection Test.** In this test, several names of a particular object are given. The correct and the exact name is to be sorted by the students. This is also a new type of test.

11.6 DIAGNOSTIC AND ACHIEVEMENT TEST IN MATHEMATICS

The aim of diagnosis is to analyse the difficulties of the student in a particular phase of work. The aim is to reveal reliable information concerning his weakness in order to overcome them by concentrated action and for remedial teaching. It can also be used as an inventory test to find out how much the student knows about a given phase of the subject-matter. Diagnostic tests are used to discover and analyse pupils difficulties with a view to setting up specific remedial measures to correct and remove difficulties.

A diagnostic test is different from the achievement test in Mathematics. The main purpose of diagnostic test is to study the nature of difficulties experienced by pupils. While constructing a diagnostic test the teacher has to consider the individual difficulties experienced by students in solving problems. The test items should also give due consideration to the varying abilities of pupils in solving different types of problems. The age-norm, the grade norm etc. should also be given due consideration. Before constructing such a test a pilot study be conducted over a given area or unit and its results statistically analysed before finalising the test.

The reliability coefficient of the test has to be calculated and then the diagnostic test can be deemed to be fit for administration over a large sample.

Appropriate remedial instructions be given and for this careful planning is essential. The causes of failure in solving a problem are to be hypothesized systematically.

The importance of diagnostic tests is due to the following:

(*i*) Nature of the subject-matter.

(*ii*) Difficulties experienced by students as a group.

(*iii*) Difficulties experienced by certain individuals.

An achievement test is used to measure the degree of mastery of skills, fundamental concepts, process and general knowledge of the subject, attained by the student. The achievement test is valid when it can measure the extent to which the purpose for which it has been constructed.

Importance of Blue-Print in Constructing Achievement Test

The **blue print** here means the plan that the teacher has in evaluating the performance of the pupils.

The blue print concerns itself to the knowledge acquired by means of study, remembering, thinking, solving problems and formulating hypothesis. It is here that the formulation of instructional objectives and their respective behavioural changes can be clearly identified.

In a **blue print** the objectives are listed out horizontally. They are knowledge, understanding, application and skill. Again horizontal forms of test items are indicated. They are essay questions, short answer questions and objective questions.

Vertically we find the content divided into sub-units. The question paper should cover all the sub-units and all the objectives. The score for each type of question viz. essay, short answer and objective type should be fixed.

Chapter—12

Mathematics Club and Recreational Activities in Mathematics

12.1 INTRODUCTION

For supplementing the teaching of Mathematics in the class-room and to widen the knowledge of his students a good Mathematics teacher can involve his students in a number of cocurricular activities such as *Mathematics club, visits and excursion, broad-casts, gramophone lectures* etc. There is no limit to such extra curricular activities and teacher is free to undertake one or more such activities in his school for the benefit of his students.

Some of these activities and their organisational set up are taken up in the next few pages.

12.2 MATHEMATICS CLUB

Importance of Mathematics Club

As in some other subjects so also in Mathematics, the students be encouraged to organise themselves into *Mathematics clubs* and *Mathematics associations*. Under the auspices of these organisation, discussions and lectures etc. are arranged. Such functions are quite helpful in creating interest in Mathematics. Under the auspices of such organisation certain games based on some concepts of mathematics and mathematical problems can also be arranged. This is likely to help the students in having an idea of the practical utility of Mathematics in addition to creating their interest in Mathematics.

The values of Mathematics clubs may be summarised as under:

(*i*) It is useful in arousing and maintaining interest in Mathematics.

(*ii*) It stimulates the active participation of the students.

(*iii*) It develops in the students a habit of selective study. This helps them to make a distinction between relevant and irrelevant material.

(*iv*) The knowledge gained by students in various functions of such club activities supplements the class teaching.

(*v*) It provides the students an opportunity of free discussion and they are benefited from one another's view.

(*vi*) Gifted students get an opportunity to satisfy their needs and interests by actively participating in the activities of such clubs and associations.

(*vii*) Studentsget an apportunity to listen to some will known and distinguished Mathematicians.

(*viii*) It gives the students basic training in organising such programmes.

(*ix*) It is helpful in making proper utilization of leisure time.

(*x*) Through participation in such clubs students get acquainted with the contribution of Great Mathematicians in their fields.

Organisation of Mathematics Club

A Mathematics club, if properly organised, will be a great help in enlivening the teaching of Mathematics. Such a club should be run by the students under the guidance and supervision of his or the teacher. For proper running of a club the most important thing is the preparation of a draft constitution of the club. This draft be prepared by the Mathematics teacher in consultation with the head of the institution. This draft constitution should provide all important details about the name of the club, aims and objectives of the club, details regarding membership and the fees etc. To be paid by members, purposes for which the expenditure can be incurred and person competent to approve such an expenditure. Various offices available to members and the procedure for filling up such offices by other relevant details.

For efficient and successful working of Mathematics clubs in expert body has suggested the organisation as under:

(*i*) Such a club should have the head of institution as its patron.

(*ii*) One of the senior maths teachers be asked to be the sponsor of the club.

(*iii*) Membership of the club be open to all the Mathematics students of the school.

(*iv*) Associate-membership may be allowed to some other students interested in Mathematics.

(*v*) The club may have an elected executive committee. The members of executive should include the following and should be elected or nominated from amongst the students:

(*a*) Chairman

(*b*) Secretary

(*c*) Asstt. Secretary

(*d*) Treasures

(*e*) One or two class representatives from each class.

The executive committee may also include a librarian, a store keeper and a publicity officer.

(*vi*) Only a nominal membership fee be charged from the members.

(*vii*) The club members be asked to tap other resources and carry out the club activities in their own locality.

Assignment of Duties to Officer Bearers of a Mathematics Club

For a cohesive and efficient functioning of a club, there must be a clear demarcation of duties to be assigned to its office bearers. Following suggestions have been made in this regard.

Patron. He is expected to take a keen interest in all the activities of the club and to extend all the possible facilities to the club.

Sponsor. He is the main force to start the club and he has to take initiative to start such a club and make it a hub of activities. His role should be that of an advisor, guide and supervisor and he should refrain from becoming a dictator. He should always be alert to avoid any mishap. He should keep a strict watch on the activities of the club members.

Chairman. He being the elected representative of the student should be asked to preside over all the formal functions organised by the club. He has also to convene and preside over the meetings of the executive committee of the club.

Secretary. He is also an elected member and is to look after and maintain a proper record of various activities of the club. He should call a meeting of the executive committee in consultation with the chairman and in accordance with the constitution of the club. He should keep a true record of the meetings of the executive committee. He is also responsible to carry out all correspondence on behalf of the club and to extend invitation to speakers and guests for various functions of the club.

Asstt. Secretary. His main role is to assist the secretary in performance of his duties. In the absence of secretary he has to carry out all the functions of the secretary.

Treasurer. He is the person who is responsible for collection of subscription/membership fee for the club. He has also to maintain a proper account of receipts and expenditure of the club. He must present his accounts of the executive for audit and scrutiny at least once a year.

Members of Executive Committee. A member of executive committee is expected to extend his active cooperation and participate actively in formation of club's policy and programme. He should use his contacts and influence to make the programme of the club a success.

Suggested Activities for a Mathematics Club

(*i*) Organising inter-class, inter-school competitions on some interesting Mathematical topics.

(*ii*) Arranging a lecture by some renowned Mathematics teacher or scholar.

(*iii*) Celebrating days and events pertaining to the history of Mathematics or men of Mathematics.

(*iv*) Organising discussions about the practical applications of Mathematics.

(*v*) Organising recreational activities in Mathematics such as puzzles, riddles, catch-problem, number games etc.

(*vi*) Making or collecting charts, models, picture, graphs etc. for the Mathematics laboratory.

(*vii*) Conducting related project activities.

(*viii*) Preparing items for wall magazine.

(*ix*) Organising mathematical exhibitions or fairs.

(*x*) Organising certain outings of mathematical interest

such as visits to post-offices, banks, market places, big business concerns etc.

(*xi*) Organising paper reading contests about certain important topics of Mathematics.

(*xii*) Making arrangements to listen to certain radio broadcasts on mathematical topics.

(*xiii*) Organising seminars and career courses relating to Mathematics.

Thus we see that Mathematics club can cover a wide variety of topics relating to the subject. If the students participate in such activities whole-heartedly, then we derive great benefit. The club can go a long way in arousing and maintaining interest of the students. They will develop love for the subject. The utility of Mathematics club depends upon the interest shown by the teacher and the extent to which the students are motivated to take part in the activities of Mathematics club.

Mathematics Club and Classroom Teaching

The activities of Mathematics club and a supplement to classroom teaching. Such clubs play an important role in making Mathematics education more meaningful and effective. Various charts, models, improvised apparatus prepared by members of the club can be used as important teaching aids for teaching of Mathematics in the classroom. References could be made to various Mathematics projects undertaken by the club members and the club members may be asked to explain their projects in the class. The explanation of a project by a student in a class may then be put to open discussion in the class which would make other students more interested in learning Mathematics.

To make best use of the trips and excursions arranged by the Mathematics club, the students be given a questionnaire so that students may be more attentive to provide their answers. Answers given by the students may then be discussed in the classroom and teacher can coordinate all the facts observed by the students into a complete lesson.

Some method can be used to correlate and coordinate various club activities with classroom teaching.

There is no doubt about the fact that if the club activities are organised properly they will never interfere with classroom teaching. Various activities of the club are expected to develop the skill of the student, his power of reasoning, understanding, his power to distinguish between relevant and irrelevant etc.

Evaluation of Mathematics Club

To find out the extent to which a club has succeeded in achieving its stated objectives it is necessary to carry out regular periodical evaluation of the activities of the club. Such an evaluation may be external or internal or it may be a mixture of both. For internal evaluation the views of patron, sponsor about the activities of the club may be obtained. They should express their views along with their suggestions for improvement in the working of the club. For external evaluation the sponsor of some other near by Mathematics club be asked to visit the club activities and express his opinion. He may also be asked to give suggestions for improvement. An effort be them made to further improve the working of the club in the light of suggestions given for improvement.

12.3 RECREATIONAL ACTIVITIES IN MATHEMATICS

Mathematics is considered as dry subject and students do not find anything interesting in it. This impression about Mathematics can be reversed with the help of recreational activities in Mathematics. It is also possible to present a lively and interesting picture of Mathematics with the help of these activities. Recreational activities bring variety and also develop taste for Mathematics.

In ancient times, Mathematics was mainly studied for its recreational value and as a leisure time activity. Playing with numbers and other mathematical problems was enjoyed by people. Riddles in Mathematics provided fun and were quite witty. Some examples of such Mathematical riddles are as under:

(*i*) A clock strikes six in five seconds. How long does it take to strike twelve?

The answer is not 10 sec, but 11 sec.

(*ii*) An oil merchant has a tank of oil and he has two measures, one of 3 litres and another of 5 litres. He is to take 7 litres from the tank.

How will he do this by using these two measures?

Aesthetic Enjoyment in Mathematics

In Mathematics we come across many number games and patterns which give aesthetic enjoyment e.g.

(*i*) *Magic Square*

In this square the digits 1 to 9 are arranged in such a manner that the sum of digits in all directions is 15.

4	9	2
3	5	7
8	1	6

(*ii*) *Some interesting number patterns:*

$0 \times 9 + 1 = 1$ $\qquad$ $9 \times 9 + 7 = 88$

$1 \times 9 + 2 = 11$ $\qquad$ $98 \times 9 + 6 = 888$

$12 \times 9 + 3 = 111$ $\qquad$ $987 \times 9 + 5 = 8888$

$123 \times 9 + 4 = 1111$ etc. $\qquad$ $9876 \times 9 + 4 = 88888$ etc.

The importance of recreational activities can be summarised as under:

(*i*) Recreational activities bring a healthy change in the class atmosphere.

(*ii*) Recreational activities develop taste for Mathematics.

(*iii*) The students learn to appreciate the power and beauty of Mathematics.

(*iv*) Recreational activities prepare the students for leisure time. They can put riddles etc. and enjoy their leisure time.

(*v*) These develop many abstract relationships which would otherwise remain vague.

(*vi*) They sharpen wit and stimulate quick thinking.

Organising Recreational Activities in Mathematics

We have already seen that recreational activities in Mathematics are a source of enjoyment and are also quite useful as leisure time activities. For deriving maximum possible benefit such activities be organised in a proper way, following points should be kept in view while organising recreational activities in Mathematics:

(*i*) The teacher should fix a period in time table for recreational activities and the students be informed about it.

(*ii*) An intelligent and active student be made incharge of the activities and be named as secretary etc.

(*iii*) The teacher should ask all the students to come prepared with some riddles or recreational work on the fixed day.

(*iv*) Those students who want to participate be asked to give their names to the student incharge of the activities.

(*v*) The participants be asked to come to the stage turn by turn and present their items.

(*vi*) Only one student be allowed to put his item before others at a time.

(*vii*) The teacher or the participant should make clear any mathematical principle or formula underlying a riddle.

(*viii*) Over use of riddles should be discouraged.

(*ix*) The teacher should choose some interesting riddles that are related to a particular topic which he is teaching. Such riddles have great motivational value.

Chapter—13

Arousing and Maintaining Interest in Mathematics and Principles of Meaningful Learning

13.1 INTRODUCTION

To arouse and maintain the student's interest in Mathematics is a major problem for the teacher. The teacher knows very well that loss of interest is the major cause of student's failure. If the student has to be taught properly, the natural curiosity should be awakened among the students. This awakening of curiosity would create interest in them and would develop their attention towards the subject. This can be safely done for elementary classes by introducing play method. Later on, according to psycho-physical requirements, other methods such as cross-words or quiz etc. may be resorted to. If by allowing them to resort to these methods, an attempt is made to explain to them the methods also, the teaching would be interesting and useful.

The teaching can be made interesting and useful by correlating the present problem with interesting things already studied by the students.

The elements of novelty, usefulness and curiosity are the first thing to awaken the interest. The teacher should always try to keep interest alive by making the teaching practical and useful for day to day life. Interest in the subject can be effectively aroused and maintained by numerous special devices and activities. Some of these are discussed here.

13.2 TECHNIQUES TO BE EMPLOYED TO DEVELOP INTEREST IN MATHEMATICS

(*i*) **Intellectual Activity**. It is possible to arouse the students interest by stimulating curiosity. The work in Mathematics should challenge the intellect of students. This stimulates their curiosity and mental powers and helps in awakening their interest. The intellectual activity is governed by (*a*) thirst for knowledge (*b*) love of truth and beauty and (*c*) desire to interpret and control environment. The interest will be maintained if it remains challenging to their mental powers. This means that we should not present mathematical facts to pupils in the readymade form as this will encourage only cramming. We should maintain heuristic attitude in our teaching. Curiosity is the powerful urge which stimulates efforts to understand and learn certain things.

(*ii*) **Emphasising Practical Application**. One is always anxious for a thing which one considers more and more valuable. Generally student's interest is aroused by pointing out the applications of Mathematics to some other field with which he is already familiar. He comes to know that Mathematics is an important subject worth learning. When he realises the utility of the subject his interest is aroused and maintained in Mathematics.

(*iii*) **Correlation with Other Subjects**. Mathematics is related to so many other subjects and the teacher should make full use of these correlations to arouse students interest in Mathematics. It is thus desirable to take up relevant problems of Mathematics from other subjects while teaching Mathematics.

(*iv*) **Recreational Activities and Mathematics Club**. These have been discussed in detail in the previous chapter. The role of Mathematics club in developing students interest in Mathematics has been discussed at length. Recreational activities such as puzzles, riddles etc. make the subject lively and interesting active Mathematics club is one of the sure signs of students interest.

(*v*) **Practical Work**. Practical presentation of matter should precede its abstract form. Small children can not understand and appreciate much at abstract level. The children like to observe and handle various objects. They may be asked to verify mathematical truths by making experiments.

(*vi*) **Variety**. A topic should not be continued for too long a period, otherwise monotony would set in and students interest will be lost. Similarly the same method or aid will lead to loss of interest. Thus the teacher should try to bring some novelty or variety in his day to day teaching.

(*vii*) **Good Teaching**. For good teaching a teacher should prepare his lesson plan and use correct method of teaching. A good teaching is sure to keep student interested in the subject (Mathematics).

(*viii*) **Use of Teaching Aids**. The teaching can also be made interesting by proper use of teaching aids. The teaching aids provide a departure from routine teaching and help in making understand even difficult ideas. Preparation of aids and applications can be a (regular) activity of the learners.

(*ix*) **Suitable Physical Conditions**. Physical discomforts should be eliminated. Distractions should be avoided. Psychological conditions for study should be observed. There should be no over crowding in the class. Rooms should be well ventilated and black-boards should be well painted.

(*x*) **Individual Attention**. The teacher should pay individual attention to various categories of students. All the students are not interested in the same things. Some can be motivated by challenging situations, some by practical work and so on. In the usual class teaching, some of the pupils may not understand certain steps, which is indicated by their blank note-books, such students begin to lose interest. The teacher should make sure that all understand what he teaches.

A reference to historical background of different mathematical terms and ideas gives a good start for learning them. The teacher should strive to make the subject-matter attractive and pleasant.

The aim of teaching Mathematics for fun and pastime should receive some attention. Organisation of a mathematical workshop can provide a combination of recreation, activity and learning.

The teacher can think of many other ways and means to arouse and maintain interest of his students in his teaching. He should himself be interested in teaching. Only then he will take pains to make his work interesting to the students. He should also try to understand his students, their general level of achievement, interests and developmental stage, this will help him in selecting and adopting better motivational procedures.

13.3 PRINCIPLES OF MEANINGFUL LEARNING IN MATHEMATICS

Meaningful learning in Mathematics can consist of Mathematical experiences as the following:

(*i*) Those experiences which are helpful in mental, emotional and social development.

(*ii*) Those experiences which have utilitarian, practical and behavioural values.

(*iii*) Those experiences which are useful in learning higher and advanced aspects of the subject.

(*iv*) Those experiences which are helpful in proper learning of other subjects.

(*v*) Those experiences which stimulate and maintains interest in the subject and which lead to development of proper attitude towards the subject.

Principles of Meaningful Learning

There are many principles of meaningful learning in Mathematics which are as follows:

(*i*) **Principle of Motivation.** It is essential that the students are motivated before they are made to learn anything. Motivation is the basic activity for creating interest. Various means such as aids, relationships, historical references, anecdotes and possible applications can be adopted to provide motivation. When learning is prompted by inner urges and motives, it is bound to be meaningful.

(*ii*) **Principle of Definite Purpose.** Learning is meaningful if it is directed by some definite aim. The aim and objective should be definite and these be made clear to the students.

(*iii*) **Principle of Utility.** When a student knows that topics or sub-topic that is being taught is useful in his present or future life, his aim becomes more definite. In this way learning becomes need based and so more meaningful. Thus teacher should tell the students about applications of the topic of teaching in various fields.

(*iv*) **Principle of Heuristic or Problem Solving Attitude.** By proceeding on heuristic lines teacher can extract out maximum information from his students. In this method students find a continuous challenge to their intellect. If this approach is adopted Mathematics never appear dull or dreary. Methods like heuristic, analytic, induction and problem solving and recommended to the teacher and those like effort, understanding, intelligent practice and problem solving are recommended for the learner.

(*v*) **Principle of Practice.** In learning of Mathematics, there is need for regular and persistent practice. The student should never lose patience, hope and self confidence. With sufficient practice, even the details become clear and the child develops in-sight into the subject. His learning becomes meaningful fruitful.

(*vi*) **Principle of Logical Thinking**. When the students work logically and systematically, the things learnt are meaningful. They exercise their thinking and reasoning powers, instead of cramming or blind memorisation. Crammed facts are always meaningless. The knowledge gained by systematic process of thinking and reasoning is a permanent and valuable assest to the pupils.

(*vii*) **Principle of Activity**. The students learn best when they are actively involved in the teaching-learning process. If they are passive listeners only, their interests will fade away and there will not be any worthwhile learning. So the teacher should develop mathematical ideas or principles with the active cooperation of students. However, activities of children should also be meaningful.

Students are influenced by the teacher's own personality and his abilities. The teacher should have a sense of humour, patience, imagination, friendliness. The teacher should have a love for the subject. The teacher's ability to relate the subject to life situations will help to a great extent in motivating the learner. The job of a teacher lies in creating a climate of pupil interaction and inspiring them to know things by themselves.

Chapter—14

Backward and Gifted Students

14.1 INTRODUCTION

Teachers must be aware of the individual differences that exist among the pupils. Whatever may be the subject, teachers are to take into account such individual differences to make his teaching effective and that is also true in case of teaching of Mathematics. Broadly speaking students may be classified as average, below average (Backward) and above average (Gifted).

14.2 BACKWARD STUDENTS IN MATHEMATICS

When a student is found to lag behind other students in his class we call that particular child as backward. Backwardness in Mathematics may be of two kinds:

(*i*) General backwardness, and

(*ii*) Specific backwardness.

(a) **General backwardness**. It is the case, when a child is backward in all the subjects. This type of backwardness is because of low I.Q. Such students can be pulled up to some extent, by the combined efforts of teachers and parents. In case a child has very low I.Q. he may be guided to take up some manual job.

(b) **Specific backwardness**. In this case, a child is backward in Mathematics, but he is quite good in other subjects. To pull up such a student, the Mathematics teacher must make efforts in a planned way. Individual cases may have to be tackled in separate classes whereas border cases may be treated in the class-room itself. The teacher must study individual cases, before applying remedial measures.

Identification of Backward Students

The teacher can identify backward students in the following ways:

(*i*) To identify students with low I.Q teacher may carry out intelligence tests.

(*ii*) To find, if a student is slow in picking up facts, teacher can put up few oral questions and observe the responses given by the students.

(*iii*) Teacher can also know about the level of understanding of a student by observing their faces. Whenever a student fails to understand some important details his face bears a blank look.

(*iv*) The score of a student in an achievement test also points to the position of the student. The score of a backward child is generally low.

(*v*) A backward child is not able to do written work in a finished style. He generally does things in a haphazard manner.

(*vi*) A backward student would prefer to be seated on a back bench or in corners.

(*vii*) A backward student is generally irregular in doing his home-work.

(*viii*) A backward student may not be very regular in attending the class.

(*ix*) A backward student is likely to remain passive for most of the time in the class.

Suggestions for Helping Backward Children

A teacher will be able to help a backward child if he can find the cause of backwardness of the child. Here we are listing some important causes for backwardness of a child. The suggestion for helping a backward child are also given alongwith the cause of backwardness.

(i) Physical Handicaps. In case of some students the cause of backwardness may be a physical cause, such as poor eye sight, defect in hearing, stomach trouble or headache. Mathematics needs special concentration and because of the physical defects the child fails to concentrate on Mathematical work.

A medical examination of such students may be advised. The cooperation of parents should also be sought. Physically handicapped children be given sympathetic but normal treatment. They should never be ridiculed by the teacher or the class-mates.

(ii) Poor Mental Health. The backwardness may be due to mental cause, inborn or environmental.

In such a case the teacher should study each case individually. An attitude of love and sympathy and preparedness to help children will be helpful. The teacher should develop in them proper reading and learning habits, power of concentration and memorisation. Serious cases of poor mental health be referred to psychologists or psychiatrists.

(iii) Lack of Interest. In some cases the cause of backwardness may be the distaste for the subject, which may be natural or acquired. The distaste for the subject may be due to faulty methods of teaching or learning, harsh and disinterested teachers, heavy syllabus etc.

In such cases a genuine taste will be developed through the teacher's patience and persistence. He should not pronounce a case as hopeless and backward. He should develop a positive attitude of the students for the subject.

(iv) Defective Teaching. If the method of teaching is defective, it is likely to create a distaste for the subject. The faulty method of teaching creates certain doubts in the student's mind, about some fundamentals of the subject. Such doubts hinder the progress of the child.

In such a case the teacher should choose some correct method of teaching keeping in view the nature of the topic and the type of students to be taught. The teacher should not hesitate to explain to students again and again if required.

(v) Teacher's Attitude. Some teachers are lenient while some are strict. The harsh and unsympathetic attitude of the teacher never pays. Teacher should be sympathetic to his students and his attitude should be encouraging.

(vi) Influence of Home. Some children may have uncongenial home conditions and so may remain disturbed. They may not be able to do their home work regularly. Some parents talk about Mathematics as a dull, dry and tough subject.

In such cases the teacher should try to understand the home conditions and should establish links with the parents. Parents be advised to talk positively about Mathematics even though they may not be good in the subject.

(vii) Irregular Work Habits. Generally the students are not very regular with their work and as the teacher proceeds furthers, they fail to pick up certain new facts because they forget certain previously learnt facts. A gap in knowledge hinders their progress in Mathematics. Such a situation is likely to be found in those students who cut their classes.

In all such cases the teacher should try to make the students more regular in their work. Such students be assigned home-work regularly. Such students can also be given tests or assignments at short intervals.

(viii) Lack of Individual Attention. Because of individual differences all the students do not understand things in the same way. The intelligent students pick up quickly but the weak students need more explanation and illustrations.

It is the responsibility of the teacher to see that even backward students follow his lesson. If required teacher should give enough drill work and the difficulties of backward students be individually attended.

(ix) Change of School or the Teacher. Sometimes the students have to change school due to parent's transfer etc. and he may find the course at new school to be different. Even in case of same courses, the coverage may be different. It is likely to hinder the progress of the child.

In such cases it would be advisable to arrange private coaching for the child.

(x) Defective Work Habits. In some cases the difficulties may arise due to difficulties in language to understand problems. They may be working in an unsystematic and haphazard manner. The lack of ability of drawing skills, poor hand writing etc. may be responsible to make the child unsystematic and irregular and thus make him a backward child.

In such cases the teacher should not insist not on neat and accurate systematic work. The student may be encouraged to improve his drawing skill and handwriting etc. The teacher can also help the students in analysing problems in analysing problems or statements so that the student is able to understand them.

(xi) Temperamental Maladjustment. Some students may be too much sentimental, or nervous. Such students fail to control their emotions. When they start work, they get impatient and get confused and fail to concentrate on Mathematics. They are likely to commit mistakes while solving problems. In this way they become backward in Mathematics.

Such students need sympathetic treatment. Teacher should try to understand the causes of their emotional maladjustment and should encourage them to work systematically and patiently.

From the above discussion we can conclude that there are various causes of backwardness in Mathematics and the teacher can do a lot in removing the backwardness in children. The concious and persistent efforts of the teacher are likely to bear fruit.

14.3 GIFTED STUDENTS IN MATHEMATICS

A student is considered as **Mathematically gifted student** if he shows consistent remarkable interest and achievement in Mathematics. The number of Mathematically gifted students in a school is generally limited to one or two However the education of gifted children is of utmost importance. Thus such gifted students in Mathematics have to be identified by the teacher.

Identification of Gifted Students in Mathematics

It has been observed that the gifted students begin to show their talent right in early stages and such students can be identified as under:

(*i*) Gifted student picks up things rapidly and easily.

(*ii*) A gifted student is quick in grasping, relationships, making generalisations and drawing conclusions.

(*iii*) He puts intelligent questions in class.

(*iv*) He is able to solve those problems which are of a higher standard.

(*v*) He shows originality in solving problems.

(*vi*) He possesses a good power of imagination, thinking and reasoning.

(*vii*) He is a liking to work at abstract levels and does not like simple practical work.

(*viii*) His achievements are remarkable in various achievement tests.

(*ix*) His assignment work is of good standard.

(*x*) He is always alert and actively participates in teaching learning process.

Enrichment Programme for Gifted Students

Since it is not possible to have separate schools for such gifted students so such gifted students be given certain enrichment programmes in the same class. The enrichment programme for such students may include:

(*i*) An enriched syllabus to provide for extensive and intensive study.

(*ii*) They should be encouraged to enrich their knowledge by the study of supplementary readers, reference books and general literature from the library.

(*iii*) They should be allowed to do their independent study in the library.

(*iv*) For teaching such gifted children the teacher should use heuristic, analytic, problem, project or discussion method.

(*v*) They should be told the history of the development of various topics and about the contributions of renowned Mathematicians.

(*vi*) Gifted students be encouraged to actively participate in various activities of Mathematics club.

(*vii*) Gifted students be encouraged to apply mathematical facts for solving their day to day problems and should be told about the practical, cultural and disciplinary values of the subject.

(*viii*) Gifted students be asked to organise seminars, exhibitions etc. concerning Mathematicians.

(*ix*) They should be asked to work on some useful projects either independently or collectively.

(*x*) They should be told that there is enough scope for research work in Mathematics.

(*xi*) The work of such gifted students should be duly appreciated by the teacher.

(*xii*) Special coaching be arranged for such students.

In a subject like Mathematics providing individual attention assumes a greater role because of the intricate skill involved and the vigorous mental and disciplinary qualities in built in the very nature of the subject.

Chapter—15

History of Mathematics

15.1 INTRODUCTION

Mathematics has been the backbone of our civilization. It is no exaggeration to say that history of Mathematics is the history of civilization. Mathematics has led to the development of various subjects, vocations and technology. Mathematics is an exact science which is still playing an important role in various walks of life.

According to J.W.L. Glaisher, "I am sure that no subject looses more than Mathematics by any attempt to dissociate it from its history."

Mathematics has been a progressive science.

15.2 VALUE OF HISTORY OF MATHEMATICS

For a teacher the utility of history of Mathematics can be summarised as under:

(*i*) It provides a glimpse of the role played by Mathematics in various walks of life.

(*ii*) It shows the correlation of Mathematics with other branches of knowledge.

(*iii*) It clearly brings out the fact that significant developments in the subject have always been prompted by human needs.

(*iv*) It makes clear the fact that Mathematics is a man-made science.

(*v*) It makes the teaching of Mathematics interesting.

(*vi*) It is easier to understand most of the mathematical topics, concepts and terms by reference to their historical background.

(*vii*) It helps in gradation of subject matter, the topics discovered earlier were simpler.

(*viii*) It makes the correlation of Mathematics with other subjects easier.

(*ix*) It helps in enhancing the reputation of the teacher.

(*x*) It provides a warning against making hasty conclusions.

(*xi*) It gives better understanding of the subject.

The history of Mathematics depicts the different stages in the development of Mathematics throughout the ages. It shows that Mathematics is a dynamic subject, not static and it should be taught as such.

15.3 HISTORICAL REVIEWS OF DEVELOPMENTS

In the history of Mathematics there have been some very remarkable developments in the form of discovery and evolution of certain ideas and processes. These ideas and processes claim special status and significance in the overall progress of mathematical knowledge. They are considered to the landmarks in the history of the subject. At this moment we shall discuss only a few of them.

1. Notation System

The origin of notation system is as old as the man himself. Number sense is some thing innate in man. It is believed that animals and birds also have number sense. The primitive man was able to differentiate one object from two but could not tell one and one are two.

The primitive man used various ways to count. He used fingers, notches, cuts in the trees, lines on the ground, pebbles, etc. for the purpose. The notation system originated and developed differently in different countries.

The numeral '1' perhaps meant one lifted finger.

'Two' was represented by two fingers or lines. If we write two lines without lifting the pen, it becomes **Z** which ultimately changed into **2**.

Or

It becomes μ the numeral used by the Arabs or Persians. Similarly if we draw three lines without lifting the pen, it becomes 3 or ϖ or 3 all numerals for three.

Babylonians

The Babylonians used wedge-shaped symbols. One was represented by V, ten was represented by < and hundred by V <.

Roman System

The Roman system is based on the idea of counting fingers or lines. Thus I, II and III represented one, two and three respectively V probably represented the whole hand. To avoid clumsy I I I I they wrote I before V.e. IV, the symbol gave rise to the idea of positional value. Then the symbols VI, VII, VIII etc. The symbol X was perhaps the combination of two fives.

Hindu-Arabic System

The notation system 1, 2, 3... can be called Hindu-Arabic System. This system was originated by Hindus, perfected and transmitted to the west through the Arabs. Some ancient symbols carved on stone are found.

I	II	+	6
One	Two	Four	Six

At some other places, some such symbols are found:

–	=	±	7	?
One	Two	Four	Seven	Nine

The symbol 0 was used to denote vacuums. The word zero comes from Arabic 'Sifar' which was translation of the Hindu word 'Shunya'. Arabs also made certain modifications in Hindu numerals. During 13th century and after the Hindu-Arabic system spread all over the world.

2. Metric System of Weights and Measures

Primitive man used different stones, seeds etc. for the purpose of weighting. In India, *Ratti* (a seed) was taken as the basic unit of weight, 'Penny' an English unit of weight was considered as equal to 32 wheat seeds, various limbs of body were used by man to measure lengths e.g. cubit, span, pace, foot etc. In England a yard was fixed as the distance from the nose to the thumb of King Henry I.

Because of lack of communication systems the units of weights and measures varied from place to place. The unit 'Pound' was used by Romans. At some places the 'pound' was considered to be of 13 ounces at another of 18 ounces. So there was a lot of confusion in the system of weights and measures. In 1960 the Eleventh General International Conference on Weights and Measures adopted a system of units that includes the original Metric units and various other units used in Science and Engineering. (For details refer *Encyclopedia Britanica* please).

The scientists took the distance from the North pole to the equator on a line running through Paris. This distance was divided into ten million parts and one such part was called a metre. As it was not very accurate, it was given up. Now the metre is defined as the length of a standard bar kept in Paris.

For smaller measurements, the metre was divided into tens using Latin prefixes as deci, centi, milli. For longer measurements, they multiplied by tens using Greek prefixes such as kilo, deca, hecto etc.

1 m = 10 dm

1 dm = 10 cm

1 cm = 10 mm

1 km = 1000 m

1 decameter = 10 m etc.

Similarly units of area were developed and we have square metres, square decimetres and square centimetres as the units of area.

Volume

In the same way, units of volume were developed and we have cubic metre, cubic centimeter etc. as units of volume.

Weight

The weight of one cubic centimeter of water at 4°C was taken as one gram. The gram was further sub-divided into decigrams, centigrams and milligrams and multiplied into decagrams, hectograms and kilograms.

Superiority over non-metric units. The non-metric units varied from place to place and there was a great confusion. Metric system has brought about uniformity of measurement all over the world. It has facilitated trade as the traders and manufacturers can deal and bargain on the basis of the same units throughout the world. Further, it is easy to remember various metric units as these are based on the scale of ten. One who knows multiplication and division by ten, can remember easily the units of weight, length, area, volume etc. The scale generally facilitiates calculations.

3. Historical Development of Logarithms

The word 'logarithm' is derived from the Greek words 'logos' and 'arithmos'. Logos means to reason, to reckon, to calculate Arithmos means a number. Thus logarithm stands for *calculations of numbers*.

Logarithms were inverted by John Napier, the famous mathematician of Scotland. In 1614, he published his logarithmic table. It took him twenty years to prepare logarithmic tables. Making use of logarithms, he converted the difficult processes of multiplication and division into simple process of addition and subtraction. This saved a lot of time and labour of the mathematicians and scientists over the world. Kepler, the famous astronomer, remarked that Napier tripled the life of an astronomer.

Henry, Briggs, professor of Mathematics in London was so much impressed by this invention that he came to Scotland to meet Napier and discuss with him his new invention. According to Briggs, Napier proceeded as under:

$$10^1 = 10, 10^2 = 100, 10^3 = 1000$$

This was written as log 10 = 1

Logarithm of 100 is 2

Logarithm of 1000 is 3 and so on.

Further he observed that 100 x 100 means simply

adding logarithm 2 and 1

$$10^2 \times 10^1 = 10^3$$

Similarly, $10^2 \div 10^1 = 10^1$

So division means the subtraction of logarithms.

Napier began to multiply, divide, square and extract square- roots of various numbers. He computed logarithms of hundreds of numbers, and computed them to several decimal places. It took him months and years. Finally in 1664 the first table of logarithms of numbers was prepared.

Thus starting with the logarithms of sines. Napier applied logarithms to numbers. The terms Mantissa and Characteristic were introduced by Briggs in 1624. The first table of logarithms of trigonometric functions to the base 10 was made by Gunter in 1620. Gauss suggested using it for the fractional part of all decimals.

4. Historical Backgrounds of Computer Mathematics

In age of automation man has invented machines for every field of life to make his function easy quick and reliable computers to help a mathematician. Computers have their origin in man's attempts to find ways and means to facilitate calculations.

Probably the earliest attempt was a table of dust and sand on which calculations were carried out with the help of stick. This was known as abacus. Erasing on the abacus consisted in smoothing out dust or sand with hand. Next attempt probably a ruled table with small stick pebbles or counters arranged in lines. Using the principle of position a single bead on a line would represent 1 in next line it would represent 10 and so on.

The next development was given by John Napier in 1617. He arranged a system of rods to represent the method of calculation. These rods were called 'Napier's bones'. In 1642 Pascal devised first mechanical computer. He attached cylinders with the notched wheels of rocks. Each wheel was divided into ten small divisions. The system was so arranged that one complete rotation of unit wheel would turn one division on the tens wheels and so on. It was an adding machine. Leibnitz introduced in this, a device to calculate multiplications and divisions.

Towards the beginning of 19th century, Charles Baves, a professor of Mathematics in the Oxford University invented a computer consisting of 18 wheels. In 1944, world's first electronic computer was invented. He was called electronic brain of the woıld. It consisted of 3500 parts. It would take 300,000 micro seconds in addition of two numbers. Then came more and more sophisticated computers.

15.4 ANECDOTES FROM THE LIFE HISTORY OF MATHEMATICS

The height which Mathematics is occupying today and the progress which it has made through the ages is all due to the dedicated and sustained work of its great students, many such students of Mathematics have became immortal because of their memorable contributions to Mathematics. They will be remembered by mankind for all times to come and mankind will always remain indebted to them for their contribution. The future scholars in Mathematics will get inspiration from the lives and deeds of these great scholars. We had many such great mathematician in past and here we will take up for consideration some of them.

Prominent Mathematicians

A comprehensive list of prominent mathematicians is given here.

Name of Mathematicians	*Period*
Thales	640 B.C. to 550 B.C.
Pythagoras	569 B.C. to 500 B.C.
Zeno	495 B.C. to 435 B.C.
Plato	429 B.C. to 348 B.C.
Euclid	330 B.C. to 295 B.C.
Archimedes	287 B.C. to 212 B.C.
Ptolemy	100 A.D. to 168 A.D.
Pappus	about 300 A.D.
Arya Bhatt	about 350 A.D.
Brahma Gupta	about 640 A.D.
Leonardo of Pisa	1175 A.D. to 1230 A.D.
Copernicus	1473 A.D. to 1543 A.D.
Napier	1550 A.D. to 1617 A.D.
Galileo	1564 A.D. to 1642 A.D.
Kepler	1571 A.D. to 1630 A.D.
Des Cartes	1596 A.D. to 1650 A.D.
Pascal	1623 A.D. to 1662 A.D.

Name of Mathematicians	*Period*
Gregory	1638 A.D. to 1675 A.D.
Newton	1642 A.D. to 1727 A.D.
Leibnitz	1646 A.D. to 1716 A.D.
Bernoulli (Jacob)	1654 A.D. to 1705 A.D.
Bernoulli (Jhon)	1667 A.D. to 1748 A.D.
De Moivre	1667-1754
Toyfer	1687-1741
Maclaurin	1698-1746
Euler	1707-1783
D'Alembert	1717-1783
Lagrange	1736-1813
Laplace	1749-1827
Cauchy	1759-1827
Gauss	1777-1855
Abel	1802-1829
Hamilton	1805-1855
Ricmann	1826-1866
Cayley	1821-1895
Weierstrass	1815-1897
Ramanujan	1887-1920

PYTHAGORAS

It is generally believed that Great Mathematician Pythagoras was a native of Samos belonging to Jonian colony of Greeks planted on western shore and island of Asia Minor. He settled at Crotona, a town in South Italy, 29 B.C. Pythagoras travelled to Egypt to gather knowledge. He used to deliver lectures on Philosophy and Mathematics. His lectures were heard by persons of all ranks. The influence of

Pythagoras on his listeners was so great that they formed themselves into a society called 'Order of Pythagoreans.' This influence was more religious than political. They bound themselves with an oath that they would not reveal the secrets and teaching of the school. A 'star' shaped pentagram was the distinctive badge of the brotherhood.

In Mathematics the Pythagoreans made great progress, particularly in the field of numbers and geometry of solids and areas. He is credited to have discovered the proof of the theorem of right angled triangle. He is also said to have discovered the harmonical progression in the notes of a musical scale, by finding the relation between the length of a string and the pitch of vibrating notes. To Pythagoras, numbers were not attributes, but they were the stuff out of which all objects we see are made—the rational reality. In Geometry 'one' was identified with the point 'two' with the line, 'three' with the surface and 'four' with the solid.

Aristotle has remarked, "The Pythagoreans first applied themselves to Mathematics, a science, which they improved and penetrated with it, they fancied that the principles of Mathematics were the principles of all things." A younger Mathematician Eardemus remarked that, "They changed Geometry into a liberal science; they diverted Arithmetic from the service of commerce."

Another kind of problem which interested Pythagoras was 'application of Areas.' He introduced the term, 'parabole', 'ellipse' and 'hyperbole'. Apollonius adopted this nomenclature which is in use even today. This classification has proved to be the key to further discoveries, one of them being the discovery of *irrational numbers*.

Pythagoreans made substantial progress in the theoretical side of arithmetic and algebra. They had a geometrical equivalent for our method of solving quadratic equations. They studied various types of progressions—Arithmetic, Geometric and Harmonic.

PLATO

The two well read philosophers of Athens are Socrates and Plato. Plato exerted a great influence on Mathematics by founding an academy in Athens. Plato has put an inscription on his lecture room which read as, "Let no one destitute of Geometry enter my doors." He believed that a man should be trained to see below the surface of things. Proclus, a Greek Commentator, remarked, "Plato caused Mathematics in general and Geometry in particular to make a very great advance, by reason of his enthusiasm for them which is of course obvious from the way he filled his books with mathematical illustrations..." It is related to the question, "what does God do?" Plato replied, "God always geometriozise."

EUCLID

Alexander of Mancedonia, the first conqueror of world, found that the city of Alexandria was the meeting place of Greeks, Jews and Arabs. Ancient Mathematics was perfected and treasured in libraries in this city. Ptolemy, the successor of Alexander, established a university and Euclid worked as a teacher in this university. He taught there for about 30 years.

Once a person, on reading Geometry with Euclid, asked, "What shall I get by learning these things?" Euclid called his slave and said, "Give him three pence, since he must gain out of what he learnt."

He wrote books. His famous works are 'Elements'. The 'Element' of Euclid consists of thirteen books. Book I, II, IV and VI on times, areas and simple figures are mostly Pythagorean. Books III on circles expounds Hippocrates. Book V in on proportions and elaborates the work of Eudoxus. Books VII, VIII and IX are arithmetical and give an interesting account of theory of numbers. Prime and composite numbers are introduced. L.C.M. and G.C.F. the theory of geometrical progressions, the theorem $a^m a^n = a^{mn}$ and the method of summing the progressions by use of equal ratios were also expounded by him. He also introduced the idea of perfect numbers, which is far harder to find than the rare postage stamps. A number is said to be perfect when it is equal to sum of its factors, such as 6,23,486. The largest perfect number so far discovered is 2^{126} (2^{127-1}).

Book X mainly deals with the doctrine of irrational numbers, specifically of the type V $(\sqrt{a} \pm \sqrt{b})$, where a and b are positive integers. Book XI mainly deals with elementary solid geometry. Book XII deals with the method of exhaustion and finding the area of a circle in the form πr^2. Book XIII gives and proves the constructions for the five regular solids, and ends with decahedron.

Except a few logical blemishes that occur in his works, much has survived unchanged. He left nothing to be desired. Firstly, he laid down carefully his definition, then his common assumptions or axioms, then his postulates before proceeding with the orderly arrangement of their consequences.

Many other writings of Euclid have come down to us dealing with astronomy, music and optics. But two of his works: 'Books of Fallacies' and 'Porisms' are lost. We have come to know of them indirectly through Pappus, another mathematician of latter era.

ARCHIMEDES

Euclid was followed by Archimedes. Archimedes was the practical man of common sense. He introduced imaginative skill and insight in Geometry and Mechanics and invented Integral Calculus. His father Phidias, was an astronomer and was related to King of Synacuse, Hlero II. Young Archimedes, spent sometime in Egypt, most probably at Alexandria, with immediate successors of Euclid.

When Syracuse was sieged by the Romans, Archimedes who was seventy five years old directed his skill against the enemy. Plutarch, the Roman leader, is said to have cried out to his men, "Shall we not make an end of fighting against this geometrical Brareus, who uses our ships like cups to ladle water from the sea, drives off our sambuca ignominiously with cudgel-blows, and by the multitude of missiles that he hurls at us all at once, out doses the hundred-handed giants of mythology." But it was of no avail. No record of all this ingenuity of Archimedes is available anywhere. But even after the fall of the city, Archimedes was thinking about a diagram on the sand lying on the ground when he was struck down by a Roman soldier.

Archimedes gave strict proofs for finding the areas, volumes, centre of gravity of curves and surfaces, circles, spheres, conics and spirals. By finding the tangent of a spiral he embarked in the subject differential geometry. In his works, he used algebraic formula such as

$$\sum_{1}^{n} r^2 = \frac{1}{6} n(2n+1)(n+1)$$

$$\sum_{1}^{2n-1} \sin \frac{y\pi}{2n} = \cot \frac{\pi}{4n}$$

He was familiar with continued fractions. He created new applications of Mathematics in Statics and Hydrostatics.

PTOLEMY

Ptolemy was a good astronomer and his treatment of astronomy was as lucid and complete as the treatment of Euclid in Geometry. He gave a comprehensive account of astronomy in his book 'Almagest'. Arabs were very much fascinated by this book. His works were based on the assumption that earth was the centre of all universe and even sun rotated around it. However, Copernicus proved that this assumption was wrong and that sun is the centre of all universe and all planets moved round sun.

PAPPUS

He was a great Mathematician. He was the founder of a new branch of Mathematics known as 'calculus of variations'. His most famous theorem states. "The volume (or area of curved surface) generated by revolution of the area (length of arc bounded by two straight lines about a straight line in its plane not intersecting it, is equal to the area (length of arc) of the curve multiplied by the length of arc of its central."

He gave a detailed account of different properties of quadrilaterals and specially those with a grouping of six points upon a line into three pairs. For the first time the word 'locus' was used, the statements like straight line is a curve of order one, conic is a curve of order two, and so on were also used for the first time by him. Particular cases of cubic and other curves were also discovered.

NAPIER

Johan Napier belonged to noble Scottish family. At that time Scotland was a country of barbarous hospitality and of baronial leaders. Their knowledge of Arithmetic was confined to counting on fingers. He lost his mother at age of 13 and in the same year, he was sent to University of St. Andrews, where his interest was aroused both in Arithmetic and Theology.

Napier acquired great reputation as an inventor. He made a sort of chart-arithmetic in which digit moved like rooks and bishops on board. He also devised a piece of such efficient artillery that it could kill all cattle within the radius of a mile. This invention horrified Napier and he refused to further develop it.

He also propounded the binary system of writing the numbers as against decimal system. By 1590, he discovered logarithm—a device which replaces multiplication by addition. His treatment of the subject shows intimate knowledge of the correspondence between arithmetical and geometrical progressions.

He could anticipate the practical benefit of logarithm in other branches of Mathematics and sciences and so he deliberately kept himself aloof of all other engagements, and started writing the tables of logarithm. This was a life-long task and these tables were published twenty-five years later. All this was done before either the theory of indices or differential calculus had been invented.

Napier was also a geometer. He devised new methods in spherical astronomy.

JOHN KEPLER

Kepler was born of parents of fair financial condition, but his early childhood was full of problems and so he left his house. He graduated from the University of Tubingen.

He became lecturer at Gratz and then turned into a thorough Copernican. He was much agitated about the fact that why there were only six planets (only six planets were known by then).

Later Kepler came under the influence of Galileo who helped to stabilise his genius. He thought of a harmony between Arithmetic Geometry and Music which could solve all mysteries of the universe. He found three laws of planetary motion. These were stated by him in 1609 and 1619. The two laws stated in 1609 are:

(*i*) The orbit of each planet is an ellipse with sun at focus.

(*ii*) The line joining the sun to the planet sweeps out equal areas in equal times.

The third laws stated in 1619 is as under:

(*iii*) The square of the period of the planet is proportional to the cube of its mean distance from the sun.

The first law made a change in the scientific outlook; the second law provides an early example of infinitesimal calculus.

Kepler used symbols analogous to I, V, X, L, but instead of number one, five, ten and fifty he selected one, three, nine, twenty seven etc. Thus he wrote

$$20 = 27 - 9 + 3 - 1.$$

In his book, "Harmonies Mundi" he had made a systematic search into the theory of Musical intervals and their relations to the distances between the planets and the sun.

DESCRATES

He was a French. He was a delicate person. He received traditional education in Mathematics, Physics, Logic and Ancient languages. He led a roming unsettled life and wandered all over the continent. In 1638, he published two books (1) Discourse on Method and (2) Meditations.

'Discourse and Method' contained important mathematical work.

His work changed the face of Mathematics because he founded Analytical Geometry. This later laid down the foundation of differential calculus which made Newton and Leibnitz immortal Mathematicians. It was Descartes who first set the fashion of denoting variable by X, Y, Z and constants by a, b, c. He also introduced indices to denote continued products of same factor. Descartes distinguished between two classes of curves: geometrical and mechanical, or as Leibnitz preferred to call them: algebrical and transcendental.

Descartes also devised a method of determining the shortest line PQ from a given point P to a given curve (this line is now called normal). He also discovered an interesting curve, called Cortesian Oval, that led to far-reaching research in geometrical analysis.

Descartes made a serious attempts to build up a system in such a way that it could appeal only to a Mathematician—by first framing his axioms and postulates. He was cold, prudent and selfish.

SIR ISSAC NEWTON

Issac Newton is one of the greatest Mathematicians ever produced. He was mechanical minded by birth. He had made a carriage that could be moved by the passenger, a sun dial which stood in the courtyard.

He studied at Cambridge and soon mastered Kepler's optics, but failed to follow books on Astrology because they contained diagrams of the universe. After taking his degree, he went on learning Mathematics and Natural philosophy. He discovered that white light consists of coloured lights. In Mathematics, his famous discovery was differential and integral calculus. In Astronomy he discovered and elaborated the law of universal gravitation. In all these works he fused the points of view of Napier and Descrates.

In 1707, his book '*Arithmetic Universals*' appeared. He also published two other books shortly afterwards. He gave one important theorem about determining the positions of roots of an equation without proof. The proof was given by Sylvester, one hundred and fifty years later.

It can be said in brief that Newton left his mark on every branch of Mathematics. He is reported to have remarked, "I keep the subject of my enquiry constantly before me, and wait till the first drawing opens gradually, by little and little into full and clear light."

BERNOULLI BROTHERS

Jacob and John Bernoulli were two brothers, who in turn became Professors of Mathematics at Bosel. Jacob was the fifth child and John the tenth child (and thirteen years junior) of a large family. At one time, elder brother had been forbidden by his father to study Mathematics or Astronomy. Among his many discoveries it is that of equiangular spiral, that is finest of them all. He was so much fascinated by this curve that it was engraved on his tomb in fulfilment of his wish.

John Bernoulli added fresh material to the store of analysis which is now a part of differential equations. His works exhibit a bolder use of negative and imaginary numbers.

EULER

Euler was the son of a clergymen and had natural aptitude for Mathematics. At an early age in the University of Bosel, he attracted the attention of John Bernoulli. He received the degree of Master of Arts at the age of seventeen wherein he submitted a dissertation on 'Comparison between Cartesian and Newtonian System.' At the age of nineteen, he transmitted two dissertations to Paris Academy. One of them was on masting of ships and the other on Philosophy of Sound. In 1733, he married a Swiss lady, the daughter of a painter who had been brought to Russia by Peter the Great. In 1735, he found the solution of a problem in three days which otherwise deemed solvable in several months. But in this attempt, he lost an eye. At the age of thirty in 1737 he was honoured by Paris Academy for dissertation upon the flux and reflux of the sea. In 1741, he was invited by King Fredrick the Great of Germany to live there. He remained there till 1766. Here he prepared a set of lessons on nature philosophy, a model of interesting teaching, for the princess of Anhalt Dessau. It is noteworthy that Euler could find time for such elementary works amid his other literary interests. A fire broke out in his house in 1771 in which all his books were burnt but his writings were safe. His ultimate aim was the perfection of analysis and calculus. In connection with one simple formula $e^2 x + 1 = 0$, Folix Klein has remarked: All analysis was centred here. Every symbol has its history— the principal whole numbers 0 and 1; the chief mathematical relations — and = ; *i* the sign for 'impossible' square root of minus over and *e* the base of Naperian logarithm.

MACLAURIN

He was educated at the University of Glasgow. He carried forward the work of Pascal. He gave a wonderful account of higher geometry. It is the Mathematics of rods and bars, constrained by pivots and guiding rail. It fascinates the geometer who likes to see the wheels go round. In this kind of Geometry, Cartesian method fails totally.

Later on he wrote essays on the equilibrium of spinning planets and also produced a great Geometrical work on fluxions. A French Mathematician Lagranze remarked, "The work of Maclaurin surpasses that of Archimedes himself, while Newton was greatest genius the world has ever seen, and the most fortune, for only once can it be given a man to discover the system of the universe."

LAGRANGE

He came from an illustrious family and at the age of sixteen became the professor of Mathematics in the Royal School of Artillery at Turin. At the age of nineteen he became famous by solving the so-called isoperimetrical problem, which had puzzled the world for more than 50 years. The method was the beginning of calculus of variations. It led to more fruitful results of Hamilton and continued in the works of Einstein and latest phases of wave mechanics.

One of his books 'Mechanic Analytique' was published in Franche. After 1787 he directed his thoughts to Metaphysics, History, Religion, Philosophy, Medicines, Botany and Chemistry. He used to say that 'Chemistry is as easy as Algebra'.

GAUSS

He was the son of a brick-layer. Gauss was known for his marvelous intuition in higher Arithmetic. In 1807 Gauss was appointed as the first director of a New observatory at Gotlingen. Gauss wrote voluminously and made an early reputation by his work in the theory of numbers.

Gauss gave a result that (a log a) gives a good approximation to the total number of prime numbers less than a, when a is large. No proof was available in his notes but Hadamard and dela Vallee Poussin gave the proof about fifty years ago.

Gauss was the last complete mathematician, and he adorned every branch of science. The beginnings of almost all his discoveries are to be found in notes written in a diary, which has been preserved. The diary reveals pioneer facts higher trigonometry, now referred to as elliptic functions.

Gauss developed the theory of surfaces, with special attention to their curvature and conditions for one surface to fit another. Because of the rigour imposed by Gauss, his Mathematics became totally different from the Mathematics of Newton, Euler and Lagrange.

The method of 'least squares' which is indispensable at present was invented by Gauss. Gauss was the first to give a Coherent account of complex numbers.

The second great stage in his career began on the first day of nineteenth century, when the planet Ceres was discovered by the Astronomers where Gauss had predicted. In 1809 he published his, "Theory of motion of heavenly bodies revolving round the sun 'in' conic section." He also made many significant advances in Geometry. Applications of Mathematics to Geodesy, Newtonian theory of attraction etc.

He is popularly known as 'Prince of Mathematics."

EINSTEIN

He was born in a Jewish family in 1879 in Germany. In 1901 he became a citizen of Switzerland because he was very much fascinated by its independent atmosphere.

In 1905 he expressed his revolutionary views in which mention was also made of principle of special relativity. In 1913 he came back to Germany as Professor of Berlin University and a Member of Royal Persian Academy of Science. The beginning of first world war interfered with his work.

In 1916 he published his 'General Principle of Relativity.' Between 1921 and 1933, he toured and lectured all over the world and was also awarded Nobel Prize.

During the regime of Adolf Hitler, a campaign was launched to convert Jews to Christianity, at that time he was on a lecture tour of America (U.S.A.). He refused to return to Germany and settled in U.S.A. and was appointed Professor in Princeton Institute for Advanced Study at New Jersey. He died on April 11, 1955 at the age of 76.

Before Einstein, Newton's system had been regarded as the ultimate solution of the fundamental problems of science. This estimation is reflected in Alexander Pope's verse:

'Nature and Nature's law lay hid in night;

God said, let Newton be; and all was light.
Then came Einstein and some one added;
But not for long. Let Einstein be the Devil, said
And to, it was dark; the light had fled."

Some people mistakenly associate his name with manufacture of atomic bomb.

INDIAN MATHEMATICIANS

ARYABHATTA I

He was the first of great Indian mathematicians. He was born near Patna in about 476 A.D. He lived near Patna from about 476 A.D. to 550 A.D.

Another person by the same name was born in 10th century A.D. and is known for his book "Maha-Siddhanta."

Aryabhatta I was a great Mathematician. He was the first person to present Arithmetic, Algebra and Geometry in his astrological calculations. He had written four books on Mathematics. These are "Aryabhatya" which is a collection of astronomical tables, "Aryastasata" which is a note on numeration in Arithmetic, "Kalakriya" which is a note on time and its measurement and "Gola" which is a note on the sphere.

In his book Aryabhatta I has given 121 shlokas which have been divided into four parts: (*i*) Gati-Paadika, (*ii*) Ganit Paadika, (*iii*) Kaal Kriyapad, and (*iv*) Ga-Pad. The last part consists of only eleven shlokas made up of a very wide matter. In his first shloka, he has mentioned five basic principles of Mathematics; in his second shloka, decimal system has been explained. Similarly in later shlokas, methods have been given to calculate the area of a rectangle, triangle, circle, curved surface of cone and volume of sphere. In one, shloka, it has been pointed out that if the diameter of a circle be 2000 units, then its circumference equals 62832 units. This gives the value of π correct to four decimal places.

In other shlokas, methods have been given for construction of a triangle, circle and quadrilateral etc.

In thirty shlokas, mention has been made of the principles of Algebra. If an attempt is made to explain each step of his book according to the present standards, a voluminous book would be prepared. In this way, it can be said that Aryabhatt-I has consolidated a very wide subject-matter in a very small book.

He gave a general solution of a linear indeterminate equation by the method of continued functions. He gave the volume of pyramid as half of the product of the base and the height and also gave the volume of a sphere. He gave almost all the formulae for knowing areas of different figures.

He gave the formula

$$(a + b)^2 = a^2 + 2ab + b^2$$

and also revealed this identities

$$1^2 + 2^2 + \ldots n^2 = \frac{1}{2}\text{n} \ (n + 1)\ (2n + 1)$$

$$1^3 + 2^3 + \ldots . n^3 = (1 + 2 + 3 + \ldots \ n)^2 = \frac{1}{2} n^2 \ (n + 1)^2$$

He also contributed to geometry and explained the famous Pythagoras Theorem as under:

"The square of the Bhuja plus the square of the Koti is the square of the Katna."

He also revealed the geometrical fact.

"In a circle the product of two Saras is the square of the half chord of the two arcs, i.e. $a \times b = c^2$, where c is half the chord and the saras (arrows) are the segments of a diameter which bisects any chord.

In addition to Mathematics he was also the master of astronomy, which is closely related to Mathematics. He wrote a book containing a collection of astronomical table. He hel that the earth is a spherical body and that it revolves round the sun. He had also made calculations of the rotation of the earth on its axis. He also had the knowledge of gravitational pull of the earth. He was one of the great Indian mathematicians of whom the country is truly proud.

BHASKARACHARYA

Bhaskaracharya was born in 1114 A.D. at some place near Bijapur in Hyderabad. His father was a learned man in Vedas and Shastras. Bhaskaracharya was very good in Astrology and served as head of the astrological laboratory at Ujjain. He compiled many books on different branches of Mathematics. Some of them are 'Siddhanta Shiromani', 'Karam Kantoohal', 'Samay Sidddhanta Shiromani' and 'Surya Siddhanta'. Siddhanta Shiromani is divided into four parts and each part is sub-divided into several chapaters. The first part is known as 'Lilavati', based on the name of his daughter. In this book, questions have been composed in a very interesting manner.

He introduced, for the first time, the idea of infinity while dividing a number by zero. He also gave many important formulae for measurements. e.g.

Area of sphere = 4 x area of circle

Volume of sphere = Area of sphere x $\frac{1}{6}$ of its diameter.

He also gave formulae for permutation and combination e.g.

Number of permutation of *'r'* things is equal to $\frac{Lt}{LkLl}$ where k and l are different objects.

He also had a knowledge of surds. He also dealt with cubic and biquadratic equations such as

$$x^3 + 42x = 6x^2 + 65$$

or $$x^4 - 3x^2 - 900\,x = 9999$$

His book "Bij Ganit" is a book on Algebra. In this he has discussed directed numbers, the negatives being designated as debt or loss and being indicated by a dot over each number, and the usual rules and formulae being stated correctly. He dismissed the imaginary by stating:

"There is no square root of negative quantity for it is not a square."

He presented a complete and systematic explanation of the Indian method of solving determinate and indeterminate problems on various topics including sale and purchase, interest, gems, gold, permutations of syllables in a stanza, military marches, excavations and the measure of grains.

He also gave a proof of Pythagoras theorem. He gave a method of deducing new sets of solutions of $x^2 + 1 = y^2$. He also discussed $x^2 + B = y^2$. C where B and C are non-square integers.

He presented complicated and abstract theorems in poetic form. He had the knowledge of the gravitational power before Newton. He has made a clear mention of it is one of his books.

The place of Bhaskaracharya is very high in the domain of Mathematicians. In a Journal of Royal Society, Dr. Stopwood has remarked, "we must acknowledge the intimate capabilities of Bhaskaracharya."

BRAHMAGUPTA

Brahmagupta is one of the most distinguished Mathematicians of ancient India. He was the son of Vishnu Gupta and was born in Punjab. He lived in Ujjain and worked in great astrological laboratory at Ujjain. He wrote his first book 'Brahm-sp-huta-Sidhanta" at this place at the age of 30. It consists of 21 chapters and contains great knowledge on arithmetic, geometry, algebra and astronomy. In his calculation he has used the value of $\pi^2 = 10$. In chapter an arithmetic, he has given a detailed account of progression, areas of triangles and quadrilaterals, volumes of trenches and slopes and amount of grains, in heaps etc. He also invented four different methods of multiplication, namely (*i*) Gan Mutrika (*ii*) Khanda (*iii*) Bheda (*iv*) Ista.

He explained the method of inversion for the first time in the following way:

"Beginning from the end, make the multiplier divisor, the divisor multiplier, make addition subtraction and subtraction addition, make square, square-root and square root-square. This gives the required quantity.

He gave the exact concept of zero. He defined it as $a - a = 0$. He gave the following rules to deal with negative numbers.

(*i*) Negative multiplied or divided by negative becomes positive.

(*ii*) Negative subtracted from zero is also positive.

He solved the equation $x^2 - 10x = -9$ by a rule which is equivalent to the quadratic formula. He multiplied the constant term by the co-efficient of x^2, added the square of half the co-efficient of x and found the square-root of this sum. He then subtracted half the co-efficient of x and divided it by the co-efficient of x^2. The quotient gave the solution of the equation.

His work on arithmetic includes integers, fractions, progressions, barter, simple interest, the mensuration of plane figures and problems on volumes.

He· found the formula for addition of geometrical progression

$$a + ar + ar^2 + \ldots\ldots n \text{ terms} = \frac{a\left(r^{n-1}\right)}{r-1}$$

In the field of geometry, he elaborated upon the properties of right angled triangles and for the first time gave the solution of a right angled triangle by giving the following value of its sides:

$$a = 2mn;\ b = m^2 - n^2;\ c = m^2 + n^2 \text{ and } a = \sqrt{m};$$

$h = \frac{1}{2}\left(\frac{m}{n} - n\right); c = \frac{1}{2}\left(\frac{m}{n} + n\right)$ where m and n are two in equal integers.

He also gave, for the first time, suggestions for the construction of a cyclic quadrilateral having its sides as rational numbers. Two of the following formulae given by him are in use even at present:

(1) Area of a cyclic quadrilateral having a, b, c and d as its sides $=\sqrt{(s-a)(s-b)(s-c)(s-d)}$ where $a + b + c + d = 2S$.

S is perimeter of the quadrilateral.

(2) Length of one of the diagonals of the cyclic quadrilateral

$$= \left(\frac{bc + ad}{ab + cd}\right)(ac + bd)$$

Length of the other diagonal $= \left(\frac{ab + cd}{bc + ad}\right)(ac + bd)$

Brahmagupta was the first Indian writer, who applied algebra to astronomy. He was a great mathematician, an astronomer and a poet.

MAHAVIRACHARYA

Not much is known about his life. He is known for his book "Ganita Saar Sangarah", "Shatrinshika" and "Jyotish Patal".

Dr. E. Smith who translated "Ganita Saar Sangrah" into English has claimed that Mahaviracharya is a greater Mathematician than Brahma Gupta and Bhaskaracharya. In his opinion the analysis of oral and written questions on trigonometry given by Mahaviracharya is far superior to that given by Brahma Gupta and Bhaskaracharya.

Mahaviracharya considered Mathematics to be the most useful subject that is used in economics, music, ayurveda, grammar and other fields of knowledge. In this books he describes additions, subtractions etc. In areas he deals with conversion of rectangles into squares and vice-versa, of circles into squares and vice-versa. He has also given details of various kinds of triangles.

He was the only Hindu Mathematician who studied different properties of ellipse.

SRIDHARACHARYA

Sridharacharya belonged to Karnataka (Mysore). He was a scholar of Sanskrit in his childhood. He was a follower of Shaiva religion and later changed over to Jainism. He compiled a book "Trin-Shatika" that consists of three hundred shlokas. In *Ganita Saar Sangrah* of Mahaviracharya, mention has also been made of Sridharacharya. His works include treatises on square root, cube root, fractions, compound practice, progressions, areas and interest.

S. RAMANUJAN

Sriniwas Ramanujan Aiyanger (briefly known as S. Ramanujan) was a member of poor Hindu family in Tanjore district of Madras Presidency. His father was a 'munim' to a cloth merchant at Kumba-Konam. He was born after a prayer to goddess Nagamiri on December 22, 1887. He first went to school at five and at the age of seven, he was transferred to Town High School at Kumba-Konam, where he held a scholarship. He was quiet, meditative and had strong memory. He entertained his friends with theorems and formulae and the square root of two to any number of decimal places.

He passed the high school examination at the age of 16. He was a great genius in Mathematics though he lived only thirty three years yet he left a lasting impression upon the field of Mathematics.

Ramanujan was one of the greatest pure mathematicians known to the world. His greatest contribution to Mathematics was in the field of numbers. In fact, he had a very original and intuitive approach to numbers. He remembered the idiosyncrasies of every one of the first 10,000 integers to an extent that each one of them became his personal friend. In the simplest arrangement of digits, he found wonderful properties, consequences, symmetries and relationships, that had escaped the notice of even the ablest of Mathematicians upto that time. He studied the highly composite numbers also which are recognised as the opposite of prime numbers.

He studied their structure, distribution and special forms. Dr. Hardy, a great Mathematician of England of his time, has remarked about Ramanujan's work on numbers. "The elementary analysis of highly composite numbers is most remarkable and shows very clearly Ramanujan's extraordinary mastery over the algebra of inequalities."

Ramanujan derived pleasure from the game of fiddling with numbers. He presented many startling statements about numbers. For example, he made the statement that every even integer greater than two is the sum of two primes, i.e. numbers having divisions. Thus, 4 is the sum of two primes 1 and 3, 6 is the sum of two primes 3 and 3 and 8 of the primes 3 and 5 and so on. It can also be said that this statement is true of all the even numbers, though the number of primes in case of large numbers may be more than two.

The partition of whole numbers is another similar problem, which engaged the attention of Ramanujan. Take the case of number 3. There are three alternative ways to write it i.e. 3 + 0, 1 + 2, 1 + 1 + 1. There are no other ways of partitioning this number. Similarly 4 can be written in five different ways i.e. 4 + 0; 3 + 1; 2 + 2; 2 + 1 + 1; 1 + 1 + 1 + 1 and there are no other ways of partitioning it, if only integers are to be used.

However, this process of partitioning is very different but Ramanujan developed a formula that is valid for any number. This formula is universally applicable, no matter whether the number is 3 or 3,000,000.

Ramanujan also investigated about divergent series. When Dr. Hardy examined his investigation, he remarked, "I had never seen anything the least like them before. A single look at them is enough to show that this could only be written by a mathematician of the highest class."

He was one of the greatest masters in the field of higher geometric series and continued fractions. He produced quite a number of results in the fields of definite integrals and elliptic functions.

Regarding Ramanujan, Prof. Hardy says, "Here was a man who could work out modular equations, work out theorems of complex multiplication, to orders unheard of, who had mastery of continued fractions on the formal side at any rate, beyond that of any mathematician in the world, who had found for himself the functional equation of the Zeta-function, and the dominant terms of many of the most famous problems in the analytic theory of numbers, and he had never heard of a doubly periodic function, or of Canchy's theorem, and had indeed but the vaguest idea of what a function of complex variable was. . . . All his results, new or old, right or wrong, had been arrived at by a process of mingled argument, intuition and induction of which he was entirely unable to give any coherent account".

"It was a impossible task to ask such a man to submit a systematic instrument to try and learn Mathematics from the beginning once more."

England had honoured him by electing him to the Royal Society and Trinity Fellowship. He did not receive any such honour from India, but every Indian is proud of this great genius of the country.

SHAKUNTALA DEVI
(The Queen of Figures)

Shakuntala Devi, the widely travelled Mathematical prodigy hails from Bangalore. She has received world-wide auclades as a Mathematical genius who could solve problems faster than they were set. She has beaten a £80,000 computer 'Utecom' in addition to many other electronic calculating machines all over the world.

If you give her any date in the last century, she could tell you what day of the week it fell on. In seconds she would add five rows of eight-digit numbers and then multiply the result by any five-digit number of your choice. All in the head.

She discovered her extraordinary talent with figures at an early age. By the time she was five she had become an expert in complex mathematical problems. Since then she has been touring the world, giving performances everywhere and entrancing the audience with her wizardy.

When she was barely thirteen, she had challenged the accuracy of a problem set by a BBC television interview, and it had turned out to the surprise of many that the little girl was dead right. When asked how she goes about the whole thing so confidently, she says, "It all depends on my practice and talent." She categorically denies the opinion of Australian author Enrich Von Daniken "Certain facts indicate a superior extra-terrestrial control of human minds." Mrs. Shakuntala Devi herself can not explain her swift ability to solve Mathematical problems involving addition, subtraction, multiplication and division, using logarithm and other shortcuts, though she has written how a normal person can do some tricks in her books, "Figuring the Joy with Numbers", "Figuring Made Easy." The other books to her credit are "Book of Numbers"; "Puzzles to Puzzle You." The God gifted Shakuntala Devi gives the performances just to popularize the interest of Mathematics in common people and make them feel Mathematics is not a boring subject but very interesting and entertaining.

D.R. KAPREKAR

Dattatraya Ramchandra Kaprekar was a high school teacher of high intellectual achievement in Mathematics. His creative contributions to Mathematics have attracted world-wide interest over the last 50 years. He lived almost like a recluse in Deolali Camp a small town in Maharashtra near Nasik, cooking his own food and washing his own cloths and devoting over 15 hours a day to the pursuit of Mathematics, till the last moment of his life.

Kaprekar's best known contribution to theoretical Mathematics is the constant 6174, popularly known as

'KAPREKAR'S CONSTANT? in international mathematical circle.

The constant 6174 is a number which comes repeatedly when any four digit number in which all digits are unidentical, is subjected to reverse subtraction process.

The procedure is as follows.

(1) Take any four digit number with all four digits unidentical.

(2) Arrange the four digit number in a descending order, reverse them to make a new number.

(3) Substract the new number from the original number.

(4) The process is repeated with remainders and in not more than eight steps, Kaprekar's constant emerges.

Example: Take 7823

	8732	—	Arranged in descending order of digits.
	– 2378	—	Reversed and new no. obtained.
I	6354	—	Subtracted new from original
	6543	—	Descending order
	– 3456	—	New number
II	3087	—	Subtracted
	8730	—	Descending order number
	– 0378	—	New number by reversing
III	8352		
	8532	—	Descending order
	– 2358	—	Rearranged number
IV	6174	—	Kaprekar's Constant

Kaprekar has not only worked out this problem with hundreds of numbers but also derived the theory on which it works. He read the first paper on the subject at Madras

(Chennai) Mathematical Conference in 1949. The American Journal *Scripta Mathematica* published his article in 1949.

Another of his discoveries has a philosophical flavour—the "self numbers" which he says are "self born" numbers. His extensive research on "Demlo numbers" has provided much food for thought the Mathematicians all over the world. Another discoveries are of 'Polindromic Numbers", "Harshad Numbers."

He also worked a lot on operations like addition, subtraction, multiplication, and their powers and discovered many interesting results.

He was also interested on magic squares, he was expert in the fascinating game of magic squares. One of the magic square which attracted the attention of many Mathematicians is known "Gandhi Shatabdi Magic Square."

2	10	19	69
64	24	12	00
16	01	63	20
18	65	6	11

Gandhi Shatabdi Year : 02.10.1969.

The total of any column across, down or diagonal or any row is 100. Many Mathematics research scholars are presently working on Kaprekar's discoveries and generalising results which will bring a major contribution to Number Theory.

D.R. Kaprekar was a B.Sc. graduate student of Farguson College, Pune. As a student he once got a Rangler Paranjape prize for a Mathematics essay.

Chapter—16

Understanding Modern Mathematics

16.1 NUMBER SYSTEM

Natural Numbers

The origin of number system is as old as human civilization. In the beginning we had an infinite series of natural numbers. In the beginning it was thought that the system of natural numbers is closed under addition. Now it extends to all integers whether positive or negative. The number '0' is used to denote nothingness.

Rational Numbers

The system of integers does not account for all numbers of the form $p/q\,(q \neq o)$. To include such quantities the number system has to be extended and this is called the system of rational numbers.

Real Number System

The quantities like $\sqrt{2}$ $\sqrt{3}$, $b\sqrt{a}$ etc. are not included in rational number. This led to the evolution of irrational number. The number system extended in this way is known as real number system.

Complex Numbers

Even the real number system is incomplete as it is inadequate to admit the solutions of problems such as $x^2 = -3$, $y^2 = -9$ etc. The numbers of the form $x + y\sqrt{-1}$ or $x + iy$ are known as imaginary or complex numbers.

Thus we have the following types of numbers:

(*i*) **Natural Numbers** 1, 2, 3, ...

(*ii*) **Whole Numbers** 0, 1, 2, 3, 4, 5.... .

(*iii*) **Integers** –4, –3, –2, - -, + 5, + 6....

(*iv*) **Rational Numbers.**Numbers of the form $\frac{p}{q}(q \neq o)$ when p and q are integers.

(*v*) **Irrational Numbers**. All such numbers which can not be written in the form of rational numbers, $\frac{p}{q}(q \neq o)$, are known as irrational numbers.

(*vi*) **Real Numbers.** The rational and irrational numbers taken together are known as real numbers.

(*vii*) **Imaginary Numbers.** The numbers of the form $x + iy$, where x and y are real numbers, are known as imaginary numbers.

(*viii*) **Complex Numbers System.** The extended system of real numbers to include imaginary numbers is called complex number system.

16.2 OPERATION

The process by which we connect one type of thing to another is known as *operational*. For example addition, subtraction, multiplication etc.

Basic Laws Governing the Algebra of Real Numbers

Following basic laws govern various operations such as addition, subtraction, multiplication etc.

(*i*) **Commutative Law**. For a pair of numbers 'x' and 'y' we have $x + y = y + x$. It means that the *operation* (addition is this case) is independent of the order of numbers. Similarly we have $x \times y = y \times x$, here the operation is multiplication which is also commutative (i.e. independent of the order of numbers).

Commutative law is true for natural numbers, integers, rational numbers, irrational numbers and imaginary numbers.

(*ii*) **Closure**. If for two numbers x and y, $x + y$, $x \times y$ are the members of the same system then the system is considered as closed for the operations, of addition and subtraction e.g. $2 + 3 = 5$, $2 \times 3 = 6$ thus 5 and 6 are also natural numbers like 2 and 3. Thus we say that the system of natural numbers is closed for the operations of addition and multiplication.

(*iii*) **Associative Law**. If we have x, y, z as three numbers, then according to associative law, we have

$$(x + y) + z = x + (y + z)$$

and $$(x \times y) \times z = x + (y \times z)$$

This law is true for natural numbers, integers, rational numbers irrational numbers and imaginary numbers. However, it is not true for operation of division and subtraction.

(*iv*) **Distributive Law**. If x, y, z are the numbers of a number system, then

$$x \times (y + z) = xy + xz \text{ (right distributive law)}$$

$$(y + z) \times x = yx + zx \text{ (left distributive law)}$$

(*v*) **Identity Elements.** If x and 0 belong to a number system such that $x + 0 = 0 + x = x$.

Then '0' is the additive identity of the system.

Similarly if $x \times 1 = x = 1 \times x$ then '1' is the multiplicative identity of the system.

(*vi*) **Inverse Elements**. If x, y, 0 are the elements of a number system, such that $x + y = 0 = y + x$, then we say 'y' is additive inverse of 'x' or 'x' is additive inverse of 'y' if x, y, 1 belong to the system and $x\ y = 1 = y\ x$, then we say 'y' is multiplicative inverse of 'x', or 'x' is multiplicative inverse of 'y' $x \neq 0, 4 \pm 0$.

(*viii*) **Order Relations**. Various natural numbers show order relations. A number is either greater than or smaller than the other. Thus both > (greater than) and < (smaller than) and order relations in a system.

16.3 SETS

Set refers to a collection of objective. We can talk about a set of books, set of vowels etc.

A set is said to be defined if the number of objects in such a set is well defined e.g. All odd integers less than 7, set of vowels of English alphabet etc.

Set Notation. A set is denoted by capital letters such as A, B, C etc. The members of the set are referred to as set elements and are denoted by small letters a, b, c ...

The sets can be described either in Roster method (Listing method) or Rule method.

Roster Method or Listing Method

In this method the objects that form a set are put within brackets and elements of set are separated by commas e.g.

A = {1, 3, 5, 7 .... 15} i.e. Set of odd integers less than 15.

Rule Method

In this method a set is described by some characteristic property that is common to all elements of the set. e.g. In case of above example we can say

A = { $x \in$ A: x is an odd integer < 15}

The symbol '$\in$' is read as 'belongs to'.

Finite and Infinite Sets

A set of which the exact number of elements is known as a finite set e.g.

A = {1, 2, 3 ... 100} is a finite set.

A set which is not finite is known as infinite set.

A = {1, 2, 3 ...} is an infinite set.

Empty Set or Null Set or Void Set

A set containing no element is called a **null set** or **void set** or **empty set**. It is denoted by ϕ. Examples

(*i*) The set of intersection of two parallel lines.

(*ii*) The set of real roots of the equation $x^3 = -6$.

Singleton. A singleton is a set that contains only one element. It is called a unit set or one point set. e.g. The set {0}. It contains only one element '0'.

Doubleton. A doubleton is a set that contains two elements.

Equal Sets. Two sets A, B are equal if they consist of the same elements or members.

Equivalent Sets. Are those two sets in which 1 – 1 correspondence can be established between their elements their elements i.e. the number elements in each set is the same.

Sub-Set. A set 'A' is a sub-set of set 'B' if each member of set 'A' is an element of set 'B'.

A sub-set which does not contain all the elements of a set is called its proper sub-set.

Power Set. The set consisting of all sub-sets of a set 'A' is known as its power set and is denoted by 2^n. The number of elements in the power set of 'A' is equal to 2^n where 'A' has n elements.

Universal Set. A set from which all sub-sets are taken for any discussion of sets is known as universal set and is denoted by U.

Complement of a Set. If 'A' is a sub-set of a universal set 'U' then the complement of 'A' is the set of all elements of 'U' which are not elements of 'A'. It is denoted by ≈ A or A^c.

Disjoint Sets. Two sets 'A' and 'B' are disjoint if they have no common elements.

Venn Diagrams. The relations between sets can be conveniently studied with the help of diagrams. John Venn, an English man gave on such representation which is known as Venn-Euler diagram or Venn diagram, For example.

The universal set U is represented by a rectangular figure.

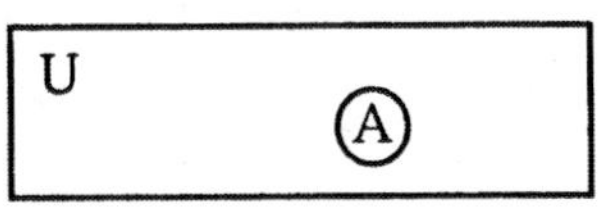

Any sub-set of the universal set is represented by a circle figure drawn inside a rectangle.

If $A \subset B$ (A is a proper sub-set of B) then it can be represented by drawing a circle inside a circle.

To represent two disjoint sets two non-intersecting circles are drawn.

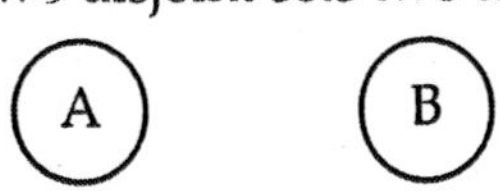

The complement of a set is represented by the shaded portion.

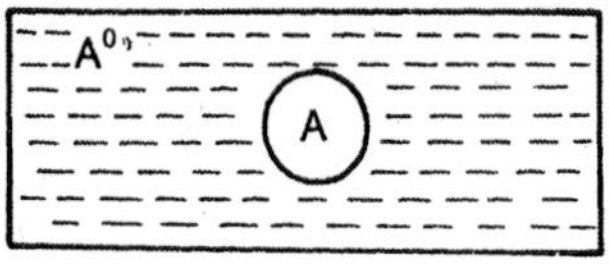

Inter Section of two sets 'A' and 'B' is the set of elements which are common to 'A' and 'B'. It is denoted by A * B and read as 'A inter section B'.

By Venn diagram it is represented as under:

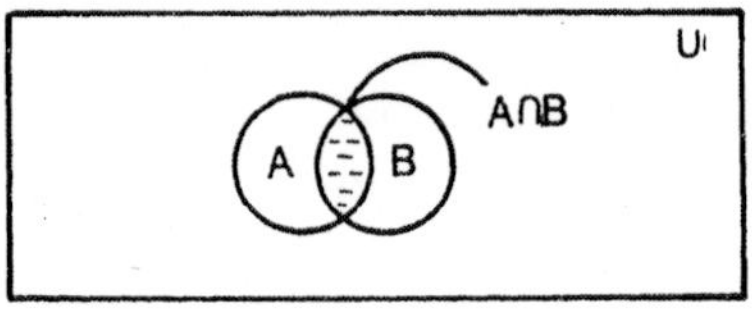

Union of Sets. Union of two sets 'A' and 'B' is the set of all those elements which belong to 'A' or to 'B' or to Both. It is denoted by A∪B and read as 'A union B'. It is represented as under:

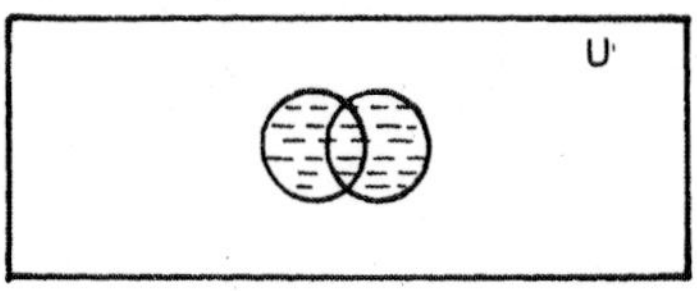

Cartesian Product of Sets

Let 'A' and 'B' be two sets. It $a \in$ A and $b \in$ B, we write (a, b) the first element taken from A and the second from B. (a, b) is called an ordered pair. In this case the order in which elements are taken is very important $(a, b) \neq (b, a)$

The set consisting of all ordered pairs obtained by choosing the first element of the ordered pair from the first set 'A' and second element of the ordered pair from second set 'B' is called Cartesian product of the sets A and B and is denoted by A × B. It is also called the **product set** of A and B e.g.

Let $\quad A = \{1, 2\}, B = \{x, y\}, C = \{5, 6, 7\}$

Then $\quad A \times B = \{(1, x), (1, y), (2, x), (2, y)\}$

$$B \times A = \{ (x, 1), (x, 2), (y, 1), (y, 2)\}$$

$$A \times C = \{ (1, 5), (1, 6), (1, 7), (2, 5), (2, 6), (2, 7)\}$$

The Cartesian product can be illustrated as under.

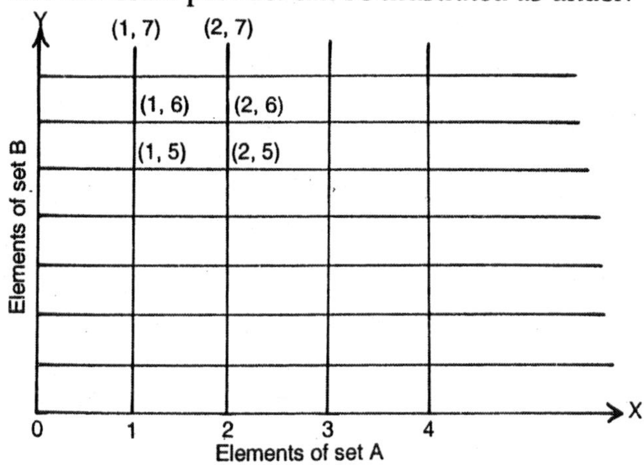

16.4 POLYNOMIALS

The algebraic expression of the type $3a$, $3a^4 + 7a$, $b^3 + 3b$, $b^2 - c^2$ etc. are called *polynomials.* In polynomials we have one or more terms connected with + or – sign and one or more terms having integral powers.

Polynomials in one variable. These are the polynomial which contain only one variable e.g. $a^3 + 7a + 8$, $2 + \frac{2}{3}a + 1/8$, etc. The first one is a polynomial with integral coefficients and the second one is a polynomial having rational coefficients.

Polynomials in two variables. These are the polynomials which involve two variables e.g. $a^2 - b^2$, $a^2 - 2ab + b^2$ etc.

Degree of a Polynomial. The degree of a polynomial in one variable, is the greatest exponent (a whole number) of the variable e.g. It is a polynomial of one degree.

Constant Polynomial. If all the terms of a polynomial except constant reduce to zero then such a polynomial is called a constant polynomial. All constant polynomial are polynomials of zero degree.

Zero Polynomial. A polynomial having all its coefficients zero is called a zero polynomial. Such a polynomial has no degree.

Monomials. A polynomial that contains only one term is known as monomial e.g. 8, $4x$, $\sqrt{3y^2}$ etc.

Binomials. A polynomial that contains two terms is called a binomial e.g. $x^2 + 3/4$, $y, + \sqrt{7}$, $x + 10$ etc.

Trinomials. A polynomial that contains three terms is known as a trinomial e.g. $x^3 + 3x^2 + x$, $x^2 + 1/7x, + 5$ etc.

Linear Polynomials. If a polynomial having one variable has a degree 1 then it is called a linear polynomial e.g. $x + 5$, $5y + 5/2$ etc.

Quadrative Polynomials. A polynomial having one variable and having a degree 2 is called a quadrative polynomial e.g. $x^2 + 5x$, $2y^2 + 3y + 1$, etc.

Cubic Polynomials. A polynomial is one variable and of degree 3 is called a cubic polynomial e.g. $x^3 + 3x^2 + 2x$, $5y^3 + 3y^2$ etc.

Biquadratic or Quadratic Polynomial. A polynomial in one variable and of degree 4 is called a quadratic or biquadratic polynomial.

16.5 EQUATIONS

Linear Equations

It is an expression involving two variables x, y in the form $ax + by + c$ where a, b and c are real numbers.

A equation in two variables of the type $ax + by + c = 0$ where a, b and c are not simultaneously zero is known as a linear equation.

Graphic Representation of a Linear Equation. Linear equation can be represented by straight lines. The two mutually ⊥ lines can be selected as axes and then one variable is represented along x-axis and another along y-axis e.g. the linear equation $2x + 3y = 6$ has ordered pairs (0, 2), (3, 0), (-3, 4) etc. Which satisfy this equation. The points can be plotted as under.

Example. (i) Draw the graph of $x = 3$. It can also be written as $1.x + 0y - 3 = 0$. The following points (3, 0), (3, 1), (3, 2), (3, 3), etc. satisfy it.

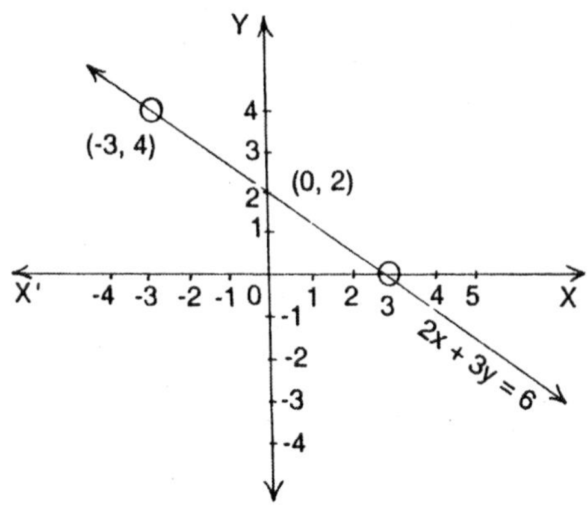

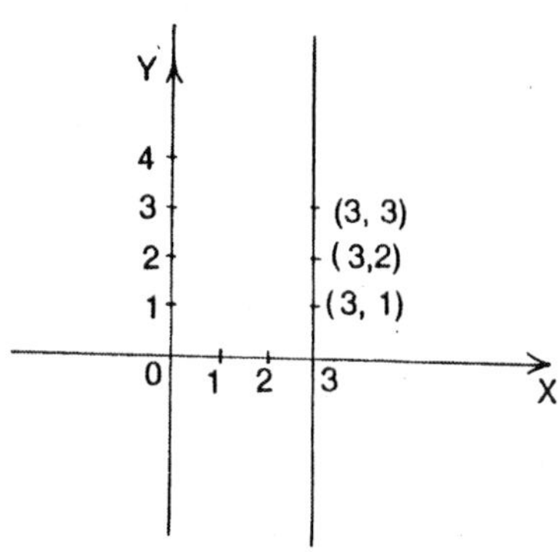

Inequations. An inequations is an equation in two variables of the type

$ax + by \leq c$ (or $< c$)

$ax + by \leq c$ (or < c)

where $a, b, c,$ are real numbers.

An ordered pair (x, y) is said to be the solution of $ax + by \leq c$ if $ax + by \leq c$. The set of all such solutions is called the solution set of the given inequation.

Such an equation can be graphically represented as under. Take the equation $x - y < 6$.

(*i*) Two angles and a side.

(*ii*) The three sides.

(*iii*) A right angle, the hypotenuse and one other side.

The equality of areas is not the same as congruence of triangles. For example, two triangles may be equal in area, yet these may not be congruent. But two congruent triangles have equal areas. Geometrical proofs of congruency can also be given.

Similarity of triangles. Similar figures have the same shape but not necessarily the same size. Similar figures are related to one another as an object and its image. Photographs of different size printed from the same negative are also similar.

There are two necessary conditions for similarity:

(*i*) The same shape (equal corresponding angles)

(*ii*) Proportionate dimensions.

Similar triangles have their sides proportional and corresponding angles equal

Similar triangles become congruent when the proportion between the corresponding sides is one. Thus congruence is a particular case of similarity. Not necessary.

16.6 TRIANGLES

Congruent Triangles

Two geometric figures are said to be congruent if they can be superimposed over one another without bending or twisting, congruent means exactly agreeing.

Two triangles are congruent if and only if all the sides and the angles of one are equal to the corresponding sides and angles of the other.

Two triangles can be shown to be congruent if the following elements are equal:

(*i*) Two sides and the included angle.

(*ii*) Two angles and a side.

(*iii*) Three sides.

(*iv*) A right angle, the hypotenuse and other side.

Please note that two triangles may have equal area but may not be congruent.

Similar Triangles

Similar triangles have the same shape but not necessarily the same size. They are related to one another as an object and its image.

For similarity the two necessary condition are:

(*i*) The same shape (equal corresponding angles)

(*ii*) Proportionate dimensions.

Similar triangles have their side proportional and corresponding angles equal.

Idea of similarity is useful in measuring heights of poles, buildings etc. It is also useful in enlarging or reducing maps.

Linear Symmetry

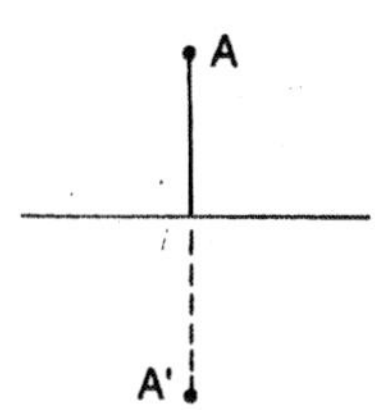

We often make use of the idea of symmetry in our day to day lives. We know intuitively what makes figures, shapes or arrangements pleasing to the eye. Often these are well balanced or well proportioned, symmetrical figures are exactly alike in all respects except one, they are right and left handed. Symmetry is the quality of balance which a figure possesses that make its appearance the same on both sides of a line, a point or a plane. Some useful results based on the idea of symmetry are as under:

(*i*) Two points are symmetric with respect to a third point if the third point is the midpoint of the line segment joining the two points.

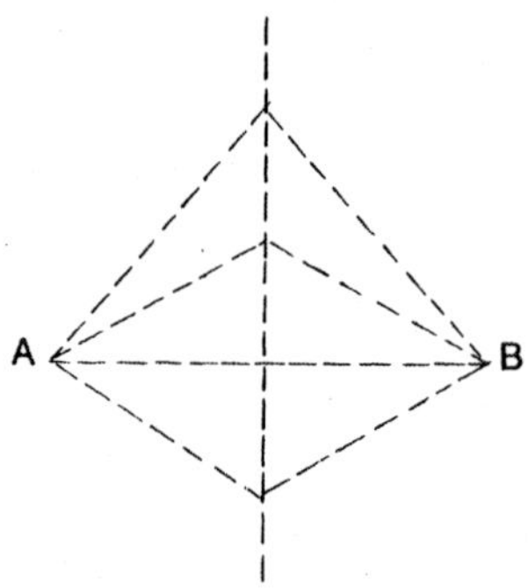

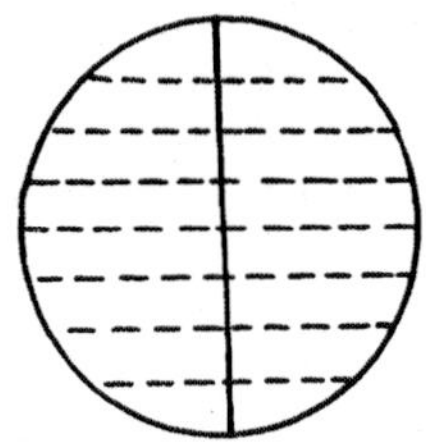

(*ii*) Line symmetry can be used in case of locus theorems as shown.

(*iii*) The chord and diameter property of a circle can be illustrated as under:

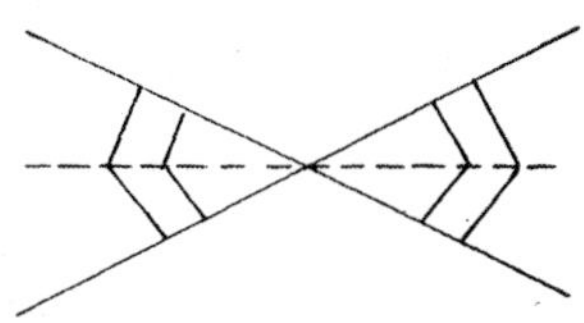

This follows from the fact that a circle is symmetrical about a diameter.

(*iii*) Circle is symmetrical about its centre also.

A pupil may be given a figure and the axis of symmetry. He may be asked to draw the rest of the figure.

(*iv*) Property of an isosceles triangle can be known by drawing perpendicular from the vertex to the base.

The idea of symmetry can be helpful in proving so many results of Geometry, and even of other branches of the subject. In our lives, symmetry has a pleasing effect. People make use of it in art, design, decoration etc.

Chapter—17

Euclidean and Non-Euclidean Geometries

17.1 IMPORTANCE OF EUCLIDEAN GEOMETRY

Geometry is the science of space and extent. It deals with position, shape and size of bodies but his nothing to do with their material or physical properties.

Demonstrative geometry deals with the shape, size and position of figures by pure reasoning, based on definitions, self evident truths, assumptions and other established geometrical truths. Euclid, a celebrated Greek Mathematician, was the father of Demonstrative geometry. Euclid devised many methods for handling its problems. His methods are intuitional, observational, inventional, constructive, formal, experimental etc. He defined basic terms such as a point, line, angle, surface, perpendicular etc. Some of these definitions are as follows:

Point. A Point is that which has no parts.

Line. A line is breath less length.

A straight line. A straight line is a line which lies evenly with the points on itself.

Surface. A surface is that which has length and breadth only.

Plane surface. A plane surface is a surface which lies evenly with straight line on itself.

Angle. A plane angle is the inclination to one another of two lines in a plane which meet one another and do not lie in a straight line.

Circle. A circle is a plane figure contained by one line such that all the straight lines falling upon it from one point among those lying, within the figure are equal to one another.

Euclid's Postulates

Some of the important postulates of Euclid are as follows:

(*i*) A straight line can be drawn from any point to any point.

(*ii*) A finite straight line can be produced continuously in a straight line.

(*iii*) A circle may be described with any centre and any distance.

(*iv*) All right angles are equal to one another.

(*v*) If a straight line falling on two straight lines makes the interior angles on the same side less than two right angles, the two straight lines if produced indefinitely meet on that side on which are angles less than two right angles.

(*vi*) There is one and only one straight line through out a point parallel to a given line.

Important Axioms or Notions

(*i*) The things which are equal to the same things are equal to one another.

(*ii*) If equals be added to equals, the wholes are equal.

(*iii*) If equals be subtracted from equals, the remainders are equal.

(*iv*) Things which coincide with another are equal to one another.

(*v*) The whole is greater than part.

With the rapid expansion of Mathematical knowledge. The Eucledean Geometry has become the subject of criticism. According to the standards of present times, Euclidean Geometry has many flaws, but it still popular.

Shortcoming of Euclidean Geometry

Some shortcomings of Euclidean geometry are as under:

(*i*) **Ambiguous and Vague Definition**. In Euclidean Geometry majority of definitions as given by Euclid are vague and ambiguous e.g. point has been defined as having no part but it is not a precise definition because point is not known by this property alone.

Length. A line is length without breadth. This is not wholly correct, viewing it in terms of a curve.

Straight line. It is a line which lies evenly with respect to its points.

This is also an ambiguous are vague definitions.

(*ii*) **Undefined terms described.** Euclid gave the definitions of terms like point, line, surface etc. intuitively and so these should be accepted as undefined objects.

(*iii*) Many a concepts that require definition or proof have been overlooked.

(*iv*) Axioms or notion have not been properly stated.

(*v*) Some assumptions or postulates are used in proofs of certain theorems though these have not been stated as axioms or postulates

(*vi*) Some of the axioms put forward are not true or are inadequate. In some cases wrong conclusion are reached if we use Euclids assumptions. The concept of betweenness has not been mentioned and so the following types of fallacies may arise:

(*a*) All triangles are isosceles.

(*b*) A point lying in the interior of a circle lies on its curved boundary.

(*c*) All obtuse angles are right angles.

(*vii*) Euclid does not use real numbers. This has led to the incompleteness of the theorem related to proportion.

(*viii*) First two theorems on congruency are proved by superposition. But this assumption in nowhere specified by Euclid.

(*ix*) There is too much dependence on figures, since the assumptions laid down were not sufficient, Euclid proved certain results with the help of figures e.g. in proving the isosceles triangle theorem, he simply assumes that the bisector of angle ∠A intersects BC and D. This is based on the assumption that there is one and only one bisector of angle ∠A which lies in the interior of that angle.

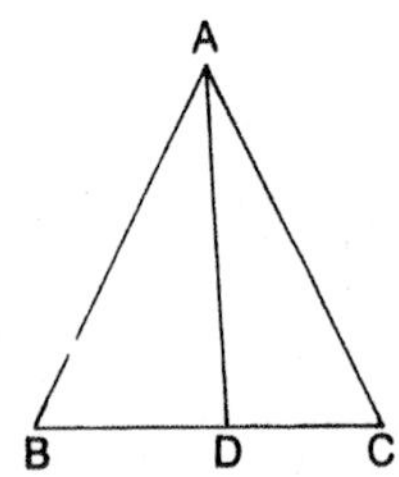

(*x*) Some of Euclid's ideas are crude e.g. he assumed that all angles must be less than two right angles.

(*xi*) It does not take into consideration the measurements on the spherical surface of earth.

(*xii*) The order of learning of Euclidean geometry is not psychological.

The views expressed by Bertrand Russel about the short-comings of Euclidean geometry are worth noting. His definitions do not always define, his axioms are not always demonstrable, his demonstration require many axioms of which he is quite unconcious. A valid proof retains its demonstrative force when no figure is drawn, but very many of Euclid's earlier proofs fail before this test."

Difference Between Euclidean and Non-Euclidean Geometries

As a consequence of the criticism of Euclidean geometry the non-Euclidean geometry originated. Later on it gave rise to two different non-Euclidean Geometries i.e. (*i*) Hyperbolic Geometry and (*ii*) Elliptical Geometry.

17.2 HYPERBOLIC GEOMETRY

John Bolyai of Hungry and Lobachevaski of Russia are considered as originators of hyperbolic geometry. They put forward the following postulates of parallel in contradiction of Euclids' parallel postulate. Gauss was the first person to express doubts about the Euclids' famous postulate of parallels i.e. there is one and only one straight line parallel to the given straight line.

The postulates put forward by John Bolyai and Lobachevaski are as follows:

(*i*) There are two straight lines that can be drawn from a point parallel to a given line.

(*ii*) In between these there are infinitely many straight lines through the point (*p*) that do not intersect the line (*l*).

(*iii*) Any line between PR and PS will intersect the line '*l*'.

∠RPM and ∠SPM are called angles of parallelism.

Following characteristics of hyperbolic geometry make clear the difference between hyperbolic geometry and Euclidean geometry.

Characteristics of Hyperbolic Geometry

(*i*) The sum of the angles of triangle is less than 180°. This sum approaches 180° as the area approaches O.

(*ii*) The sum of the angles of a quadrilateral is less than 360°.

(*iii*) Two parallel straight lines coverage towards the direction of parallelism and diverge in the other direction.

(*iv*) Similar triangles are congruent. If the three angles of a triangle are congruent to each of the three angles of another triangle, then the triangles are said to be congruent.

(*v*) The angles constructed in a semi-circle is not equal to 90°.

(*vi*) The result of Pythagorus theorem is not true, but it becomes more and more true as the area of a right angle triangle approaches O.

(*vii*) There is no existence of squares.

17.3 ELLIPTICAL GEOMETRY

It originated in 1854 and the credit for it goes to Reiman. It takes into consideration the spherical surface of the earth. A surveyor used the formula of Euclidean geometry to measure the area of a farm of fields. Theoretically he should use spherical geometry because his measurements are made on the spherical earth.

Characteristics of Elliptical Geometry

(*i*) Parallel lines do not exist.

(*ii*) A straight line has finite length.

(*iii*) The property of betweenness does not hold in the system of Elliptical Geometry.

(*iv*) There is at least one line through two given points.

(*v*) A triangle may have two right angles.

(*vi*) The sum of the angles of a triangles is greater then 180°. It approaches 180° as the area approaches O.

(*vii*) It is not true that one and only one perpendicular may be drawn on a line from a point outside it.

(*viii*) The exterior angle theorem of a triangle does not hold good in this geometry i.e. If one side of a triangle is extended to form an exterior angle, the sum of two opposite interior angles is equal to the exterior angle.

The evolution of non-Euclidean geometries brought about a radical change in the concepts of axioms and postulates. Now these are considered as basic assumptions in many Mathematical systems. All this has made the Euclidean geometry more clear and exact. Attempts have been made for removal of short comings of Euclidean geometry.

Chapter—18

Teaching of Geometry

18.1 GEOMETRY TEACHING

Geometry is a combination of two words—Geo + metry which means measurement of earth. It has two fold values. It provides knowledge and enables students to do things logically and to develop logical thinking without which geometry cannot be understood.

The geometry teaching provides a mass of geometrical facts. The geometric principles of equality, symmetry and similarity are implanted in the nature of things. It develops the ability to draw accurate plans. It is useful in engineering, machine shop, construction industries, landscape architecture, interior decorations etc. It is the key to mathematical thinking.

Beginning of Teaching of Geometry

Teaching of geometry should not be taken up before junior high school stage. Normally it should begin in class VII and go upto higher secondary stage. At the higher secondary stage there may be more of advanced geometry.

Teacher should proceed from simple to complex and from concrete to abstract problems.

Stages of Teaching of Geometry

Teaching of geometry should be divided into the following three stages:

(*i*) Experimented stage.

(*ii*) Deductive stage.

(*iii*) Systematic stage.

The above division is based on the content material of subject and psychological requirements of the students.

Experimental Stages of Teaching of Geometry

This stage begins from class V and goes upto class VII. In this period the child is taught to recognise figures, draw simple figures and measure them. An effort be made to link the teaching of geometry with every day life of the child. This stages should stop at the age of 12 or 13 years.

At this stage an all out effort be made to provide knowledge to the students through observations, recognition, inspection etc. At this stage an attempt be also made to lay foundation for the study of more advanced geometry or demonstrative geometry at the deductive stage.

Deductive Stage of Teaching of Geometry

This stage should start from class VIII and should end by class IX. After the age of 15 geometry should not be taught by the methods that suit this stage of education.

At this stage, various theorems, that are fit from psychological point of the view for the students be taught.

The function of middle school geometry is to systematize the information received by the pupils at the pre-school and primary school stage from nature and practical arts, which are permanent sources of geometric learning. At this stage the emphasis is on the understanding of fundamental concepts and techniques such as the meaning, drawing and use of lines, angles, triangles and polygons. The primary object is not to teach the pupils the geometry but to lead them to think of geometry. The practical side of geometry will thus dominate at the middle school stage.

The functions of geometry at middle school stage can thus be summarised as under:

(*i*) To systematise the information received by the child in the pre-school stage and primary stage of education.

(*ii*) To extend this knowledge to the broader and more general aspects of daily life.

(*iii*) To enlarge geometric vocabulary.

(*iv*) To help the pupils in understanding fundamental techniques involving the use of ruler, compass, protractor.

(*v*) To train them in methods of verifying geometrical facts by practical work.

(*vi*) To develop a taste for geometry.

Systematic Stage of Geometry

This is the higher secondary stage of teaching of geometry. At this stage geometry teaching should be done in a systematic and logical manner. Students be trained in proper reasoning and thinking and they should be given proper practice in logical reasoning. In this stage, which may continue till the child attains the age of 17, the major part of teaching of geometry is done.

The major purpose at this stage will be to inculcate in pupils an appreciation for logical demonstration, to acquaint them with effective methods of clear and impartial thinking; critical evaluation and intelligent generalisation to train them in the discovery of youth; and to introduce them the meaning of geometrical vigour and precision.

Function of geometry teaching at high school stage can thus be summarised as under:

(*i*) to instil in the pupils an appreciation for the significance of geometrical truths.

(*ii*) To provide training in analytical reasoning.

(*iii*) To stress exactness and accuracy in mathematical reasoning.

18.2 TEACHING OF GEOMETRY TO THE BEGINNERS

Early introduction in Geometry should be based on practical work. The subject-matter should arise out of the real problems. Pupils must be made to experience the symmetry, regularity and beauty of forms in nature.

At this stage the teaching of geometry should be based on the psychological principle of 'learning by doing'. The students be allowed to observe and handle objects, figures, shapes and learn their names. It is through practical work that the students grasp fundamental ideas. First lessons should be based on practical work. There should be no oral teaching of definitions and memorisation of abstract things. Some examples of practical work that can be done in the beginning stages are as under:

(*i*) **Handling of models etc**. The pupils be allowed to handle the geometrical models like cube, cuboid, cone, pyramid, prism, square, etc. They may be asked to count their faces, edges, corners etc.

(*ii*) **Observing familiar objects**. The pupils may be allowed to examine the corners of rooms, desks, tables, books etc. They will get the idea of points, parallel lines, perpendiculars, rectangles etc.

(*iii*) The pupils be asked to make models of geometrical figures and draw figures on paper.

(*iv*) Idea of angles can be given by taking a compass, hands of a watch, a pair of scissors, opening of a door etc.

(*v*) Various geometrical properties can be verified by actual measurements e.g. Measuring the angles of a Triangle etc.

(*vi*) Concept of an area can be made more clear by counting unit squares in geometrical figures.

The students should generalise and deduce geometrical properties by drawing, construction, superposition, experiments etc. and not be logical proofs. The practical work should precede and clarify logical work. Practical work should gradually lead to the deductive stage.

18.3 ASPECTS OF TEACHING OF GEOMETRY

In addition to the three stages of geometry discussed in Art. 18.1, the teaching of geometry may also be divided from the point of view of the subject under the following two heads:

(*i*) Modern Geometry which includes conic section and some parts of solid geometry.

(*ii*) The philosophy of geometry in which philosophical or non-Euclidean aspects of geometry should be explained.

18.4 DIFFERENT TOPICS OF GEOMETRY

Different Topics of Geometry. Teaching of Geometry includes many topics on which various theorems, problems and corollaries are based. In the following discussion an attempt will be made to explain the teaching of different aspects of Geometry in a chronological order.

Scale Drawing. When the students have been taught about the use of different instruments of Geometry, like compass, protector etc., they should be taught to draw different figures according to some scale.

Importance of Neatness and Accuracy. Before starting the teaching of Geometry, the importance of neatness and accuracy in the subject should be explained to the students. They should also be encouraged to draw lines etc., accurately. If they learn about these things, they shall be able to learn Geometry in a correct and proper perspective.

Angles. Students be told about angles and they should be asked to draw angles and measure their degrees beginning from straight angle and then the right angles etc. After they have learnt about it, they should be told about different types and kinds of angles like right angle, acute angle, obtuse angle etc.

This is, one of the basic concepts of Geometry and should be properly explained.

Parallel Lines. The students are familiar with the concept of lines so they may be taught parallel lines. This may be done by taking certain concrete examples e.g., of the rails, the lines of the answer-book etc.

The students should be asked to draw parallel lines on their exercise books with the help of the scale and set-square. Then, they may be taught about the angles drawn by vivisection.

Congruency. Knowledge of congruency of figures be imparted with the help of the pieces of paper or such other objects. Triangles may be drawn and then on the basis of those triangles, congruency may be taught.

After it has been made clear, definitions can be taken-up.

Similarity. The similarity between different figures be explained to the students.

To start with things should be made clear with the help of certain concrete examples. After the concept has been made clear, definitions and other things be taken-up. Then the practical utility of these things in life may be taught.

Locus

This is another important concept of geometry and is useful to explain many a things in geometry. It has practical utility about doors, walls etc. To start with the students be given concrete examples and afterwards problems based on this concept be taken up.

Teaching of Theorems

To teach theorems the teacher should follow the maxim 'from simple to complex'. To start with the theorems about angles and parallel lines may be taken up and afterwards theorems about right angles and other things may be taken up.

Theorem of Pythagorus

This theorem be taught only after the students have learnt a good deal of various concepts of geometry. It is better if it is taken up at higher secondary stage of education.

Teaching of Definitions

Definitions be taught at a later stage and not in the beginning. In the beginning main emphasis be put on making clear the various concepts.

Teaching of Construction

We find that in geometry many problems could be solved with the help of constructions. Students be taught construction at junior high school stage and it should continue upto higher secondary stage.

Teaching of Proposition

Propositions be taught at a later stage. In the beginning simple propositions be made clear and afterwards difficult propositions be taken up.

Teaching of Problems

The solution of a problem becomes easier if the student be trained to draw a rough figure and do the rough work.

The students be taught about the system of writing the proof or solution of the theorems or the problems. To start with the pupils be asked to give an analysis and then they be asked to put it in black and white. Finally the corollaries may be taken up.

Exercises in geometry provide opportunity to apply the knowledge of geometrical results in different situations. The following points be kept in view in teaching of exercises:

(*i*) Draw the most general figure e.g. if it relates to any triangle, draw scalene triangle.

(*ii*) Draw the figure as accurate as possible.

(*iii*) Read the exercise carefully to understand the meaning of words used.

(*iv*) Use capital letters for vertices and small letters for the sides of plane figures.

(*v*) Try to recall the axioms, postulates, theorems and corollaries which will help in finding the solution of the exercises.

(*vi*) To start with take the given statement as true and see what follows from it.

(*vii*) Alternately start by assuming the statement as incorrect and then prove it wrong.

(*viii*) It is desirable if a reference to certain theorem is given by the teacher.

Following points are quite helpful in solution of exercises:

(*i*) Equality of lines or angles is generally proved by showing them to be corresponding angles or lines of two congruent triangles.

(*ii*) If the lines which we wish to prove equal are not parts of two triangles, then draw some additional lines.

(*iii*) To prove congruency of two triangles, prove first some other pair or pairs equal. This will help us in proving the equality of the original pair.

(*iv*) To prove that angle is right angle, we generally prove that it is equal to its supplementary adjacent angle.

(*v*) If angles are to be proved equal, show that they are angles of an isosceles triangle.

(*vi*) Two straight lines can be proved parallel if it can be proved alternate or corresponding angles are equal.

(*vii*) If a line or angle is to be proved double the other line or angle, we may double the latter or bisect the former and then prove the result.

18.5 REQUISITES FOR THE TEACHING OF GEOMETRY

To make teaching of geometry easy the following points be kept in mind while teaching geometry:

(*i*) **Proper Symbolic Notion**. The students be taught about it from the very start. Proper practice be given to the pupils in this regard so that they learn things properly and then the whole concept be clear to them. It is helpful throughout the study of Mathematics. It also saves labour and helps comprehension and retention.

(*ii*) Students be also taught to translate the exercises into figures. Figures should be neatly drawn and they should be of a fair size.

(*iii*) **Accuracy of Language**. The language that is used, should be accurate and the students should be trained in understanding and correct use of the language. If students are able to learn the subject quite easily and clearly.

(*iv*) **Directions in Regard to Theorems**. Theorems are quite important in Geometry. Students should be trained in the following manner to enable them to have proper understanding of the theorems and to prove them correctly:

(*a*) The students should be asked to read the theorem carefully, so that the meaning of the words should be clear to them.

(*b*) Then they should be asked to determine the hypothesis and the conclusion.

(*c*) The figure should then be drawn on the basis of the hypothesis and the letters plotted on the figures as required.

(*d*) Then what is to be proved should be written.

(*e*) A method for the proof of the theorem should be selected and then the proof should be written systematically and properly.

18.6 DEFECTS IN TEACHING OF GEOMETRY

Teaching of Geometry in our schools is far from being satisfactory. The pupils memorise the proofs of theorems mechanically without any understanding. The main defects in its teaching may be mentioned as under:

(*i*) Aims of teaching Geometry are generally ignored by the teachers. Various concepts are terms used are not clear. The teachers generally rush through important ideas.

The teacher shouuld be clear about the aims of the subject. He should explain with illustrations important concepts and ideas.

(*ii*) Demonstrative Geometry is started without any concrete base. Abstractions come right from the beginning.

The teacher should prepare the pupils by giving knowledge of elementary geometrical ideas through experimental or inductive Geometry. He should proceed from concrete to abstract.

(*iii*) Geometry is not correlated with life, or other school subjects, not even with other branches of Mathematics.

Wherever possible, the teacher should correlate the teaching of Geometry with other subjects or topics so that the pupils develop a sense of appreciation for it.

(*iv*) It is better if teacher used analytic method and accounts for various steps taken because in synthetic method various steps are done mechanically and are not accounted for.

(*v*) We generally put more emphasis on theorems and neglect exercises and riders. Teacher should ask students to solve exercises side by side and should provide hints for such solutions whenever need arises.

(*vi*) The teacher uses same method for all types of students without taking into consideration the individual differences. It is desirable that the teacher pays individual attention to the students.

(*vii*) In most of the cases the subject-matter has been organised logically and the psychological approach has been totally neglected.

(*viii*) Lack of understanding of geometrical concepts and vocabulary in the beginning gives the impression to the students the geometry is difficult subject. It is thus desirable if the teacher makes things clear in the beginning.

(*ix*) Some teachers simply write various steps on black-board and take little pains to clarify these steps. It is desirable that the teacher should take pains to clarify various steps.

Chapter—19

Teaching of Algebra

19.1 WHAT IS ALGEBRA?

Algebra is a method of calculation by using letters and signs with integers e.g. *4a, 3b, 6ab, 5c* etc. It helps in solving many difficult and complicated problems of other branches of Mathematics. The word Algebra has been derived from the Arabic word 'Al Jebr -At Muqabulah'. In Arabic system of Mathematics it was a device of solving the sums of force. With the passage of time it has assumed new dimensions and new concepts. "It represents a radical, new and different approach to the study of quantitative relationship, characterised by new symbolism, new ćoncept, a new language. A much higher degree of generalisation and abstraction than has been encountered previously, by the fact that in contrast to Arithmetic. Algebra is more concerned with the concious examination and study of processes than with particular answers to particular problems, and by the essential dissociation of many of its parts form institution and concrete experience."

Sometimes algebra is referred to as "Generalised Arithmetic'.

19.2 AIMS OF TEACHING OF ALGEBRA

The major aims of teaching of Algebra are as under:

1. Removal of Ambiguity and Deficiencies of Language

In teaching of Algebra an effort is made to provide the student the numbers and figures in a method that is free from ambiguity and deficiency of language.

2. It Helps of Solving Difficult Problems of Arithmetic

Various formulae or algebra are quite useful to the students in solving even difficult problems of Arithmetic. Such methods also save time and labour.

3. Simplification of Calculations

Algebraic methods help in simplifications of calcualtions and save time and labour.

4. In Algebra We Present Abstract relationships in New Language and New Symbols

In algebra certain abstract relationships are presented in a new language and new symbols which is more concrete and understandable.

5. Practical Value

The knowledge of algebra is of Practical Value in various aspects of life. It provides such a mental training that may be used and applied in various life situations.

6. Checking of Results

Algebraic knowledge can be used to check the results in a satisfactory and simple manner.

7. Use of Inductive Method

Teaching of algebra emphasises inductive method which is more concrete and helpful.

19.3 IMPORTANCE OF TEACHING OF ALGEBRA

The advantages of teaching of Algebra are as under:

(*i*) It creates a concrete interest in the pupils.

(*ii*) It induces students to study certain pupils.

(*iii*) It provides the students with better opportunities to study certain topics.

19.4 THE SUITABLE TIME TO START TEACHING OF ALGEBRA

It is now accepted that teaching of Algebra should start at the Junior High School Stage of Education. Its beginning should be formal and concrete. In the beginning all out efforts be made to correlate Algebra with Arithmetic.

Drills and **Exercises** are very important in teaching of Algebra. The students be given a good deal of exercises which help in strengthening their knowledge.

19.5 METHODS OF TEACHING OF ALGEBRA

The following three methods are generally used for teaching of Algebra:

(*i*) Formal Method.

(*ii*) Equation and Problem Method.

(*iii*) Teaching of Algebra and Literal Numbers of Quantities.

(i) Formal Method of Teaching of Algebra

In it we simply teach four basic arithmetical operations (i.e. addition, subtraction, multiplication and division). In place of numbers here we use letters.

(ii) Equation and Problem Method of Teaching of Algebra

These two methods are difficult to distinguish in teaching of Algebra. To start with problem and equation method be used because it helps to develop interest in the subject.

(iii) Teaching of Algebra and Literal Numbers of Quantities

In Algebra we use letter or literal numbers instead of numbers.

19.6 ORDER OF OPERATIONS

In Algebra we teach certain mathematical operations and a definite order be followed in teaching these operations. We should start with addition and subtraction are should then take up multiplication and division.

Use of Brackets

Brackets occupy an important place in the teaching of Algebra. So it is very important to explain the use of the brackets and the method of their removal. It is essential to explain the following things about the brackets:

(*a*) The students should be given a clear idea of the meanings of the brackets.

(*b*) The students be trained as to interpret correctly mathematical expressions wherein the brackets are used.

(*c*) The students be trained to use the brackets correctly. They should know when the brackets are to be used and when they shall be helpful.

(*d*) The students be trained to transform expressions involving brackets into equivalent expressions which do not have brackets.

(*e*) The terms that are enclosed within a pair of brackets are one quality just as a packet of biscuits or a bundle of boxes etc.

(*f*) Brackets are like containers or the limits or areas that confine certain things. The students should be given a thorough training in removing the brackets.

Teaching of Addition in Algebra

It is an operation with directed numbers. It should begin with concrete examples. A line may be drawn and its centre may be marked as zero. On the left negative numbers may be indicated and positive numbers, may be indicated on the right. Then the solutions of problems may be taken up.

Following four are the possible cases:

(*a*)	+4	(*b*)	+4	(*c*)	−4	(*d*)	−4
	+3		−3		+3		−3
	+7		+1		−1		−7

The students be told that when plus quantities are to be added, movement should be to the right and when minus quantities are to be added the movement should be to the left of the sign of equality.

From the above examples teacher can lead the students to the following rule:

"To add two numbers with like signs, prefix the common sign to their numerical sum, otherwise prefix the sign of numerically larger number to their numerical difference."

By Collecting Like Terms

e.g. $4a^2b^2 + 3a^2b^2 - 7a^2b^2 = -2a^2b^2$

$4a^2b^2 + 3a^2b^2 - 7a^2b^2 + 2a^2b^2 = 0$

$9a^2b^2 - 7a^2b^2 = 0$

$2a^2b^2 = 0$

By Taking Common Factors

e.g. $xa^2b^2 - ya^2b^2 + za^2b^2$

$= a^2b^2 (x - y + z).$

2. Teaching of Subtraction

In comparison to addition it is a bit difficult to learn. It is the reverse of addition.

In teaching of subtraction the teaching should start from simple problems and gradually take up complex problems.

The subtraction is actually the process of addition but with reversed sign.

e.g. $(5x^2 + 3y - 3x^2y^2) - (3x^2)$

$= 5x^2 + 3y - 3\,x^2y^2 - 3x^2$

$= 2x^2 + 3y - 3x^2y^2.$

In Algebra '+' and '–' signs do not only indicate addition and subtraction but certain other things as well. In some times indicate time, some times rise and fall etc. The students be explained about this so that they manipulate these signs properly.

3. Teaching of Multiplications

The sign for multiplication is '×'. Following points should be noted during multiplication

$$+ \times + = +$$

$$- \times - = +$$

$$+ \times - = -$$

$$- \times + = -$$

Multiplication Operation

$$3ab^2c^3 \times 5a^2bc$$

$$= 3 \times 5a^{1+2}\, b^{2+1}\, c^{3+1}$$

$$= 15a^3b^3c^4.$$

The teacher can lead the students to the following rules:

(*a*) In multiplication the exponents of the same letters are combined together.

(*b*) Numerical coefficients are multiplied together.

4. Division Operation

Sum (for example):

$$\frac{9a^4b^5c^3d}{3a^2b^3cd}$$

Solution: $\dfrac{9a^4b^5c^3d}{3a^2b^3cd}$

$$= \frac{9}{3}a^{4-2}b^{5-3}c^{3-1}d^{1-1}$$

$$= 3a^2b^2c^2d^0$$

$$= 3a^2b^2c^2 \textbf{ Ans.}$$

The teacher can lead the students to the following rule.

The exponent of divisor is subtracted from the exponent of dividend in case of same letters.

Teaching of Factors

Factorising means the method of finding factors of an expression when the given expression is a product of two or more expressions each of the letter expression is known as a factor e.g. x is a factor of $x^2 + xy$.

Since factorisation is a difficult operation its teaching must not start before class VIII. It is essential for a teacher to give practice in the factorisation of expression of the following forms.

(*i*) *Quadratic Equation*

Factorise $x^2 - 7x - 18$

By finding the sum and product of roots

Sum of roots = – 7

Product of roots = – 18

Thus the roots are –9 and 2

$x^2 - 7x - 18 = (x - 9)(x + 2)$

By Completing the Squares

e.g. Factorise

$= x^2 - 10x$

$= x^2 - 2.5x + 5^2 - 5^2$

$= (x - 5)^2 - (5)^2$

$= (x - 5 + 5)(x - 5 - 5)$

$x(x - 10)$

By Grouping

e.g. Factorise

$x^2 + xy + xz + yz$

$$= (x^2 + xy) + (xz + yz)$$
$$= x\,(x + y) + z\,(x + y)$$
$$= (x + y)\,(x + z)$$

(*ii*) Factorization using remainder theorem.

(*iii*) Factorization of cyclic order etc. etc.

Teaching of Equation

Equation is a symbolic expression showing one expression equal to another. It is very helpful in solution of the problem. The teacher should clearly explain the meaning of equation by taking the example of balance. If the height in both the pans of a balance are equal then it will neither tilt towards left nor towards right. If they are different it will tilt towards one side.

While teaching equations following four axioms be kept in mind:

(1) If equal quantities are added to equal quantities, the results are equal.

(2) "If equal quantities are subtracted from equal quantities, the results are equal."

(3) "If equal quantities are multiplied by equal quantities, the results are equal."

(4) If equal quantities are divided by equal quantities, other than zero, the results are equal.

Problems and Equations. In the problems of Algebra, some statements are translated into algebraic numbers and statements. The teaching of equations and problems should start from translation of such statements into algebraic figures. Then the procedure should go on.

In teaching of equation we should proceed from simple to complex.

Simple Equation

Simple equations are those in which two sides are equal and which are connected with sign of equality (=). e.g.

if $x + 5 = 12$ find the value of x.

Its solution gives $x = 12 - 5 = 7$

Some More Examples

Example. If $y - 4 = 9$, find the value of y.

The question arises from which number 4 may be subtracted to get 9.

Out of 9 + 4 or 13, 4 can be subtracted to get 9?

$\therefore y = 13$

Example. If $5x + 3 = 28$, find the value of x.

Here question arises with which integer 5 may be multiplied to get 28 when 3 is added to the product

$5x + 3 = 28$

$5x = 28 - 3$

$x = \dfrac{28-3}{5} = 5$ **Ans.**

Hence 5 may be multiplied by 5 to get 28 by adding 3 to the product.

Example. If $5y - 3 = 17$. Find the value of y.

Solution. The question here arises with which integer 5 may be multiplied to get 17 after subtracting 3 from the product

$5y = 17 + 3$

$y = 4$ **Ans.**

Example. If $3x + 4 = 2x + 5$. Find the value of x.

Note. The teacher should tell the students that in such type of simple equations, all the terms containing x are to be taken on one side and without x to other side.

Solution. $3x - 2x = 5 - 4$

$$x = 1 \text{ **Ans.**}$$

Simultaneous Equations

It is a system of two First Degree Equations in two unknowns:

e.g.

$$3x + 4y = 9$$

$$4x + 3y = 5$$

Solution

Multiply both the numbers of each equation separately with such integer that the coefficients of the unknown (x and y) may have same absolute value:

$$3x + 4y = 9 \quad ...(i)$$

$$4x + 3y = 5 \quad ...(ii)$$

Multiply equation (*i*) by 4 and equation (*ii*) by 3.

we get

$$12x + 16y = 36 \quad (iii)$$

$$12x + 9y = 15 \quad (iv)$$

Subtracting (*iv*) from (*iii*)

$$7y = 21 \text{ or } y = 3.$$

Putting the value of y in (*i*), we get

$$3x + 4y = 9$$

$$3x + 12 = 9$$

$$3x = -3 \text{ or } x = -1.$$

Solving Arithmetical Problems

To solve arithmetical problem it should first be translated into the language of Algebra. An Algebraic equation is formed to find the unknown value. e.g. the sum of two numbers is 36 and their difference is 12. Find the numbers.

$$x + y = 36 \quad (i)$$

$$x - y = 12 \quad (ii)$$

Adding (*i*) and (*ii*), we get.

$$2x = 48 \text{ or } x = 24$$

Substituting the value of x in (*i*), we get

$$24 + y = 36$$

$$y = 12.$$

Conditional Equations. In conditional equation, there is only one or a limited number of values. In such an equation, there is a condition and, therefore, it is called a conditional equation. Given below is an example of the same:

$$3x + 4 = 13.$$

It shall be true only when $x = 3$. In other conditions, it shall not be true. Here the condition is that x has the value of 3.

Different Types of Equations. Other than the equations given above, equations are also of the following types:

(*i*) Linear equation.

(*ii*) Quadratic equation.

Graphical Method of Solving Problems or Equations. In this method the solution of the problems or the equations is found out by plotting the figures on the graphs. It is not a general method, but is sometimes used. It is more often used in factors are square-roots.

Teaching of Graph

Graph is simply a line or line drawn on squared paper to show changes in quality. With the help of graphs process of teaching can be made clear and easy.

General Principles of Graphic Representation of Data

Plotting or graphing is carried out with reference to two

lines called coordinate axis. One is vertical line called y-axis and the other horizontal line, known as x-axis. These two lines are perpendicular to each other. The point of intersection of these two lines is called origin and is denoted by O in general.

As for example the figure below shows a system of co-ordinate axes:

1. The origin serves the purpose of zero point of reference for both axes.
2. Distances measured to the right of O along x-axis are known as positive.

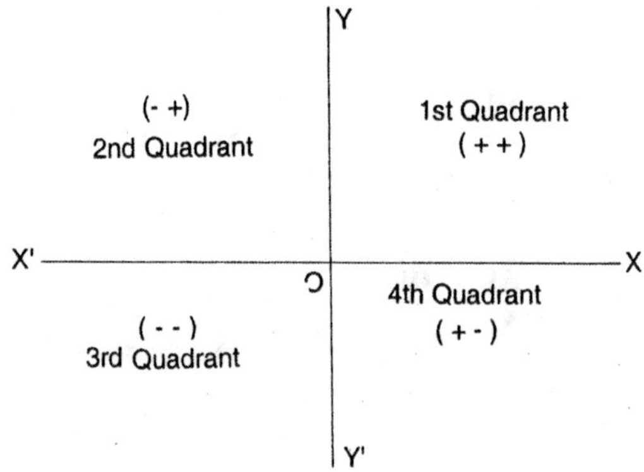

3. Distances measured to the left of O along x-axis are known as negative.
4. Distance measured above O on y are positive.
5. Distances measured below O on y are negative.
6. The intersection of x-axis and y-axis at O forms four quadrants or divisions.
7. In the first quadrant both x and y are positive.
8. In the second quadrant x is negative and y is positive.
9. In the third quadrant both x and y are negative.

10. In the fourth quadrant x is positive and y is negative.

Plotting of Points

Suppose the coordinates of the points A are (x = 5, y = 2). Taking O as the starting point we will move five units towards right on the x-axis and from the origin O upward two units on the y-axis.

Similarly the point B whose coordinates are (x = – 4, y = –6) can be plotted on the third quadrant by moving 4 units left from O on x-axis and then down 6 units along y-axis.

Similarly points C and D can be plotted.

Need for Teaching of Graph. It helps in illustration of certain abstract thoughts and figures. Through the graph, it is possible to present things is more concrete manner.

When to Teach Graph? Teaching of graph should not start before class VIII. Graphs may be about area, about circle and such other things. The students may be taught to draw graphs neatly and correctly. Unless they are taught to draw it in this manner, its utility shall be exhausted.

By graphical method, the students should be told how to solve two simultaneous equations of first order, or one equations of first order and the second order; plotting of data of temperature of a patient, production of a country in different years, imports and exports etc. The students should be taught how these graphs can be plotted and how relevant information can be gathered from them.

Teaching of Formulae in Algebra. Formula is a short form of a long statement. It is a method that economise the efforts. It has been defined as below:

"It is a statement of a general rule applicable to anyone of a definite class of problems; and the statement is expressed in a conventional form for its properties of consciousness and comprehensibility."

Importance of Formulae. The knowledge of a formulae is very important in the teaching of Algebra. It is very helpful in the solution of different problems.

Teaching of Indices

The word indices in the plural of the word index

$$9 = 3 \times 3 = 3^{1+1} = 3^2$$

$$27 = 3 \times 3 \times 3 = 3^{1+1+1} = 3^3$$

we see 3^2 means two times 3

3^3 means three times 3

The power of 3 in each case is known as index of 3 and the integer 3 is called base.

We also see that $a \times a = a^{1+1} = a^2$ and $a \times a \times a = a^{1+1+1} = a^3$

Thus we find that when the bases are the same the powers are added up. This means

$$3^2 \times 3^3 = 3^{2+3} = 3^5$$

Similarly $a^3 \times a^2 = a^5$ and $a^m \times a^n = a^{m+n}$

Operation of Division

To understand the operation of division let us consider the following examples:

$$3^5 \div 3^2 = 3^5 \times \frac{1}{3^2} = 3^5.3^{-2} = 3^{5-2} = 3^3$$

Note: When 3^2 from denominator is taken to numerator sign of indices is changed.

Let us take '*a*' in place of 3

$$a^5 \div a^2 = a^5 \times \frac{1}{a^2} = a^{5-2} = a^3$$

Put $5 = m$ and $2 = n$

$$\therefore\ a^m \div a^n = a^m \times \frac{1}{a^n} = a^{m-n}$$

Hence during the process of division the index of the quotient is equal to the difference of the power of the dividend and divisor provided the base is the same.

Correlation Between Algebra, Arithmetic and Geometry. These are the three branches of Mathematics and have a strong correlation. Their correlation should be utilised properly. This correlation can make certain concept more clear. Through Arithmetic and Geometry, it is possible to make certain Algebra in concepts clear. Similarly, through the method of Algebra, it is possible to solve certain complicated sums of Arithmetic as well as Geometry.

19.7 REASONS FOR COMPARATIVE DIFFICULTY IN ALGEBRA

Algebra is thought to be the difficult and abstract of all the branches of Mathematics. It is related to various other branches of Mathematics and is generally referred to as 'Generalised Arithmetic'. It may be related to geometry by saying that Algebra is only written Geometry and Geometry is merely pictured Algebra.

The reasons for comparative difficulty in Algebra are summarised below:

(*i*) It starts from deductive analysis of facts.

(*ii*) All the students may not possess the quick manipulative skills which are essential to solve problems.

(*iii*) Algebraic sums and other operations, through similar to Arithmetical operations have their own intricate details and special characteristics.

(*iv*) Intuitive thinking is essential in solving problems.

(*v*) Modern and abstract Algebra depends heavily on the power of logical analysis.

(*vi*) A sound knowledge of Algebra is essential to understand further theories.

Methods that Can be used to Overcome the Difficulties of Pupils

Following methods are helpful to some extent to overcome the difficulties of the pupils:

(*i*) To overcome too much memorization of ruler and formulae, some amount of oral work and drill may be given.

(*ii*) To reduce the abstractness, a few examples from arithmetic may be given.

(*iii*) Teacher should pay individual attention and take necessary remedial action in each case.

(*iv*) When ever possible, similarities between Algebraic operations and Arithmetical operations be drawn.

(*v*) The students be helped to gain a thorough mastery over various Algebraic operations and principles otherwise they would not be able to follow higher Algebra.

Chapter—20

Teaching of Arithmetic

20.1 INTRODUCTION

The part of Mathematics that deals with numbers and counting or calculation is known as Arithmetic. For a person belonging to any profession, knowledge of Arithmetic is essential to cope with the needs of daily life.

"The need of a good command of Arithmetic in a skilled mechanic, by the up-to-date farmer, by the progressive professional man, by the successful merchant and by the efficient housewife, is so obvious as to need no discussion."

20.2 VALUE AND UTILITY OF THE TEACHING OF ARITHMETIC

While talking about the importance of the teaching of Mathematics and the causes of its being an important place in the school curriculum, we have seen that it has a lot value in day-to-day life. In fact, it is the Arithmetic which has greater value in day-to-day life. Most of the fundamentals of the numerical works etc., are guided by Arithmetic and its principles.

In addition the practical value, Mathematics also has cultural and disciplinary value. In India and Egypt, we find in importance of the Mathematics even in the centuries before Christ. However, the same is true about the teaching of Arithmetic even today.

20.3 MAJOR OBJECTIVES OF THE TEACHING OF ARITHMETIC

The two major objectives of teaching of Arithmetic are as under:

(*i*) Ability to perform various number-operations skillfully.

(*ii*) To provide variety of experiences, which will enable the students to apply quantitative procedure effectively in society.

These objectives may be further divided as under:

(1) To lay the foundation for the understanding of higher Mathematics.

(2) To equip the students with the competence to enable them to understand the mathematical statements.

(3) To develop the ability to have correct analysis and reach proper conclusions.

(4) To develop a proper idea of weights and measures.

(5) To develop the ability of performing computational jobs with speed and accuracy.

(6) To give the students a clear idea of practical utility of Arithmetic in daily life.

(7) To enable the students to make dependable estimates and approximations.

(8) To develop amongst students the quality of resourcefulness and ingenuity.

20.4 GENERAL RULES FOR TEACHING OF ARITHMETIC

The following rules be followed in teaching of Arithmetic. It will help the students in understanding the subject in a better way:

(*i*) Before teaching a lesson the teacher should explain to the students the general principles underlying the topic.

(*ii*) Students be allowed to work independently.

(*iii*) Enough drill be given.

(*iv*) Teacher should do the correction work very carefully.

(*v*) An effort be made to develop orderliness, accuracy and speed.

(*vi*) Students be given enough training in oral Mathematics.

(*vii*) The interest of students should not be allowed to diminish.

(*viii*) Students be encouraged to do their written work systematically.

(*ix*) Students be encouraged to write figures neatly and correctly.

(*x*) They should be encouraged to use a simple, understandable and correct language.

(*xi*) The teacher should follow the maxim of proceeding from simple to complex.

(*xii*) The value of orderliness be taught to the students.

20.5 AIMS OF TEACHING OF ARITHMETIC

The following are the aims of teaching of Arithmetic:

(*i*) To develop Mathematical thinking in the students.

(*ii*) To arouse interest in the quantitative side of world.

(*iii*) To give knowledge of the practical utility of Arithmetic in everyday life.

(*iv*) To prepare students for study of higher Mathematics.

20.6 DIFFERENT APPROACHES IN TEACHING OF ARITHMETIC

The following four approaches are generally used in the teaching of Arithmetic:

1. **Incidental Approach**. This approach is opposed to the traditional or drill approach. In this approach the teaching is done in a rational and incidental manner.

2. **Drill Approach**. In this approach, the teacher continues to repeat a thing before the students till it gets fixed in the mind of the students.

3. **Social Approach**. In this method, the experiences of the child occupy an important place. The teaching of Arithmetic is done in such a way that it is linked with the experiences of the child in his daily life.

4. **Meaningful Approach**. In this approach, the whole programme of the teaching work is systematically worked out.

Fundamental Thing to be Kept in Mind While Teaching. One basic thing that has to be kept in mind while teaching Arithmetic is that it is 'a means of developing the child's natural ability' and so the teaching should lead to the method or the results that bring accuracy and speed. The best thing in the teaching of Arithmetic is that too much of emphasis should not be put on theory. The students should be made to do things in a practical manner and their ability should be tested.

20.7 PLACE OF DRILL IN TEACHING OF ARITHMETIC

The students must be given a good drill to make the teaching of Arithmetic effective and successful. Drill enables them to have the repetition of the knowledge that ultimately strengthens their experiences. Drill is nothing but exercise. However a careful and systematic planning of the exercise and the work is needed. Attempts should be made to correlate the drill of the exercises with the facts of life. Such a correlation will have permanent and lasting effect.

Following points be kept in mind about the exercises and drill:

(1) It should be clear and vivid.

(2) It should have association with the past and attempt and association in future.

(3) There should be the element of motivation.

(4) There should be no scope for guess work.

20.8 WHEN SHOULD THE TEACHING OF ARITHMETIC START?

The teaching of Arithmetic should start at the pre-primary stage or infant stage. An infant should be made to learn things about Arithmetic through playway method. In other words, it means that teaching of Arithmetic should start with the beginning or education.

20.9 IMPORTANCE OF NUMBERS IN TEACHING OF ARITHMETIC

Number is the basic element of Arithmetic. Without number nothing is possible in arithmetic. For this reason Arithmetic teaching should start with numbers. At the infant stage the students may be taught about numbers, their different combinations, method of numeration etc. After this they will be able to proceed further.

20.10 TEACHING OF VARIOUS TOPICS IN ARITHMETIC

1. Teaching in Numeration

Child mind is full of curiosity as regards numbers. The teacher should provide higher understanding of numeration through practical work, play-way methods or learning by doing.

Sense of numbers and counting can be developed by some article e.g. place one piece of marble on one side and write integer 1 on the other side. Similarly place two pieces of marbles on one side and write integer 2 on the other side and so on.

1 ●

2 ● ●

3 ● ● ●

It helps the child to learn the symbolic form of integers and their meaning. Any other object like balls of beads etc. can be used in place of marble.

Practical Work

The child should be given drill about the concept of number and quantity through recognising and memorising different integers. Then he should be asked to write different integers on slate or paper.

TEACHING FOUR FUNDAMENTAL RULES

1. Teaching of Addition

The teaching of addition should start at pre-primary stage and should continue upto primary stage.

For this first of all the students should be trained in the counting of numbers and then they should be trained in the combination of numbers. Then the students be given training of addition of one digit, then two digits and so on. In teaching of additions the teacher should proceed from simple to complex. The teacher may take help of figures and other concrete object to explain the process.

Addition is simply a process of counting in the forward direction. If a child has to add two and three. The child may be asked to represent the integers two and three with the help of lines as under:

11
111

Then ask the child to count all the lines. He will count upto 5. Then ask him to write as under:

$$\begin{array}{r} 2 \\ +\ 3 \\ \hline 5 \end{array}$$

Similarly he can be given a good practice in the process.

In the same way method of adding the numbers of two or more digits can be taught.

It we are to find the sum of 287 and 465. Then first of all arrange the given, numbers in columns of hundreds, tens and ones. The students be then told the method of 'Carry over' if the sum of integers in a particular column is more than 9.

	H	T	O
	1	1	carry over
	2	8	7
+	4	6	5
	7	5	2

Step. I. Adding integers in the column of ones we get

7 + 5 = 12 ones

12 ones = 1 ten, 2 ones

Write 2 in one's place and carry over 1 ten to ten's column to add with tens.

Step II. Adding tens we get

1 + 8 + 6 = 15 tens

15 tens = 1 hundred, 5 tens.

Write 5 in tens place and carry over 1 hundred to hundred's column to add with hundreds.

Step III. Adding hundreds we get 1 + 2 + 4 = 7 hundred.

Hence the sum is 7 hundred, 5 tens 2 ones = 752 **Ans.**

Similarly the sum of two numbers going up to thousands or more than that can be found.

Oral Work in Teaching of Addition

Oral work is quite important in teaching of Arithmetic and it is also important in teaching of addition. Through oral work it is possible to do the things more accurately. Oral work also provides a good practice.

2. Teaching of Subtraction

In subtraction we teach the students to take out numbers from one another. Only smaller number can be taken out from a bigger number. The teaching of subtraction should begin at pre-primary stage and should not go beyond primary stage.

As in teaching of addition so also in teaching subtraction teacher should proceed from simple to complex. In the beginning, the teacher should take help of concrete things such as balls, coloured pieces of wood, beeds etc. The system of borrowing and returning may also be explained and the method of changing coirs may also be explained.

Process of Subtraction

Subtraction is simply a process of counting in the backward direction. Suppose the child is to subtract 3 from 5. Ask him to write integer 5 and then integer 3 below it with sign (—). Represent the integer 5 in the form of lines. Cross the lines equal to the integer, which is to be subtracted and then write the remainder in the following way:

$$\begin{array}{r} 5 \\ -\,3 \\ \hline 2 \end{array} \qquad 11\,x\,x\,x$$

Similarly for the numbers consisting of two, three, four digits etc.

52	1 x
– 21	111 x x
31	

Subtract separately the integer of each column and repeat the process.

Then, question arises what to do it the integer of upper row in a particular column is less than the lower integer of the same column. This type of subtraction is done by the method of 'borrowing' as under:

Suppose we are to subtract 1732 from 5620.

Solution. Arrange the numbers as below:

	Th	H	T	O
Borrow		1	1	10
	(4)	(15)	(11)	
	5	6	2	0
–	1	7	3	2
	3	8	8	8

Since it is not possible to subtract 2 ones or O ones. Hence we borrow a ten from ten's column.

Step I. 10 ones – 2 ones = 8 ones

Hence write 8 in one's place.

Step II. We can not subtract 3 tens from 1 ten left with us, so we borrow 1 hundred (10 tens) from 6 hundreds, leaving 5 hundred and making 10 + 1 = 11 tens. Hence

11 tens – 3 tens = 8 tens

Write 8 in tens place.

Step III. We are left with 5 hundreds. We can not subtract 7 hundred from 5 hundred, so we borrow 1 thousand (10 hundreds) from 5 thousand, leaving 4 thousands and making 10 + 5 = 15 hundreds.

Hence 15 – 7 = 8, thus write 8 in hundreds place.

Step IV. Finally one thousand is subtracted from thousand i.e. 4 – 1 = 3, thus write 3 in place of thousands.

Hence 5620 – 1732 = 3888.

3. Teaching of Multiplication

It is a short method of 'addition of equal quantities'. In this method there is addition of more than one group. It is quick method of addition. It helps and simplifies the process of addition. It is therefore, advisable to teach it at the primary stage of education and then take it in more difficult and complex form at Junior High School or pre-secondary stage of education. In the beginning the students should be made to learn the multiplication tables of 2's, 5's and 10's. Then they should be made to learn multiplication tables of 4's, 8's, 3's, 6's and 9's. In the end, the multiplication of 7's should be taught. Learning of multiplication tables is very helpful in future life.

Process of Multiplication

Suppose 1 is to be multiplied by 2, draw 1 times two lines and count them. If 2 is to be multiplied by 2, draw two lines two times and count them. Similarly proceed for other cases.

In multiplication you should always remember that the product of a number and zero is equal to zero.

Steps of Teaching of Multiplication. To teach multiplication successfully, the teacher should take-up the following steps:

(1) Teacher should proceed from simple to complex.

(2) First of all, multiplication of one digit may be taught and then the multiplication of digits that have 'carry-over.'

(3) While teaching multiplication, the knowledge of multiplication of students should invariably be put to test.

(4) While teaching multiplication, the students should be explained that in multiplication any of the digits may be used as a multiplier and the result shall be same. For example, $7 \times 8 = 56$. Similarly, $8 \times 7 = 56$.

(5) While teaching multiplication, the teacher should determine the difficulties and the drawbacks of the students. If certain basic difficulties are removed, it shall be possible to teach them the process quickly and scientifically.

Checking the Result of Multiplication. Suppose two numbers have been multiplied and their result obtained. The problem is "Does there exist any method by which it can be ascertained that the result obtained is correct."

Suppose, for example, that the numbers 9573 and 3058 have been multiplied and the result obtained is 29,274,234. How can we be sure that the result obtained is correct? To check the results following method may be adopted.

Draw two lines intersecting one another in the form of a cross.

(i) Add all the digits of numbers which are being multiplied and reduce the sum to a number lying between zero and nine.

Thus

$9 + 5 + 7 + 3 = 24$ and $2 + 4 = 6$

$3 + 0 + 5 + 8 = 16$ and $1 + 6 = 7$

Write 6 on one side of cross and 7 on other side of cross.

(*ii*) Multiply now 6 and 7. The result obtained is 42. Add the digits of this number i.e. $4 + 2 = 6$.

(*iii*) Lastly add digits of the result obtained.
Thus $2 + 9 + 2 + 7 + 4 + 2 + 3 + 4 = 33$ and $3 + 3 = 6$.

This number 6 is equal to the result to the number 6 obtained by adding $4 + 2 = 6$. Hence multiplication is correct.

To strengthen the knowledge and experiences it is advisable to give them more of practice and drill in multiplication tables.

4. Teaching of Division

It is easy and shortened way of subtraction. It is reverse of multiplication while teaching division following things be given due consideration:

(*i*) The students be discouraged from using rote method and they should be encouraged to discover and assimilate the rules. For this they be given repeated exercises.

(*ii*) Teaching of division should be done with the help of concrete problems.

(*iii*) Students be made to practice in different situations which will be quite helpful in strengthening their knowledge and experience.

(*iv*) To start with divisions without 'carry over' should be taught and then complex ones with 'carry over' be taken up.

(*v*) Students be encouraged to write down the answer in the form that they may write down the dividend and the remainder.

Process of Division

Suppose we want to divide 15 by 5. Here we have to see how many times 5 can be subtracted from 15.

Illustrations

$$\begin{array}{rl} 15 & \\ -5 & \rightarrow \text{one time} \\ \hline 10 & \\ -5 & \rightarrow \text{two times} \\ \hline 5 & \\ -5 & \rightarrow \text{three times} \\ \hline 0 & \end{array}$$

It shows 5 can be subtracted from 15 repeatedly three times. Thus quotient of 115 divided by 5 in 3. Quotient means the number of times 5 can be subtracted repeatedly from 15. The number 15 is known as dividend and 3, the divisor.

This means 15 ÷ 5 = 3

Suppose we divide 10 by 3. In this case 3 can be subtracted 3 times, from 10 and 1 left over at the end. In this case 1 is known as remainder. It is written as 10 ÷ 3 = 3 – 1.

Division with Carrying

Suppose we want to divide 45 by 3

```
             15
Solution  3) 45
              3
            ----
             15
             15
            ----
              0
```

Step I. We start with tens. 3 in 4 goes one time, so 1 is written in the quotient. Three tens are subtracted from 4 tens leaving one ten as remainder.

Step II. Convert one ten into 10 ones and add 5 ones to get 15 ones. This can be done by placing 5 on the right hand side of 1.

Step III. Divide 15 ones by 3 *i.e.* 15 ÷ 3 = 5.

Write 5 in quotient in one's place. As no remainder is left by dividing 15 by 3, we write zero as remainder.

Teaching of Fraction

The teacher should explain that fractions mean the parts. If whole is divided in two equal parts, each of part is called a half of the whole and is written as 1/2. Similarly we have 1/3, 1/4, 1/5 and so on.

When two of the three equal parts of the whole are considered, it means 2/3 of the whole. Similarly we have 3/4, 4/7 etc. Numbers like 1/2, 1/3, 1/4, 1/5, 2/3, 3/4 etc. are called fractional numbers or common fractions. The number below the line represents the number of equal parts in which the whole is divided. This number is known as denominator. In 3/4, 4 is the denominator of the fractional number. The number above the line is known as numerator. Here 3, is the numerator.

Things to be Explained in Teaching of Fraction. The teaching of fractions in Mathematics requires the explanation of the following technical terms:

(1) Numerator.

(2) Denominator.

(3) Proper fraction.

(4) Improper fraction.

(5) Reduce.

(6) Invert.

(7) Subtracting the same number from the numerator and denominator.

(8) Multiplying the fraction with the reverse numbers.

Definition. Fraction is a division or a part of a unit or a whole.

Denominator is the divisor or the number which is below the line in the fraction. It indicates the number of the part into which the unit or the whole is to be divided.

Numerator is the dividend or the number above the line in fraction. It indicates the number or parts which are to be taken out of the parts into which a unit has been divided.

Improper Fraction is that in which the numerator is equal to or greater than denominator. e.g. 2/2 or 7/3 etc.

Proper Fractions

Fractions having numerator less than the denominator are called proper fractions, e.g. 3/4, 4/5, 7/8 etc.

Mixed Number

Mixture of a whole number and a fraction is called mixed number e.g. $1\frac{4}{5}$, $2\frac{7}{12}$, $4\frac{5}{19}$ etc.

Equivalent Fractions

Two or more fractional numbers representing the same part of a whole are termed as equivalent fractions. e.g. 1/2, 2/4, 4/8 etc.

Before teaching addition and subtraction of fractions, the students be taught the method of finding the L.C.M, of the denominators. For this, we might have to factorise the denominators. Some of the hints for factorising are given below which should be given to the students:

(*i*) If in units place a number has 2, 4, 6, 8, 0, then 2 will be a factor.

(*ii*) In the sum of all digits of a number is divisible by three, then 3 will be a factor.

(*iii*) If we take the digits at units and tens places of the given number and if the number so formed is divisible by four then 4 is a factor of the number.

(*iv*) If in units place we have 0 or 5 then 5 is a factor of the number.

(*v*) If the number formed by taking digits in units, tens and hundred place of the given number is divisible by 8 then 8 is a factor of the number.

(*vi*) If the sum of all digits is completely divisible by 9 then 9 is a factor of the number.

Since understanding fractions is a bit difficult so student be taught to learn them scientifically and properly.

Addition of Fractional Numbers

(*i*) If they have same denominator then we have simply to add the numerators.

e.g $\frac{2}{9}+\frac{3}{9}+\frac{4}{9}=\frac{2+3+4}{9}=\frac{9}{9}=1$

(*ii*) In case the denominator is not same then we should make the denominator same by finding out the equivalent fractions. e.g. $\frac{1}{6}+\frac{2}{3}$ will be changed to $\frac{1}{6}+\frac{4}{6}$ and then we get $\frac{5}{6}$.

Subtraction of Fractional Numbers

(*i*) If the two fractional numbers to be subtracted have same denominator then the answer could be found by subtracting lesser numerator from greater numerator e.g. $\frac{3}{4}-\frac{1}{4}=\frac{3-1}{4}=\frac{2}{4}$

(*ii*) If they have different denominator then change them into fractions of equal denominator and then carry out the subtraction as above. e.g. $\frac{1}{4}-\frac{1}{8}$ can be written as $\frac{2}{8}-\frac{1}{8}=\frac{1}{8}$.

Multiplication of Fraction Numbers

The teacher should tell the students that multiplication is simply a process of repeated addition. Thus

$$\frac{2}{3}\times 2=\frac{2}{3}+\frac{2}{3}=\frac{4}{3}=\frac{2\times 2}{3\times 1}=\frac{\text{Product of Numerators}}{\text{Product of Denometators}}$$

Decimal Fractions

In our country coins, weights and measures are based

on this principle so the decimal fractions must be understood carefully.

Use of Brackets. Brackets are very commonly used in Arithmetic and Algebra and have a very great importance. Simplification of sums in brackets require patience and clarity of concepts. Generally three types of brackets are used:

Small brackets: denoted as ( )

Curly brackets: denoted as { }

Larger brackets: denoted as [ ]

Sometimes a continuous line is drawn over certain terms occurring within small brackets. This signifies another brackets and in all simplification, this has to be given the first priority. Terms within small, curly and large brackets should be subsequently simplified.

In higher Mathematics, however it should be kept in mind that these brackets may have some different meanings, and there it depends upon the context: At some places [ ] denotes closed interval, ( ) denotes open interval, while at other places [ ] denotes scalar triple product of vectors.

It should be the duty of the teacher to acquaint the students with the process how these brackets can be removed, and what precautions should be taken in each case. First of all, terms within small brackets should be simplified, then curly brackets should be taken-up, and lastly large brackets should be simplified. This order has to be maintained at all costs.

Sometimes the word 'of' is to used between two numbers besides the symbols +, −, ×, ÷. In such a case, within certain brackets first priority is to be given to numbers involving 'of' between them. Second priority should be given to symbols of multiplication and division. The terms containing the sign of addition and subtraction should be simplified in the last.

Measurement. In our country, now there is metric system of measurement as well as weight. All these things have the bearing on decimal fractions. This things has to be taught, therefore, with greater caution, keeping in view its utility to the people of the country.

Teaching of Ratio and Proportions

Ratio. It is a relationship of one quantity to another. It is indicated like this

$$6 : 1.$$

Ratio of one number to another is nothing but the quotient of the first number divided by the second. The two numbers, that are used in a ratio, are called the terms of the ratio. The first one is called Antecedent and is the dividend. The second digit or number is called Consequent and is the divisor.

Teaching of Ratio. Normally, it should begin at the Junior High School of education, i.e. from class VI and should go on upto class VIII. In secondary classes, more complicated sums of ratio may be taught and explained.

Comparison of Two Ratios

Suppose we are to compare two ratios 3 : 4 and 1 : 3,

3 : 4 means 3/4 and 1 : 3 means 1/3.

In order to compare fractions 3/4 and 1/2, make an equal denominator of each fractions.

$$\frac{3}{4}=\frac{9}{12} \text{ and } \frac{1}{3}=\frac{4}{12}$$

$$\frac{9}{12} > \frac{4}{12} \text{ or } 3 : 4 > 1 : 3 \textbf{ Ans.}$$

Proportion. To understand the idea of proportion, let us consider there are four quantities 6, 18, 8 and 24, such that 6 : 18 = 8 : 24 i.e. 6, 18, 8, 24 are in proportion, which means that the first quantity is the same multiple or part of the second as the third is of the fourth. It can be expressed as 6 : 18 : : 8 : 24. The first two quantities should be of the same nature, but it not necessary that all the four quantities may be of the same kind.

Each quantity of proportion is called term. The first and fourth terms are known as extremes, whereas the second and third terms are known as means.

Suppose there is a proportion 4 : 8 : : 3 : 6

The product of the means 8 x 3 = 24.

Hence the product of the extremes of a proportion is equal to the product of its means.

Proportions may be simple or compound. Proportions may be direct as well as inverse. In direct proportions both the figures rise and diminish simultaneously while in inverse proportion one number goes up while the other number comes down.

The teaching of proportions should be taken up at the junior high school or middle school stage of education. More complicated problems may be taken up at high school stage.

Teaching of Percentage

The teacher should tell the students that hundred is such a term, which is quite easily understood by everyone. Thus percentage is connected with the easily understood term hundred. It means 'out of the hundred', e.g. 10 per cent means 10 ones of hundred. It is represented symbolically as %. Thus 10% means 10 out of 100 and is equivalent to 10/100.

It has a bearing on decimal as well. Once the decimal has been understood, it would not be difficult to calculate percentage.

Teaching of percentage should also start at the Junior High School stage of education and go in a complex form upto the High School stage of education. Here the teacher should again proceed from simple to complex problems. This is the most psychological method of teaching of the subject.

Interest: Simple or Compound. Percentage has an important bearing on the question of interest. Interest, as we all know, is surcharge on many lent or money-giving. It is of two types:

(*a*) Simple; and

(*b*) Compound.

Simple interest is an addition to the capital in the simple form. For example, simple interest on Rs. 100/- at the rate of 5% per annum shall be Rs. 5/- only. The formula for finding out simple interest is given below:

$$\textbf{Simple Interest} = \frac{\text{Principal} \times \text{Rate} \times \text{Time}}{100}$$

The teaching of simple interest should start from simple to complex problems. In other words, in the beginning, the students should be taught about simple questions on simple, interest and then difficult sums may be taken-up.

Teaching of this topic should start at the Junior High School stage of education and go upto the High School stage.

In compound interest, the interest is also charged on the interest that falls due at the end of the year. In other words, if somebody has taken a loan of Rs. 100/- at 5% of interest at the end of the year, the amount shall grow to 100 + 5 and then the interest shall be charged not on Rs. 100/- but on Rs. 105/-.

Compound interest should be taught after teaching simple interest. The formula for finding out the compound interest is like this

$$\text{Compound interest} = \text{Principal}\left(1 + \frac{\text{Rate}}{100}\right)^{\text{time}} - \text{amount}$$

given out as principal.

Discount. This too has the bearing on the percentage. It is, in fact, a reduction in the diversed price or the price at which the thing is to be sold. It is, in fact, the present worth of the actual amount. Discount is equal to interest on present worth.

Profit and Loss. Profit and loss is the principle of everyday life. Students are well aware of everybody sale and purchase of things. They should, therefore, be told this in the following manner:

Profit or gain is the selling price minus cost price.

Similarly, loss is the cost price minus selling price.

In the profit, selling price is more than the cost price but in loss, selling price is less than the cost price. Sometimes the question of percentage is also involved.

This topic should start at Junior High School stage and may continue upto Higher Secondary Stage. In teaching this topic the teacher should proceed from simple to complex problems.

To Teach Method of Average

The teacher should give the students the following concrete example of average:

Suppose there are four friends. They have pocket money Rs. 4, Rs. 6, Rs. 2, and Rs. 4 respectively. If we add the pocket money of all the four friends, it comes to 16. If we give Rs. 4 to each student, the amount of Rs. 16 is divided equally among the four. Thus amount of Rs. 4 is known as Average Value.

$$\text{Hence, Average} = \frac{\text{The sum of various quantities}}{\text{Number of quantities}}$$

Then with the help of this method the students be taught about average of rail fall, temperature etc. and the knowledge be correlated to Geography.

In teaching this topic the teacher should proceed from simple to complex. This topic should be introduced at Junior High School stage and may continue upto higher secondary stage.

Stock and Share

When there are a number of partners in a company then the capital subscribed by each partner is known as his share and the persons having such a share is called a shareholder. The profit earned by a company is divided amongst share holders in proportion to their shares and is known as dividend.

Stock is the capital of the company.

This topic can be dealt along with profit and loss at Junior High School level and may be allowed to continue upto secondary or higher secondary stage.

Square Root. This is more applied in Algebra. But its basic concept lies in Arithmetic. The object of the teacher should be to make the students perfectly clear about the squaring or finding out the square etc. square root of a particular number.

In finding out square root, it is not necessary that the square root may be in a positive number. It may also be negative number such as square root of 9 is + 3 and also – 3.

Teaching of Square Root. Here again the teacher should not try to be formal and theoretical. What is required is the clarification of the idea of square and square root. Here geometrical method may be applied and a particular figure may be drawn on the black-board. That figure may be divided into different squares and on the basis of that division, the square root may found out. This would help the teacher to make the subject perfectly clear to his pupils.

It should be emphasised on the students that if a number contains 3, 2, 7, 8 in units place, it cannot have a whole-number as its square root.

Sometimes, the application of square root finds application in factorisation of numbers. This should be told to the students with suitable examples. It is also the duty of a teacher to explain the method of factorisation and division or finding the square root of a given number and their utility in each case with suitable examples.

The teaching of this topic should start at the Junior High School stage of education and go upto Higher Secondary stage. The principle of proceeding from simple to complex problems should also be applied here. Without this, it shall not be possible to make the concept clear.

Teaching of Area

To teach this topic the teacher should start with some concrete example. Some figures should be drawn and the concept of area be clarified with the help of these figures. The students be then told that area of a rectangle is equal to the product of length and breadth. The units of area are square metres or square centimetres.

Area of a Triangle

Let us take x some rectangular sheet of the metal, say ABCD. Join AC. This line AC will divide the sheet into two equal parts (*i.e.* into two equal right angles triangles.)

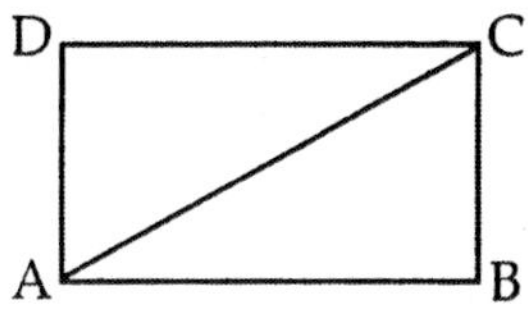

Therefore area of each triangle = $\frac{\text{Area of rectangle}}{2}$

or area of rt. ∠ d ΔABC = 1/2 AB × BC

= 1/2 Base × Height

Again, suppose we divide the same rectangular sheet into two parts by joining the mid-points of AB and CD. Let E and F be the mid-points of AB and CD respectively. Now there are two equal rectangles i.e. AEFD and EBCE. Join AF and BF to divide each rectangular part into two equal parts, forming an acute angled ΔFAB.

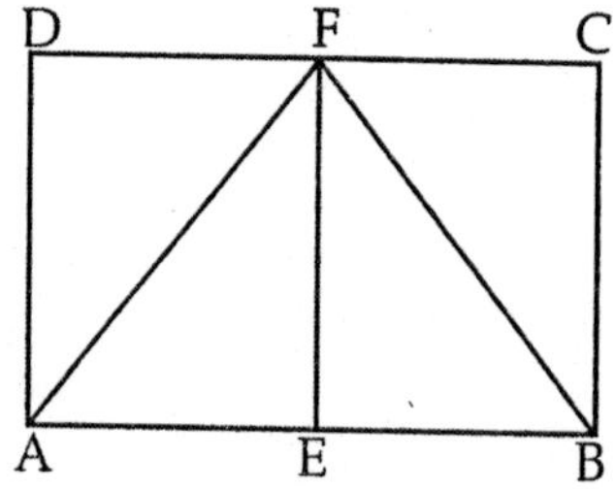

$$\therefore \Delta FAB = \frac{\text{Rectangle ABCD}}{2}$$

$$\text{or Area acute angled } \Delta FAB = \frac{\text{Area of Rectangle ABCD}}{2}$$

i.e $= 1/2 \text{ Length} \times \text{Breadth}$

$= 1/2 \text{ Length} \times \text{Height}$

BC= EF = AD.

Similarly let us consider there be a sheet of metal in the form of a parallelogram ABCD. Join BD. This divides the ll gm. into two equal parts, forming two equal abtused angled Δ DAB and DCB.

$$\text{Area of abtused angled } \Delta \text{ DAB} = \frac{\text{Area of ll gm. ABCD}}{2}$$

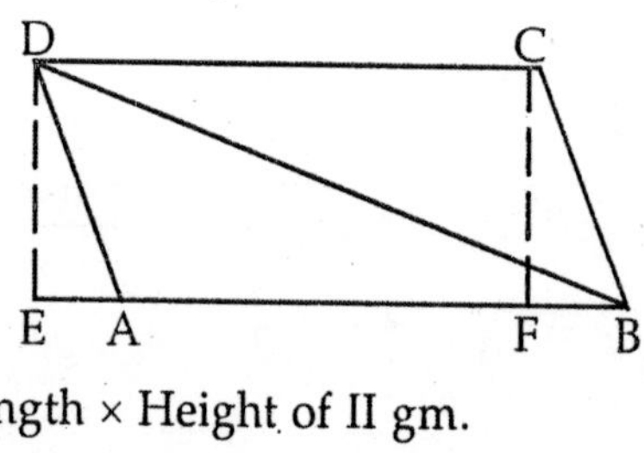

$= 1/2 \text{ Length} \times \text{Height of II gm.}$

$= 1/2 \text{ Base} \times DE$

$= 1/2 \text{ Base} \times \text{Height}$

Thus Area of $\Delta = 1/2 \text{ Base} \times \text{Height.}$

The topic of area should be introduced at the Junior High School level and should go upto Higher Secondary stage of education. The teacher should start the simpler sums and then more difficult and complicated sums should be taken-up.

Teaching of Volume

The teacher should tell the students that anything which occupies space is called solid e.g. a Box, Book or Brick etc. The outer boundaries of these solids are called surface. We see that Book, Brick, Box etc. have six surfaces which are rectangular in shape and these bodies have three dimensions, Length, Breadth and Depth (Height). Such solid is known as CUBOID.

In case the length, breadth and height is equal, the solid is known as CUBE.

Volume. Volume is equal to length × breadth × height. It should not be told in the form of a definition to the students. They should be given a concrete idea about it. The figure or the thing whose volume is to be found out should be divided into several units. Then on the basis of those units, the volume of the figure may be found out. Normally, volume is indicated by cubic measures. If the volume of a particular object is 27 units and measurement of a unit is a metre, it should be written as 27 cubic metres.

While teaching the sums about volume, the teacher should again start from simple to complex problems. The basic object is to make the concept of the volume clear to the students. The process of the classification of the concept of volume should start at Junior High School stage of education and it should go upto the Higher Secondary stage.

Chapter—21

Teaching of Number System

21.1 INTRODUCTION

We are familiar with the number system in which an ordered set of ten symbols 0 to 9, known as digits, are used to specify any number. This is commonly used in Mathematics, allied subjects and in our day to day working. It is the most famous system because fingers are most convenient natural way for human beings to use them for counting. This system is known as 'Decimal System'. The radix or base of this number is 10. It is a positional number system. The Roman number system is not a positional number system and it has no base.

Similar to 'Decimal Number' system there are other number systems known as 'Binary'; 'Octal', and 'Hexa-decimal' number systems. The base of radix of 'Binary System' is 2, the base or radix of 'Octal System' is 8 and the base or radix of 'Hexadecimal System' is 16.

21.2 AIMS OF TEACHING NUMBER SYSTEM

Decimal system is introduced and taught to the students rights from the beginning of their schooling. If these systems are introduced in High School from VIII standards. Students will know there are other systems which are similar to decimal system. Though decimal system is popular and in common use it is very useful it is not very convenient and useful in electronics and computers. For these fields 'Binary System' is very much useful because its base is 2 and used only two digits 0 and 1.

21.3 IMPORTANCE OF TEACHING DIFFERENT SYSTEMS AND 'BINARY SYSTEM' IN PARTICULAR

In high school class students are curious to know new things. They will learn the relation between different systems and because the advanced field of electronics and computers is developing day by day and it is based on binary system. The working of binary system, different operations in binary system, its relation with other systems, must be known to the students. The knowledge of conversion of numbers from one system to another system, particularly from decimal to binary and vice versa will create interest in the students and the drill of conversations will also improve the skill of calculations.

21.4 TEACHING OF DIFFERENT NUMBER SYSTEMS

Students are familiar with 'Decimal System' of number, and their fundamental properties and operations like addition, multiplication, subtraction and division on parallel lines we can introduce the other systems.

In general any number system has a set of symbols known as digits, with rules defined for addition, multiplication etc. A collection of these digits makes a number which has two parts integer and fractional separated by radix point (.) that is

$$(N)_b = \underbrace{d_{n-1}\, d_{n-2} \ldots d_1 d_0}_{\text{Integer part}} \;\underset{\text{Radix point.}}{\downarrow}\; \underbrace{d_{-1}\, d_{-2} \ldots d_{-m}}_{\text{fraction part.}}$$

Where N = a number.

b = radix or base of number system.

n = no. of digits in integer part.

m = no. of digits in fraction part.

d_{n-1} = most significant bit.

d_{-m} = least significant bit.

$$\text{and } 0 \leq d_i \text{ or } d_f \leq b_{-1}$$

The digits in the number are placed side by side and each position is the number has a weight in powers of base or radix.

21.5 COMMONLY USED NUMBER SYSTEM

Number Systems	*Base or Radix*	*Symbols d_f or d_i*	*Weights to Position*	
			i	*f*
Binary	2	0, 1	2^i	2^{-f}
Octal	8	0, 1, 2, 3, 4, 5, 6, 7	8^i	8^{-f}
Decimal	10	0, 1, 2, 3, 4, 5, 6, 7, 8, 9	10^i	10^{-f}
Hexadecimal	16	0, 1, 2, 3, 4, 5, 6, 7, 8, 9 A, B, C, D, E, F	16^i	16^{-f}

21.6 BINARY NUMBER SYSTEM

The number system with base or radix 2 is known as Binary Number System. Only two symbols 0 and 1 are used to represent numbers in this system. This is a positional number system i.e. every position has a weight in powers of two.

21.6.1 WHY BINARY NUMBER SYSTEMS ARE USED?

The basic element in first generation of computers were relay and switches. The operation of a switch or relay is bistable or binary in nature i.e. switch is either (ON) or (OFF), the symbols are respectively 1 or 0. The modern computers used in two states, saturated conduction or non-conduction (OFF).

Since large number of the electronic parts are used in computers. They should be used in such a way that slight changes in their characteristics will not affect their performance. The best way of achieving this is to use circuits which has two stable states i.e. bistable and represent these states with binary number system which uses two digits 0 and 1.

21.6.2 BINARY TO DECIMAL CONVERSION

Binary number has only two digits 0 and 1. Therefore the integer no. For example

11001010

This is a position number system. Therefore each digit has a weight in powers of 2 (the base of the system)

$$\begin{array}{cccccccc} 1 & 1 & 0 & 0 & 1 & 0 & 1 & 0 \\ \downarrow & \downarrow & \downarrow & \downarrow & \downarrow & \downarrow & \downarrow & \downarrow \\ 2^7 & 2^6 & 2^5 & 2^4 & 2^3 & 2^2 & 2^1 & 2^0 \end{array}$$

The weights are written from Least Significant Bit (LSB) to Most Significant Bit (MSB).

21.6.3 METHOD OF CONVERSION

(i) *Integer number in Binary System to decimal equivalent no.*

(a) Write the binary number.

(b) Write weights under the binary digit.

(c) Cross out the weight under the digit 0.

(d) Add the remaining weights.

Example

$$\begin{array}{llllll} 1 & 1 & 1 & 0 & & \text{—Binary number} \\ \downarrow & \downarrow & \downarrow & \downarrow & \rceil & \\ 2^3 & 2^2 & 2^1 & 2^0 & \rfloor & \text{—Write weights} \\ 8 & 4 & 2 & 1 & & \\ 8 & 4 & 2 & 0 & & \text{—Cross out weights under the digit 0.} \end{array}$$

$8 + 4 + 2 + 0 = 14$ —Add the weights.

Binary Number	Decimal Number
$(1110)_2$	$(14)_{10}$

(ii) *Conversion of fractional number in Binary System to Decimal Number*

(a) Write the Binary No.

(b) Write weights in negative power of 2.

(c) Cross out weights under the digit 0.

(d) Add the weights.

Example

0.1101 $2^{-1}\ 2^{-2}\ 2^{-3}\ 2^{-4}$	]— Binary fraction
0.5 .25 0.125 0.0625	—Write the weights
0.5 0.25 0 0.0625	—Cross out weight under the digit 0.

0.5 + 0.25 + 0.0625 = 0.8125.

Binary Number		Decimal Number
$(0.1101)_2$	=	$(0.8125)_{10}$

21.6.4 DECIMAL TO BINARY CONVERSION

(i) Integer Conversion

To convert decimal to binary number 'Double Dabble' method is used. In this method the decimal number is progressively divided by 2 and remainder is written after each division. The remainder taken in reverse order is the binary equivalent of the given decimal number. The number is divided until the division becomes zero, if the last remainder is 1, the last step is $1 \div 2 = 0$

Example: Consider $(60)_{10}$

	Remainder
$60 \div 2 = 30$	0
$30 \div 2 = 15$	0
$15 \div 2 = 7$	1
$7 \div 2 = 3$	1
$3 \div 2 = 1$	1
$1 \div 2 = 0$	1

$\therefore\ (10)_{10} = (111100)_2$

Verification

1	1	1	1	0	0
2^5	2^4	2^3	2^2	2^1	2^0
32	16	8	4	0	0

$32 + 16 + 8 + 4 = (60)_{10}$.

(ii) Fraction Conversion

For integer conversion we divide by 2 but for fraction conversion we multiply by 2 and record the carry in the integer position.

Example: Consider (0.625)

0.625 × 2	=	1.250 with a carry	1
0.25 × 2	=	.50 with a carry	0
0.5 × 2	=	1.0 with carry	1 ↓

Carry taken in the forward order give the binary equivalent no.

$(0.625)_{10} = (.101)_2$

Example 2. $(0.45)_{10}$

0.45 x 2	=	0.90	With a carry	0
0.9 x 2	=	1.8	"	1
0.8 x 2	=	1.6	"	1
0.6 x 2	=	1.2	"	1
0.2 x 2	=	0.4	"	0
0.4 x 2	=	0.8	"	0
0.8 x 2	=	1.6	"	1 ↓

∴ $(0.45)_{10} = (0111001)_2$ approximately.

21.7 BASIC OPERATIONS IS BINARY NUMBER SYSTEM

21.7.1 BINARY ADDITION

The binary addition has same basic rules on the decimal operations. Following are the rules for binary addition

$0 + 0 = 0$

$0 + 1 = 1$

$1 + 0 = 1$

$1 + 1 = 0$ a carry over of 1.

Carry over is performed in the same manner as in decimal arithmetic. To add many bit binary number carry is given to higher order columns.

Example

	Binary	Decimal
	111011	52
+	011100	28
	1010111	87

64, 0, 16, 0, 4, 2, 1   64 + 16 + 4 + 2 + 1 = 87

The binary addition is done column-wise starting with LSB, similar to decimal addition.

If we find the decimal equivalent of each binary number and add the we get a decimal number which is the equivalent decimal number of the addition result.

21.7.2 BINARY SUBTRACTION

Subtraction is inverse operation of addition. To subtract it is necessary to establish a procedure for subtracting a larger number from a smaller number. The only case in which it occurs is when 1 is subtracted from 0 the remainder is 0, but it is necessary to borrow one from next column to the left.

The basic rules for binary subtraction

$0 - 0 = 0$
$1 - 0 = 1$
$1 - 1 = 0$

$0 - 1 = 1$ with a borrow as 0 becomes 10 with borrow

$\therefore$ $0 - 1$ becomes $10 - 1 = 1$

Example

	Decimal Equivalent
10001	17
− 1001	− 9
01000	8

Example 2

101010	42
− 11110	− 30
001100	12

21.7.3 BINARY MULTIPLICATION

Binary multiplication has following rules:

$0 \times 0 = 0$

$0 \times 1 = 0$

$1 \times 0 = 0$

$1 \times 1 = 0$

Example 1

		Decimal
1011		11
× 1010		× 10
0000		110
1011+		
0000++		
1011+++		
1101110	→	64 + 32 + 8 + 4 + 2 = 110

21.7.4 BINARY DIVISION

Binary division has following rules:

$$0 \div 1 = 0$$

$$1 \div 1 = 0$$

Example 1.

Decimal

$1100 \div 101$

```
       101                 5
101) 11001               5)25
      -101
     -----
     00101
      - 101
     -----
       000
```

Example 2. $110110 \div 1001$

Decimal

```
        101                6
1001) 110110             9)54
      - 1001
      ------
       01001
      - 1001
      ------
       00000
```

21.8 EQUIVALENT NUMBERS IN THE DIFFERENT NUMBER SYSTEMS

Decimal	*Binary*	*Octal*	*Hexadecimal*
0	0000	0	0
1	0001	1	1
2	0010	2	2
3	0011	3	3
4	0100	4	4
5	0101	5	5
6	0110	6	6
7	0111	7	7
8	1000	10	8
9	1001	11	9
10	1010	12	A
11	1011	13	B
12	1100	14	C
13	1101	15	D
14	1110	16	E
15	1111	17	F

Similarly operations and conversions in other systems can be taught. Conversion of any system to decimal and vice versa. Conversion of numbers from any system to other systems and vice versa can be taught. This will definitely enrich the calculation skill if sufficient drill is gives to the students.

Chapter—22

Teaching of New Mathematics

22.1 INTRODUCTION

Mathematics is fast expanding and today we are quite familiar with certain branches of Mathematics which are referred to as New Mathematics. In this chapter an attempt will be made to learn about teaching of Trigonometry, Logarithms and theory of sets. A passing reference will also be made to teaching of computers.

22.2 TEACHING OF TRIGONOMETRY

Trigonometry is the branch of Mathematics that deals with the solution of triangles i.e.. computing the angles of a triangle with the help of given sides, and computing the sides of a triangle from the area and two angles.

Before starting the teaching of trigonometry the teacher should familiarise the students with certain important and elementary terms used in trigonometry.

The first basic important things to be told in trigonometry is the measurement of an angle in terms of radians. The students should be told that:

$$180^\circ = \pi \text{ radians}$$

and one radian equals 57° approximately.

Another important things to be taught in **Trigonometric Functions**.

The ratio of different pairs of the sides of a right angled triangle are termed trigonometric functions.

The names of trigonometric functions with respect to acute angle (θ) are as follows:

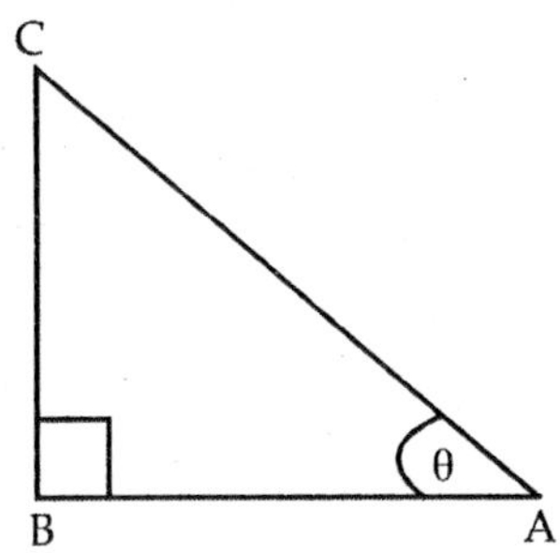

$$\frac{BC}{AC} = \frac{\text{Perpendicular}}{\text{Hypotenuse}}$$

$$= \sin\theta \text{ (sin means sine)}$$

$$\frac{AB}{AC} = \frac{\text{Base}}{\text{Hypotenuse}}$$

$$= \cos\theta \text{ (cos means cosine)}$$

$$\frac{BC}{AB} = \frac{\text{Perpendicular}}{\text{Base}}$$

$$= \tan\theta \text{ (tan means tangent)}$$

Similar relations for cot θ, sec θ and cosec θ are as under:

$$\cot\theta = \frac{BA}{BC} = \frac{\text{Base}}{\text{Perpendicular}}, \text{ (cot means cotangent)}$$

$$\sec\theta = \frac{AC}{AB} = \frac{\text{Hypotenuse}}{\text{Base}}, \text{ (sec means secant)}$$

$$\text{cosec}\theta = \frac{AC}{BC} = \frac{\text{Hypotenuse}}{\text{Perpendicular}}, \text{ (cosec means cosecant)}$$

It is necessary at this stage to tell the students the basic formula of trigonometry:

$$\sin^2 A + \cos^2 A = 1$$

and its two deductions

$$\sec^2 A = 1 + \tan^2 A$$

and $$\text{cosec}^2 A = 1 + \cot^2 A.$$

The students should then be given some exercises which involve the use of the above formula together with the following:

$$\tan A = \frac{\sin A}{\cos A}, \cot A = \frac{\cos A}{\sin A}$$

$$\sec A = \frac{1}{\cos A}, \text{cosec } A = \frac{1}{\sin A}.$$

The students be then asked to find the values of the trigonometrical ratios of 0°, 15°, 30°, 45°, 60° and 90° and to memorise them. At this stage students will be able to find the solution of a right angled triangle if at least one side is known.

After this the students be told certain other important trigonometrical relations and they will be able to deduce many more trigonometrical relations.

Solutions of Identities by Trigonometrical Formulae. Meaning of Identities

All the trigonometrical equations which hold good for all numerical values of the letters in them are called identities.

e.g. $\text{Sin}^2\theta + \text{Cos}^2\theta = 1$

If $\theta = 60^\circ$

$$\text{Sin}^2 60^\circ + \text{Cos}^2 60^\circ = \left(\frac{\sqrt{3}}{2}\right)^2 + \left(\frac{1}{2}\right)^2$$

$$= \frac{3}{4} + \frac{1}{4}$$

$$= 1$$

$\therefore$ L.H.S = R.H.S.

Teaching of Functions of Two Angles

By function of two angles we mean to deal with sum or difference of two angles, a double angle or a half angle.

If once we have proved that

$\text{Sin}(A + B) = \text{Sin } A \text{ Cos } B + \text{Cos } A \text{ Sin } B$

Geometrically, all other formulae can be derived. Some of these are as under:

$$\sin (A - B) = \sin A \cos B - \cos A \sin B$$

$$\cos (A + B) = \cos A \cos B - \sin A \sin B$$

$$\tan (A - B) = \frac{\tan A - \tan B}{1 + \tan A . \tan B}$$

$$\sin 2A = 2 \sin A \cos A = \frac{2 \tan A}{1 + \tan^2 A}$$

$$\cos 2A = 2 \cos^2 A - 1 = \cos^2 A - \sin^2 A$$

$$= 1 - 2 \sin^2 A = \frac{1 - \tan^2 A}{1 + \tan^2 B}$$

$$\tan 2A = \frac{2 \tan A}{1 - \tan A}$$

$$\sin 3A = 3 \sin^2 A - 4 \sin^3 A$$

$$\cos 3A = 4 \cos^3 A - 3 \cos A$$

$$\tan 3A = \frac{3 \tan A - \tan^3 A}{1 - 3 \tan^2 A}$$

$$2 \sin A \cos B = \sin (A + B) + \sin (A - B)$$

$$2 \cos A \sin B = \sin (A + B) - \sin (A - B)$$

$$2 \cos A \cos B = \cos (A + B) + \cos (A - B)$$

$$2 \sin A \sin B = \cos (A - B) - \cos (A + B)$$

$$\sin C + \sin D = 2 \sin \frac{C+D}{2} \sin \frac{C-D}{2}$$

$$\sin C - \sin D = 2 \cos \frac{C+D}{2} \sin \frac{C-D}{2}$$

$$\cos C - \cos D = 2 \sin \frac{C+D}{2} \sin \frac{D-C}{2}$$

$$\cos C + \cos D = 2 \cos \frac{C+D}{2} \cos \frac{C-D}{2}$$

Measurement of Angles in Radians (Circular Measure)

Consider a circle with centre O and Radius r. Join OA and cut off arc AB equal to OA (the radius of the circle), then $\angle AOB = \theta = 1$ radian

Thus 1 Radian is the angle sub-tended at the centre of the circle with an arc whose length is equal to the radius of a circle.

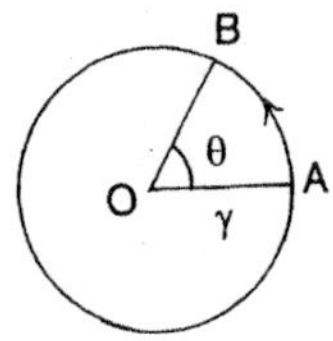

Relation Between Radian and Degrees

$$2\pi \text{ radian} = 360^\circ$$

$$\therefore \quad 1 \text{ radian} = \frac{360^\circ}{2\pi}$$

$$= 57^\circ \text{ approx.}$$

$$\text{or} \quad 1^\circ = \frac{\pi}{180} \text{ radians.}$$

Solution of Triangles, when

(*i*) Three sides *a, b, c* are given.

(*ii*) Two sides and the angle between them is given.

(*iii*) Two angles and one side is given.

(*iv*) Two sides and the angle opposite to one of these sides is given.

(*i*) Three sides are given

One of the three angles can be found out by applying law of cosines.

$$\cos A = \frac{b^2 + c^2 - a^2}{2bc}$$

The second angle say B can be found out by the law of sines

Third angle C = 180 – (A + B).

(*ii*) Two sides and the angle between them is given

Solution of Triangle in 2nd case.

Sides can be found by law of cosines

$c^2 = a^2 + b^2 - 2ab \cos c$

Angle A can be found by the law of sines

Third angle = 180 – (A + B).

(*iii*) Two angles and one side is given

Angle C = 180 – (A + B)

Sides *a* and *b* can be found by applying law of sines

$$a = \frac{c \sin A}{\sin C}$$

$$b = \frac{c \sin B}{\sin C}$$

(*iv*) Two sides and angle opposite to one of these is given

Angle A opposite to a given side can be found by the law of sines

$$\sin A = \frac{a \sin B}{b}$$

Third angle C = 180 – (A + B)

Third side can be found by law of sines

i.e. $$c = \frac{b \sin C}{\sin B}$$

Trigonometric Equation

An equation having unknown quantity under the sign of a trigonometric function is termed as trigonometric equation:

e.g. $\sin x = \frac{\sqrt{3}}{2}$ is an trigonometric equation.

Example. Solve $4 \sin^2\theta - 3 = 2 \cos\theta$

Solution. $4 \sin^2\theta - 2 \cos\theta - 3 = 0$

$\sin^2\theta = 1 - \cos^2\theta$

$$\therefore \qquad 4(1-\cos^2\theta) - 2\cos\theta - 3 = 0$$

or $$4\cos^2\theta + 2\cos\theta - 1 = 0$$

It is quadratic equation in $\cos\theta$

$$\cos\theta = \frac{-2 \pm \sqrt{4+16}}{8}$$

$$= \frac{-1 \pm \sqrt{5}}{4}$$

Distinction Between Trigonometric Equations and Identities

A trigonometric equation is an equation involving one or more trigonometric functions of the unknown angle and is true only for the particular values of the unknown where as *trigonometric identities* are trigonometric equation which are true for all values of unknown.

22.3 TEACHING OF LOGARITHMS

The students are already familiar with laws of indices (taught in Arithmetic). As a particular case we can tell the students the following laws:

$$a^0 = 1, a^{-m} = \frac{1}{a^m}, \; a^{p/q} = (a^p)^{\frac{1}{q}} \text{ etc.}$$

Generally at school stage by logarithm we mean logarithm with base 10.

$$\text{Let } a^m = x \qquad \ldots(i)$$

Where *a*, *x* and *m* are certain numbers.

Equation *(i)* can also be written as

$$\log a^x = \text{m} \qquad \ldots(ii)$$

In equation *(ii)*, the base is *a*,

We now know that

$$10^o = 1, 10^1 = 10, 10^2 = 100$$

$$10^3 = 1{,}000, 10^4 = 10000, \text{ and so on.}$$

Similarly,

$$10^{-1} = 0.1,\ 10^{-2} = 0.01,\ 10^{-3} = 0.0001$$

$$10^{-4} = 0.0001, \text{ and so on.}$$

In the language of logarithm, the above equations can be written as

$$\log_{10} = 0,\ \log_{10} 10 = 1,\ \log_{10} 100 = 2,$$

$$\log_{10} 1000 = 3,\ \log_{10} 10000 = 4 \text{ and so on.}$$

Similarly,

$$\log_{10} 0.1 = -1,\ \log_{10} 0.01 = -2,$$

$$\log_{10} 0.001 = -3,\ \log_{10} 0.0001 = -4 \text{ and so on.}$$

Since we are concerned only with common logarithm, where the base is always taken as 10, we omit in all our calculations to write 10 in suffix to log.

We have seen that log 1 = 0 and log 10 = 1. Hence the logarithm of any number between 1 and 10 will lie between 0 and 1. Similarly, logarithm of any number between 10 and 100 will lie between 1 and 2, and so on. On the other hand logarithm of a number between 1 and 0.1 will lie between 0 and –1, that logarithm of a number between 0.1 and 0.01 will lie between –1 and –2, and so on.

This indicates that logarithm of a number consists of two parts:

(1) Characteristic (Integral part).

(2) Mantissa (Decimal part).

The characteristic of any number can be found simply by observation of the number while mantissa of a number is obtained by means of a table. It is, however, convenient to commit to memory the logarithms of 2, 3 and 7. They are,

log 2 = 0.3010300

log 3 = 0.4771213

log 7 = 0.8450987.

At this stage the teacher should prove the following formulae:

(i) $\log ab = \log a + \log b$.

(ii) $\log \frac{a}{b} = \log a - \log b$.

(iii) $\log a^m = m \log a$.

(iv) $\log_b a = (\log_c a)(\log_b c)$

(v) $(\log_b a)(\log_a b) = 1$.

The main utility of these formulae is that (*i*) they reduce multiplication and division to simple operation of addition and subtraction (*ii*) they reduce the calculation of logarithm of all numbers to simply the numbers lying between 1 and 99.

The students be given sufficient practice in the calculations using logarithm tables.

22.4 TEACHING OF STATISTICS

Statistics finds wide applications in Economics, Sociology, Education, Psychology etc. At the school stage it is desirable to give a basic idea of statistics to the students. Thus they may be taught to arrange the data in a systematic form of frequency, distribution, its diagrammatical representation by figures, calculations of mean, mode and median, calculations of mean deviation and standard deviation etc.

For arranging the data following points be given due consideration:

(*i*) Choose the length of class interval in such a way so as to abridge the whole data in 10–15 class intervals.

(*ii*) All class intervals should be of equal length.

(*iii*) The total of frequencies of all class-intervals should be equal to the number of data given.

Class interval in abbreviated as C.I. and length of each class interval as i. The middle point of class interval is denoted by x and the frequency by f, cumulative frequency is represented by C.F.

The students may then be taught to prepare histograms, frequency polygon, cumulative frequency curve etc.

To illustrate these let us consider the following example:

In frequency polygon the point A, B, C, D, E, F and G, correspond to the middle points of respective class-interval 0 – 10, 10 – 20, 20 – 30, 30 – 40, 40 – 50, 50 – 60 and 60 – 70.

Along Y-axis the two diagrams (*i.e.* histogram and frequency polygon) and drawn to different scales.

C.I	*Frequency (f)*	C.F.
0—10	2	2
10—20	4	6
20—30	7	13
30—40	10	23
40—50	12	35
50—60	9	44
60—70	6	50

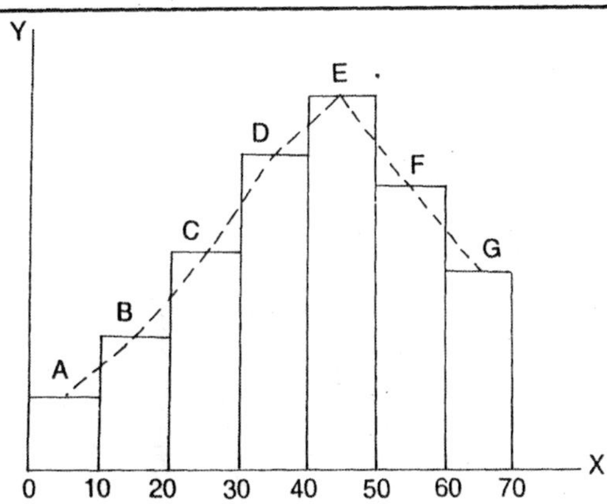

Histogram and frequency polygon super-imposed on one another.

A cumulative frequency curve is generally S-shaped (see Fig. below).

At the third stage of the topic, the students should be told to find mean, median and mode of a given data. Great emphasis must be laid on their calculation, specially while calculating mean, because median and mode are of very little importance in further study of the subject.

In case of only a few numbers (10 to 15) the mean is same as average but for a data given in frequency distribution from average has on meaning.

Merits in Calculation of Mean

(*i*) Mean is quite rigidly defined.

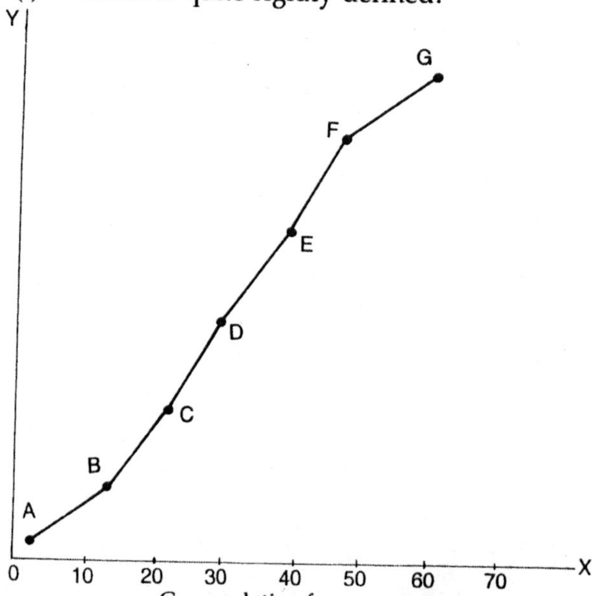

Cummulative frequency curve.

(*ii*) Mean is based on the whole of the given data.

(*iii*) In calculations of mean equal weightage is given to the whole of the given data.

(*iv*) Mean has a fixed value.

(*v*) It is possible to calculate mean mathematically.

(*vi*) Fluctuations of sampling show least effect on mean.

Demerits of Calculations of Mean

(*i*) Sometimes mean does not fully represent the given data.

(*ii*) Predominant frequencies are more emphasised in mean.

(*iii*) Sometimes mean may come out to be a number which does not occur in any class-interval because it fails to be a whole number.

(*iv*) It is not possible to find mean simply by inspection.

(*v*) The truth of mean will be effected if certain data is missed.

(*vi*) Sometimes mean does not give the correct picture of prosperity.

Deviations from Mean

Mean deviation is the deviation of the given data from the mean.

Standard deviation is obtained if we find the square root of the sum of the squares of deviations of the data from their mean.

For finding out whether a group analysed consists of homogeneous or heterogeneous elements it becomes essential to calculate deviations.

In any discrete sequence the mean deviation is given by

$$\text{Mean deviation} = \frac{\sum(x-M)}{N}$$

where x is one of the given numbers, M is the mean of the data and N the total of all frequencies.

For continuous sequence mean deviation is

$$= \frac{\sum f(x-M)}{\sum f} = \frac{\sum f(x-M)}{N}$$

where x is the mid-point of a certain class-interval, M is the mean of the whole data, f the frequency of the class-interval in which x occurs and Σf of the total of the frequencies.

Standard deviation for discrete series is given by

$$\frac{\sum f(x-M)^2}{N}$$

For a continuous series, it is given by

$$=\frac{\sum f(x-M)^2}{\sum f}=\frac{\sum f(x-M)^2}{N}$$

where the letters have the same meaning as given above.

Coefficient of Dispersion is obtained on dividing the standard deviation by the mean of the given data.

Coefficient of Variation is obtained on multiplying the coefficient of dispersion by 100.

22.5 TEACHING OF COMPUTER MATHEMATICS

Importance of Computer in Mathematics

In the present times the importance of computers is increasing quite rapidly and as a matter of fact computers have now become indispensable. We are highly dependent on computers in our everyday life. The work-force in present times mainly depends on computers.

Since computer is important so it is desirable that students be given the idea of potentialities of this work-force. To cope with new work-force a new mathematics is evolved which is referred to as *Computer Mathematics*. This new Mathematics i.e. computer Mathematics has been evolved because of Man's attempt to devise ways and means to facilitate calculations.

In India, a programme was launched for Computer Literacy and Studies in schools.

Electronic Computer

In the beginning we had mechanical computers which were just like mechanical calculators. They were provided with rotatory circular discs. Afterwards, mechanical computers using wheels were introduced. This type of computers were able to operate to calculate the results of addition, subtraction, multiplication and division in a very short time.

The first Electronic computer known as 'Electronic Brain' was designed in 1944. It was able to make computer calculations in a fraction of a second.

Modern Electronic Computer

Modern Electronic Computer is actually an electro-mechanical device which carries out the work of Mathematical calculations accurately and quickly.

Modern Computer can be defined as:

A computer is an electric, auto machine, which presents data and works on the data to give results upto 100% accuracy, provided input data is error free.

Applications

Computer has a wide-spread practical fields of life e.g. entertainment, games, music, home-appliances, preparation of budget, whether forecasting, news net working, railways, and air ways services, banking services, defence services, industrial activities, preparation of university examination result etc. In fact, there is no end to the use of computer in modern life.

Computer in Schools

Computer-education courses have been introduced almost in all universities of India. They are offering computer education upto degree level. Besides this, I.I.T. (Indian Institutes of Technology) are offering computer course upto M. Tech. and Ph.D. level. Many polytechnics in the country are offering computer education upto Diploma level. Computer Mathematics is the main part of computer education.

The computer education has also been introduced in schools today. The beginning for this project was made in 1984 with the launching of the progamme for Computer Literacy and Studies in schools in 1984. A workshop was organised at NCERT, New Delhi on March 26 and 27, 1984, in which representatives from various resources centres, I.I.T. Engineering Institutions, Central Board of Secondary Education, Kendriya Vidyalay Sangathan and some selected schools participated. This workshop laid a great stress on computer education in schools.

The National Policy on Education has also laid great stress on computer education in schools. The Programme of Action announced by the Ministry of Human Resource Development laid down a concrete programme for introducing computer education in schools.

According to the Programme of Action of Government of India computer education has been made a part of education in selected schools all over the country 75% Secondary and Higher Secondary schools have been provided with micro-computers to familarise students and teachers with the range of computer applications and their potential as a learning medium.

Programme of Action of the Government has announced the following measures for introducing computer education in school:

1. Introduction of elective computer course at higher secondary level during the coming years.
2. Extension of computer programme to cover all higher secondary schools in 1991, secondary schools by 1995 and elementary school in the long-term.

As computer education in schools will mainly consist of Computer Mathematics. It is essential that computer

Mathematics is taught in all schools and Secondary, Higher Secondary and Senior Secondary stages.

The students should be imparted elementary knowledge of computer Mathematics. They should be taught the skill of using computers for steedy calculation process. They should also be taught the working mechanism of computers.

In all developed countries of the West and Japan in the east, computer Mathematics has been included in the school syllabus. In fact, Japan has made a great progress in the development of computer Mathematics and its students make free use of computer for calculation work. Japan had invented in 1980 the first pocket computer. It is known as Sharp PC. The students in Japan do not make brain calculations during the study and practice of Mathematics. They solve all sums and problems of Mathematics involving calculations with the help of pocket computer which they carry to their schools and even examinations halls.

In India also the students are allowed to have pocket-computer with them in schools as well as examinations halls, but they very few students make use of them upto this time, because pocket computers are not within the easy reach of all students as yet and most of the students do not know the method of using them. But time is not far when all the students will use computers and Computer Mathematics will become a very popular subject in schools.

Chapter—23

Lesson Plan in Teaching of Mathematics

23.1 INTRODUCTION

A proper planning of the lessons is key to effective teaching. The teacher must know in advance the subject-matter and mode of its delivery in the class-room. This planning will give the teacher idea of how to introduce the topic, how to develop the key concepts, how to correlate the concepts to real life situations and how to conclude the lesson.

L.B. Stands conceives a lesson plan as 'Plan of Action' implemented by a teacher in the class-room. G.H. Green says, "The teacher who has planned his lesson wisely related to his topic and to his class will be in a position to enter the class-room without any anxiety, ready to embark with confidence upon a job he understands and prepared to carry it to a workmanable conclusion. He has forseen the difficulties that are likely to arise, and prepared himself to deal with them. He knows the aims of his lesson in intended to fulfil, and he has marshalled his own resources for the purposes. And because he is free of anxiety, he will able cooly to estimate the value of his work as the lesson proceeds, equally aware of failure and success and prepared to learn from both."

23.2 FEATURES OF A LESSON PLAN

In writing a lesson plan the following points be written down:

1. Data.
2. Period.
3. Class.
4. Duration of period.
5. Subject.
6. Topic.
7. General objectives.
8. Specific objectives.
9. Previous knowledge of the students.
10. Teaching aids and materials to be used.
11. Introduction.
12. Statement of object.
13. Presentation.
14. Generalisation.
15. Recapitulation.
16. Black-Board summary.
17. Home work.

23.3 STEPS OF LESSON PLANNING

Important steps are discussed below:

(*i*) **Introduction**. It is the most important part of lesson plan. It pertains to preparing and motivating students to the lesson content by linking it to their previous knowledge, by arousing curiosity, and by appealing to their senses. For this the teacher used the method of questions and answers having bearing on the previous knowledge of the students. This should not take more than 7–8 minutes.

(*ii*) **Presentation**. It involves stating of the object of the lesson. The teacher should state the object in such a way that it may not pose a problem before the students. This statement should be short, definite and attractive. The teacher should then expose the students to the new information. While writing this part the teacher may divide his plan in two parts. In one part, the subject or topic to be taught should be presented in a systematic manner. In the second part, the method of teaching may be stated. Use of teaching aids should be made during presentation of learning material along with students participation in the lesson through questions. An attempt be made to associate the learning material to daily life situations by citing examples and by drawing comparison with the related concepts.

(*iii*) **Generalization**. When the topic has been made clear to the students, the teacher should make an effort to draw generalisation with the help of definition, principles etc. The students may be encouraged to draw generalizations themselves. In other words, the students must realise that they have got new knowledge and are able to apply it.

(*iv*) **Application**. In this step an effort is made to apply the knowledge gained to certain situations. This is likely to result in reinforcing the new knowledge on students.

(*v*) **Recapitulation**. Recapitulation is assessing the effectiveness of your lesson by asking the students the questions on the contents of the lesson. The questions should be pointed ones.

(*vi*) **Blackboard Summary**. After finishing the topic, the teacher should write down the summary of the topic or the lesson on the blackboard. This should be done with the help of the students. Summary should be short and definite.

(*vii*) **Home Task**. In order to strengthen the knowledge and the experiences, the students should be given some home task. The students should be asked to write out certain things or do some practical experiments.

23.4 SOME MODEL LESSON PLANS

LESSON PLAN—1

Class: XI	Time: 40 minutes
Date:	Period:
Subject: Mathematics	Topic: Number System.

General Objectives

(*i*) To develop the reasoning power of the students and to bring about their intellectual development.

(*ii*) To impart to students the knowledge of Mathematics so that it can be used by them in their actual life.

(*iii*) To enable the students to solve different situations in life wherein the knowledge of Mathematics is required.

Specific Objective

To acquaint the students with the number system.

Apparatus

Ordinary class-room, chalk, duster etc.

Pervious Knowledge

The students know certain numbers and are also familiar with elementary operations.

Introduction

To introduce the lesson and to test the previous knowledge of the students, following questions will be put to them:

(*i*) Write two numbers, one before and another after 6.[5 and 7]

(*ii*) Write a number lying between 2 and 3. [2.5]

(*iii*) What is (2–5) equal to? [–3]

(*iv*) What type of number is this?

When no satisfactory answer is given to question (*iii*) and (*iv*) the teacher will introduce the topic by announcing, today we shall study about number system in detail.

Presentation

Matter	*B.B. Summary*
What are natural numbers?	The numbers 1, 2, 3, 4 .... are called natural numbers.
Is zero a natural number?	No, zero is not a natural number and it denotes nothingness.
What are whole numbers?	When the natural numbers include zero, these are called whole numbers.
What is 2–5?	It is not a positive whole number.
What do you mean by system of integers?	If the number system includes negative integers it is called system of integers. –5 –4... 0, 1, 2...
What are rational numbers?	In a system of integers, division is not always possible and we sometimes have numbers of the type p/q where q≠0 and p, q are integers. All such numbers are called rational numbers.
What type of numbers are included in system of rational numbers?	It includes all positive and negative integers including zero. It also includes fractional numbers.

Section Recapitulation

(*i*) What type of numbers are the following?

(*a*) 1, 2, 3, ...60, 61 (Natural numbers)

(*b*) 0, 1, 2....50 (Whole numbers)

(*c*) –55, –54...0, 1, 2, 3, 4, 5 (Integers)

(*d*) –40, –39...3/2, 7/2... (Rational numbers)

Step 2

Can we represent rational numbers on a straight line	Yes, they can be represented by points on a straight line? Fix the point 'o' as origin on a line 'l' The length OA can be fixed equal to a unit length (OA = 1) and can plot various points (–1, –2..., 1, 2, ...) on the line.
How can a rational number 4/5 be represented on this line?	To represent 4/5 divide OA in 5 equal parts and take 4 such parts to right of A to get the required point.
How to get $-\frac{4}{5}$?	Similar procedure as above be carried out but to left of 'o'.
Is $\sqrt{2}$ a rational number?	No, it is an irrational number.
What is the system of real numbers?	The enlarged system of numbers which includes irrational numbers also, is called the system of real numbers.

Recapitulation

Real Numbers

↓ Rational Numbers ↓ ↓ Irrational Numbers

↓ Integers ↓ Whole numbers ↓ Natural numbers

Integers: –4, –3, ...0, 1, 2,...

Whole numbers: 0, 1, 2, ...

Natural numbers: 1, 2, 3, ...

Home work. Solve the sums 1, 3, 5, 6 of exercise 2.

LESSON PLAN–2

Class: IX Time: 40 minutes

Date: Period:

Subject: Mathematics Topic: Factorisation

General Objectives

(*i*) To develop in pupils the power of comprehension about general rules in Algebra.

(*ii*) To develop the reasoning power in the pupils.

(*iii*) To develop the interest of students in Algebra.

(*iv*) To develop in the pupils the capacity to solve their actual life problems.

Specific Objectives

To teach the pupils the rules of factorisation, method of factorisation etc.

Teaching Aids

No specific teaching aid is needed.

Previous Knowledge. The students already know the process of multiplication.

They also know about division and multiplication. They are also aware of the fractions and divisions. It shall not be difficult to explain the factorisation to them.

Introduction. The topic can be introduced with the help of the following questions and propositions:

(1) Find the number which when multiplied give 25. (5×5)

(2) What is meant by multiple? When certain parts are multiplied, the result is known as multiple.

(3) What shall be the factorisation of

$$(x - y)^2 = (x^2 - 2xy + y^2)$$

$$(x^2 - y^2) = (x + y)(x - y)$$

$$(x - y)^2 = (x^2 - 2xy + y^2)$$

These principles will be told in detail and in a proper manner.

Statement of the Objects or Statement of the Teacher. The teacher should then say, "Today, I shall teach you about Factorisation."

Presentation. He will present the following problems before the students:

$$(a + b)(a - b) = a^2 - ab + ab - b^2 = a^2 - b^2$$

Similarly $(a + b)^2 = (a^2 + 2ab + b^2)$

$$(a - b)^2 = (a^2 - 2ab + b^2)$$

and $(a + b)(a + c) = a^2 + (b + c)a + bc$

From this, it follows that coefficient of a is the sum of b and c, while the last term is their product.

He will ask the students to find the factors of

$$a^2 - 5a + 4.$$

After this the students will be asked to find out two digits or numbers whose addition shall come to 5 and whose multiple shall be 4. These figures shall be 1 and 4. Therefore the above mentioned problems shall work out as given below:

$$a^2 - 4a - a + 4$$
$$= a(a - 4) - 1(a - 4)$$
$$= (a - 4)(a - 1).$$

The things will be written and explained to the students as under:

(1) What numbers will give $-5a$ when added' is the first step of question. $(-4a, -a)$

(2) Now, what shall be the form of the question? $(a^2 - 4a - a + 4)$

(3) Why has it been done so? (In order to facilitate the factorisation).

(4) Now, what are the two groups out of which the common factor or quotient may be found out? $a^3 - 4a$ and $- a + 4$.

(5) What shall be the common factor or quotient of the first group? (a).

(6) What is the remainder of the first group? $a(a - 4)$.

(7) What common factor or quotient may be taken out from the second group that the remaining or remainder may be equal to one factor of the first group? $-1\ (a - 4)$.

(8) What shall be the second step of the question now? $[a\ (a - 4) - 1\ (a - 4)]$.

(9) What shall now be the two factors? $(a - 4), (a - 1)$.

Factorise: $8b^2 + 51b + 55$.

(1) What thing is to be done first in this direction. Find out two numbers whose sum is 51.

(2) What should be the relationship of these numbers? 51 should be divided into two such parts that their sum or addition may be 51 and their product may be $55 \times 8 = 440$.

(3) What are those numbers or digits whose product is 440 and additon 51? $40 + 11$

(4) What shall now be the form of question number 1? $(8b^2 + 40b + 11b + 55)$.

(5) What are the required groups now? $(8b^2 + 40b)$ and $(11b + 55)$.

(6) What common factor should be taken out from first group. $(8b)$.

(7) What shall then be the remainder? $(b + 5)$.

(8) What shall then be the form of the first group? $8b\ (b + 5)$.

(9) Similarly, what is to be seen in the second group while taking out the common factor? $(b + 5)$ should be the remainder taking out the common factor.

(10) What shall be its form? $11\ (b + 5)$.

(11) What shall then be the new form of the whole question? $\{8b\ (b + 5) + 11\ (b + 5)\}$.

(12) What is the common factor of the groups that is to be taken out? $(b + 5)$.

(13) What shall be the remainder of the two groups? $(8b + 11)$.

(14) What shall now be the form of the question?

$(b + 5)\ (8b + 11)$.

(15) What are the two factors? $(b + 5)\ (8b + 11)$.

Blackboard Summary. The teacher may then, with the help of the students, put down the following on the blackboard:

$8b^2 + 51b + 55$

$= 8b^2 + 40b + 11b + 55$

$= 8b\ (b + 5) + 11\ (b + 5)$

$= (b + 5)\ (8b + 11)$. This shall be the answer.

Revision and Home Task. The teacher may give the following questions to the students for the revision work and to test the knowledge of the students:

(1) $3a^2 + 18a + 24$.

(2) $6b^2 + 95b + 75$.

(3) $72b^2 - 145b + 72$.

(4) $24a^2 = 76a + 40$.

LESSON PLAN —3

Class: X — Time: 40 minutes

Date: — Period:

Subject: Mathematics — Topic: Frequency Distribution Tables

General Objectives

(i) To develop in students the power of comprehension of statistics.

(ii) To develop the reasoning power in the students.

(iii) To develop the interest of students in statistics.

Specific Objectives

To enable the students to represent the statistical data in the form of frequency tables.

Introduction

To introduce the topic the teacher will draw the attention of the students to the difficulties faced in drawing conclusions from a numerical data which are too large. To overcome this difficulty we have to systematise the data and put it as briefly and neatly as possible.

Announcement of Aim

Teacher will then announce that today we shall learn about the method abridging and systematising the given data.

Presentation

The marks obtained (out of 25) by 50 students of Class X are as under:

16, 15, 5, 2, 3, 16, 5, 18, 2, 5, 0, 0, 3, 3, 3, 1, 11, 9, 8, 10, 7, 4, 3, 3, 0, 14, 0, 12, 6, 15, 7, 4, 3, 9, 19, 13, 1, 19, 1, 7, 6, 20, 6, 12, 11, 20, 3, 14, 2.

From this raw data or ungrouped data we can not get any idea about the achievements of students.

To condense the data

(*i*) First of all we determine the range i.e. the difference between the maximum and the minimum number. Here it is 20–0 = 20.

(*ii*) Then the range is divided into classes. These classes may be between 5 and 15. Here we may have 7 classes.

(*iii*) We determine the size of the class interval by dividing the range by the number of classes.

Here we have $\frac{22}{7} \approx 3$ ($\approx$ means approximately)

(*iv*) Then we set up class limits.

(*v*) We take each item of the data, place a tally mark against the class interval.

For convenience after four tally marks we put the fifth one diagonally to cross the other four as shown below:

Class Interval	*Tally Marks*	*Frequency*
0—3	~~IIII~~ ~~IIII~~ I	11
3—6	~~IIII~~ ~~IIII~~ III	13
6—9	~~IIII~~ II	7
9—12	~~IIII~~	5
12—15	~~IIII~~	5
15—18	IIII	4
18—21	~~IIII~~	5
Total		50

This is known as **frequency distribution table** or **table** or **briefly frequency table**.

Application

Ages of 24 boys in class X of a school are as under:

15, 15, 14, 18, 17, 15, 14, 15, 16, 16, 17, 18, 15, 14, 13, 14, 16, 16, 13, 14, 14, 15, 19, 16.

Construct a frequency table for it.

Appendix 1

M.D.U. & Kurukshetra Syllabus 1991 and Onwards

TEACHING OF MATHEMATICS

Time: Three Hours | Marks: 100

Unit 1. (*a*) Element of new Mathematics.

(*i*) Ideas of undefined terms, axioms; postulates and methods of reasoning and proof.

(*ii*) Sets and their elementary operations.

(*iii*) Structures of number systems.

(*iv*) Shortcomings of Eucledean Geometry and Characteristics of Non-Eucledean Geometries.

(*b*) History of the notation system and Computer Mathematics.

(*c*) Contributions of Aryabhatta, Bhaskaracharya and Ramanujan in Mathematics.

Unit 2. (*a*) Importance or value of teaching of Mathematics.

(*b*) Aims and objectives of teaching Mathematics at the secondary stage.

(*c*) Translation of objectives in behavioural terms.

Unit 3. Curriculum in Mathematics

(*a*) Principles of curriculum construction.

(*b*) Formulation of curriculum.

(*i*) Formulation of objectives.

(*ii*) Selection and organisation of the content and topics.

(*iii*) Suggesting appropriate learning experiences.

(*iv*) Suggesting suitable methods and technique for evaluation.

Unit 4. Method and techniques of teaching Mathematics.

(*a*) Methods: Inductive, deductive, analytic-synthetic, Heuristic, laboratory and project.

(*b*) Techniques: Oral work, written work, drill work, Home-work and self study.

Unit 5. Equipments for teaching Mathematics.

(*a*) Text-books: function, selection and evaluation.

(*b*) Audio-visual aids in teaching of Mathematics.

(*c*) Organisation of

(*i*) Mathematics laboratory.

(*ii*) Mathematics library.

(*iii*) Mathematics club.

Unit 6. Evaluation in Mathematics, Preparing objective based test items in Mathematics.

Unit 7. (*a*) Backwardness in Mathematics—Diagnosis and Remedial teaching preparing a diagnostic test in Mathematics.

(*b*) Enrichment programmes for the gifted.

Unit 8. Lesson planning in Mathematics.